Voice
of
CBI

Attention Authors

'We Convert Fighters into Writers'. That's the motto of Manas Publications since more than four decades. Our message to the world is that India can win the battle not only by the bullet but also by the pen. There is no dearth of intellectuals in our country, but their knowledge is confined to them only. No sincere effort has been made by any other publisher to channelise their knowledge in national interest. That is why the talent of a large number of intellectuals remains latent. An author transforms his knowledge into a manuscript, and it is our job to spread his/her knowledge by converting it into a beautiful book. For over four decades, Manas has been motivating the intellectuals by publishing their manuscripts and would like to publish your manuscript too. If you or your colleagues have any manuscript ready for publication or are working on it, kindly contact us with detailed synopsis and list of contents. We will transform your work into a valuable publication. If you wish, we can also suggest you the suitable subjects for writing the books related to your area of expertise. Manas is known for its publishing quality and commitments. We take utmost care in production and give wide publicity to the book as well as its author through our national and international distribution network.

Voice of CBI

M Narayanan
Former Jt Director : CBI

Manas Publications
(We Convert Fighters into Writers)
New Delhi- 110002 (INDIA)

MANAS PUBLICATIONS
(We Convert Fighters into Writers)
(Publishers, Library Suppliers, Importers & Exporters)
4402/5-A, Ansari Road (Opp. HDFC Bank)
Darya Ganj, New Delhi-110 002 (India)
Off. ✆ 011-23260783, 23265523, Res. ✆ 011-23842660
Fax: 011-23272766
E-mail: manaspublications@gmail.com
manaspublications@yahoo.com
Website:www. manaspublications.in

ISBN 978-81-7049-467-6
₹ 595/-

Designed at
Manas Publications

Printed in India at
RK Offsets, Delhi
and published by Mrs Suman Lata for
Manas Publications, 4402/5-A,
Ansari Road, (Opp HDFC Bank),
Darya Ganj, New Delhi-110 002 (INDIA)

Contents

Preface

Over the last four years, since I retired in January 2009, there have been many a request, coming to me from some retired officers and as well as the serving professionals of Central Bureau of Investigation for recording some of my experiences and observations, during my long career in the organisation. The regard to and reputation of the organisation are the two factors, which required consideration, while trying to do so. Experience varies from person to person and cannot be generalised. Official life has a bearing on the personal life and therefore, any two persons' responses may always differ on some or all the incidents and issues. Individually and collectively, we contribute to the success of an organisation, but the degree of such contribution varies from individual to individual. This organisation, and in fact all organisations, survive on the sincere contributions of those, who work dedicatedly and honestly, irrespective of others' contribution and response. It would not be an exaggeration if I say that the system works only on account of the services rendered by a few. This is so everywhere. It is also not strange that those who work dedicatedly and honestly with accountability and responsibility, encounter problems and still become answerable.

Recently, two retired senior most officers of the Central Bureau of Investigation came on the TV's national network channel and said that the CBI remained under constant pressure from outside. But the exact nature of pressure or demand and in what manner the cases were handled by those good officers are not available. Such information would have been of help to the present and future Directors. It is high time that such instances are exposed which itself will definitely help in making the CBI autonomous and independent, because such demands or interferences will surface, if not exposed. There should be transparency. Well, having served for more than 38 years, in various capacities and handled important cases, I do subscribe to the view that many times the investigation or other matters get derailed, because of such instances. The pressure is from different type of authorities and institutions — public, media, Government, Parliamentarians and so on. All legitimate pressures are alright. But investigation takes time. Quality suffers, if there is pressure. All inappropriate or illegitimate pressures require to be exposed and condemned. Orders, instructions and directions from the Constitutional courts are in public interest and interest of justice and are destined to render justice, wherever required, according to law.

I read in newspapers that U.S. Misra, former Director has expressed that there was pressure on him in the case against Ms. Mayawati and the CBI of the day denied it saying that it is only the personal opinion of Shri Misra. How can it be? He was the Director then, and he is the only right person to express so because he was under pressure. Such a denial is incorrect. Where should we search for the guts? I recollect, when I went and told Shri Misra, the then Director, that Amit Jogi, who was called to the office for interrogation should be arrested, as his involvement in the case had come up, he thought for a minute and said all right you go ahead. Similarly, in the case of fake encounters in Anantnag by the Army, killing civilians, though there was some difficulty, Vijay Shanker, the then Director said that on facts, we should prosecute. A right and impartial decision was the need of the day. Many such examples are there.

Suicide by Hari Dutt, Additional Superintendent of Police, CBI, Trivandrum branch, clearly exposes the existence of such external as well as internal threats, interferences and manipulative attempts — pressures which the honest officer could not bear or adjust with. Earlier, Inspector Sultan Singh had also committed suicide on account of similar reasons. The method adopted is not the correct or approvable one. They should have protested and dragged the concerned accused or suspects and or officers into public exposure through the media etc. Hari Dutt was investigating a fake encounter case in which some senior officers of Kerala police were reportedly involved. Normally, such cases are given to some of the Central branches in Delhi as it becomes difficult for the local branch to handle these. The situation is serious. A number of Investigating Officers used to come and tell about several internal and external pressures. Only same advice to all of them, is to protest strongly and bring it on record for your safety, be fair, just and honest in all your acts and or dealings. If you are not able to handle, then ask for transfer of the case to another officer. Fear of transfer to a distant place and thereby disturbing the family including children's education and adverse report in the form of Annual Confidential Report are some of the factors, which force the subordinates to keep quiet and adjust with the environment. Discipline is another major factor in this and other organisations of this nature. The result may be that sometimes its becomes suffocating. The case of Hari Dutt demands appropriate action against those involved. Only impartial inquiry will bring out the truth, perhaps. Facts may become clear. As a supervising officer, it should be my duty to look after and encourage the subordinates to do their duties properly. I recollect, when I was DIG, on the orders of High Court, I was asked to investigate some sensitive cases, relating to Dera Sachha Sauda and complete the same within two months. The Joint Director and the Special Director supervising these cases came to my room and told me that the cases were given to me for closing and so I should wind up. The person was politically influential. He had large number of followers. He was head of Dera Sachcha Sauda. I told them that I investigate cases according to law and evidence and do not take instructions from anybody. The case was handled according to law and the accused involved were chargesheeted. Every Investigating Officer should perform his duties in accordance with law and nothing else.

The CBI has been in existence for decades, with a reputation of its own. It has developed into a highly technical institution, capable to handle not only scams but varieties of cases, like economic frauds, Human trafficking, child trafficking, drug trafficking, arms trafficking, smuggling, money laundering, counterfeiting cases, antique related offences, cyber crimes, murder cases, kidnappings, dacoities, rape cases, fake encounter cases, custodial death cases, bomb blasts, terrorist crimes, organised crimes, serial killings, necrophilic killings and so on, using the latest scientific aids. The esteemed courts of law have been appreciating the work done by the CBI from time to time and have been giving sensitive cases to the CBI. There is continuous demand from the State governments and the public for entrusting sensitive cases to the CBI. If the CBI forms a different opinion about involvement of some persons in a case or about the offences committed, then the Courts are there to review them in accordance with law and modify them and or interfere in the matter. Actions of the CBI are subject to judicial reviews. Well, CBI is also expected to perform in accordance with law and discharge its duties properly and impartially. Deviations in some cases and mishandling of cases, for any reason, will naturally invite criticism. Such acts damage the institution. Vested interest always result in inappropriate decisions.

Some senior retired officers are of the opinion that the CBI should be given Constitutional powers and therefore should be brought under the Lokpal so that it is independent. My opinion is that the CBI is practically independent except in cases, where it has to obtain clearance for initiating action against Joint Secretaries and above. It will not apply to trap cases. It is again independent on receipt of such permission. The point is that it should function independently. The organisation should handle all assignments impartially, boldly and take appropriate decisions, according to law and should not play politics. The provision requiring to seek prior permission to conduct investigation against Joint Secretaries and above, needs an amendment as it indirectly supports corruption at higher levels. It may be pointed out here that before conducting investigation, the CBI makes enquiries to find out whether there is *prima-facie* material for any such investigation by the CBI. Well, if an FIR already registered is transferred to CBI or when the Constitutional courts order for a CBI investigation, then the case is registered immediately and investigation is taken up. Many times the law officers also scrutinise the material and give opinion as and when required.

The cry for CBI Act to strengthen the hands of the organisation has gone overboard. It should take care of all weaknesses in the present Act, including the power to conduct enquiries and investigation against senior officers. Yes, the question of impartiality and functioning according to law, stands answered with reference to the quality of leadership, the organisation has, from time to time. If the leader or boss does not compromise, then the subordinates will also not. Therefore, independence to work should or could only mean that one should work independently, without succumbing to pressures and nothing more. One should protest, resist and if the working atmosphere becomes or gets polluted, then he should resign in protest.

There were instances, when some police officers did that. Constitutional power is dangerous specially because it will do away with the existing judicial review mechanism also. Here again, the power or the trend of issuing orders by Magistrates to Director CBI and senior officers to appear and answer, should be stopped. If every Magistrate starts questioning the CBI, the criminal justice system will collapse, because the investigating agency gets little time to complete the investigation, whereas the courts keep them for years and go on analysing, hearing other parties etc. So many things may come up. Instead, the courts have their own power and procedure to be adopted and that should be followed and the cases should be disposed of, in accordance with law.

What is needed is to have an honest leader, who can safeguard the interest of the organisation only and not that of anybody else. A boss who will only think about his two years tenure as Director and nothing more than that. One who does not crave for any assignment after his tenure, as a matter of routine is credible. One who can insulate the organisation from external influences and spread confidence among the subordinates down the line through his individual, unbiased and impartial leadership and decisions irrespective of the status of the persons involved in the matter under scrutiny by the organisation is also adorable. A person who can bluntly say no to any request or favour must be respected. It will be difficult to find such persons, but it may not be impossible. I may, personally, say that I did not have the opportunity of enjoying working under such a leader. Well, such a nature of approach, attitude and quality was found, to a large extent, in Ashwani Kumar, the then Director under whom I worked for six months only. I found that most of the staff had the same opinion about him. He was clear in his mind and was very quick in taking decisions. I recollect his instructions that we should be fair in our investigations and should not favour anybody involved in the case. When I became Joint Director some orders passed by the courts to initiate action against the Investigating Officers under Section 217 of the Indian Penal Code for not chargesheeting some of the persons in some cases, came up for consideration. It was found that the Investigating Officer had recommended, but the final order received from the Directors, earlier, did not show such persons as accused. Well those orders of the courts were challenged in the higher courts. Even though the final order in a case is passed by the Director, the report under Section 173 CrPC is filed in the court under the signature of the Investigating Officer and he gets all the blame, many times. But, it is only the opinion of the Investigating Officer and the court while taking cognizance of the report, has the power to disagree with the opinion of the officer and frame a judicial opinion.

It is my considered opinion that, when, we have to function within the parameters of the law of the land, how does it matter whether you have Constitutional powers or not. You have the legal powers. Only thing is that it should not be misused. In the anti-Sikh riot cases when I informed Ashwani Kumar that the investigation has brought out evidence of involvement of some leaders including Sajjan Kumar, Member of Parliament, he said that it is the right approach not to make any difference with regard to the status of the accused in any case. The role of Jagdish Tytler whose case was closed earlier was also discussed.

Of course, it was a horrible incident and as we were present in Delhi at that time, we were witnesses to many of the incidents. Nobody can deny the incidents and therefore the truth should come out, otherwise it will be injustice to the victims if we fail to probe the involvement of these two and other leaders in these crimes. He expressed that rendering justice to the victims should be our priority and in this regard nobody should be spared. We also took a quick and right decision in the cases, relating to police atrocities on agitating public in Nandigram, West Bengal. There are so many other such instances.

The recommendation of the former Director, CBI to maintain the *status quo* of the CBI, is the right approach. Keep the CBI as it is. Strengthen it and make it more accountable and transparent, as far as the law permits. Expand it and allow it to grow. Fill up the vacancies and provide more Investigating Officers and Law Officers. Provide more scientific and technological support and other facilities for better output. Provide more and sufficient funds for an independent existence, rather than making the agency to approach the Government for getting funds from time to time. An independent investigating agency will be in the interest of the country. When Vijay Shanker was the Director, Management experts were hired to review the CBI working system to make it more accountable and effective in its functioning and also to modernise it. The idea was to make it fit to cope up with the work load and pressures. The experts submitted their reports and subsequently, geographical expansion was made and some branches were opened in some states and areas. A lot needs to be done after proper analysis. Infrastructural facilities and atmosphere for professional investigation are the basic needs of the organisation for better and impartial output.

The recent submission of the Goverment refusing to strengthen the hands of the CBI by giving it more funds and financial power to develop its infrastructural facilities and operating network, skills as well as freedom to operate against criminals, corrupt public servants including Ministers, according to law, is unfortunate. If one is honest and impartial, he will definitely say let the CBI investigate it properly, according to law. It is high time that the CBI exercises its legal powers to deal with corrupt public servants from top to bottom in scams whether 2G Scam, Coalgate, Railway scam and or any other scam. Permission is required to save the honest officers not the corrupt officers or criminals. To commit crime is not part of official duty or in discharge of official duties. Even otherwise Section 6-A of DSPE Act (as amended) refers to joint secretaries and above but not of equivalent or higher rank. Exert your powers, rest will fall in line.

Author

Chapter 1

Professional Basics

Investigation is a complex subject that includes a number of professional basics to be understood well. As defined in Section 2(h) of the Code of Criminal Procedure, 1973 (CrPC), it includes all the proceedings under the Code for the collection of evidence conducted by a police officer or by any person (other than a Magistrate) who is, authorised by a Magistrate on his behalf.

In fact, investigation starts with registration of the case or FIR under Section 154 of the Code and ends with Section 173 of the Code including the power to conduct further investigation under Section 173(8) CrPC. Besides, there is a power to arrest under Section 41 of the Code, power to summon documents under Section 91 and conduct search for recovering incriminating material under Section 93 of the Code with search warrant issued by the court. The police have the power to conduct searches even without such court warrant as per Section 165 of the Code. The Supreme Court of India in the case of *H.N. Rishbud vs. State of Delhi*, 1955 AIR 196 has defined investigation as consisting generally of the following steps:

(1) Proceeding to the spot;

(2) Ascertainment of the facts and circumstances of the case;

(3) Discovery and arrest of the suspected offender;

(4) Collection of evidence relating to the commission of the offence which may consist of *(a)* the examination of various persons (including the accused) and the reduction of their statements into writing, if the officer thinks fit and *(b)* the search of places for seizure of things considered necessary for the investigation and to be produced at the trial; and

(5) Formation of the opinion as to whether on the material collected there is a case to produce the accused before a Magistrate for trial and if so taking the necessary steps for the same by filing a chargesheet under Section 173.

These steps are confirmed subsequently in most of the cases. A police officer making an investigation is enjoined to enter his proceedings in a day-to-day case diary. Where such investigation cannot be completed within the period of 24 hours and the accused is in custody, he is enjoined also to send a copy of the entries in the diary to the Magistrate concerned. It is important to notice that when the investigation is conducted not by the officer in charge of the police station but by a subordinate officer (by virtue of one or the other of the provisions enabling him to depute such subordinate officer for any of the steps in the investigation), such subordinate officer is to report the result of the investigation to the officer in charge of the police station. If, upon the completion of the investigation it appears to the officer in charge of the police station that there is no sufficient evidence or reasonable ground, he may decide to release the suspected accused, if in custody, on his executing a bond. If, however, it appears to him that there is sufficient evidence or reasonable ground, to place the accused on trial, he is to take the necessary steps under Section 170 of the Code. In either case, on the completion of the investigation, he has to submit a report to the Magistrate under Section 173 of the Code in the prescribed form furnishing various details. There is a provision for further investigation as per Section 173(8) CrPC. The scheme of the Code also shows that while it is permissible for an officer in charge of a police station to depute some subordinate officer to conduct some of these steps in the investigation, the responsibility for every one of these steps is that of the person in the situation of the officer in charge of the police station, it having been clearly provided in Section 168 that when a subordinate officer makes an investigation, he should report the result to the officer in charge of the police station. It is also clear that the final step in the investigation, *viz.* the formation of the opinion as to whether or not there is a case to place the accused on trial is to be that of the officer in charge of the police station. There is no provision permitting delegation thereof but only a provision entitling superior officers to supervise and/or participate under Section 36.

Investigation is thus, to collect evidence to ascertain the crime committed and identify the culprits. Evidence may be:

- Oral
- Documentary
- Circumstantial
- Audio-video, digital evidence
- Scientific evidence
- Recoveries
- Dying declaration
- Confessions
- Extra-judicial confessions
- Electronic data records, mobile phone printouts, etc.

In this era of sophisticated crimes and crime-literate criminals, concentration, on collection of scientific evidence is of more importance. Scene of crime is very important as it may provide:

- Information on the *corpus delicti*
- Information on the *modus operandi*
- Evidence to link a suspect with a victim
- Evidence to link a person to the crime scene
- Information to disprove or support a witness's testimony
- Evidence to identify a suspect
- Investigative leads, and
- Evidence to identify a substance

You are not here to crave for publicity and appear before the camera. Such a step is dangerous. Do your job properly according to law and leave. At the same time, do not cave in to criticisms if you have done your job properly and without any bias. One or the other party is bound to criticise you. There is a new trend of bringing and showing the accused in custody before the electronic media and forcing him to confess. This is not correct. If the accused himself goes and admits before the media voluntarily, before arrest, then it is admissible. Once your job of investigation as per the provisions of Chapter 12 of CrPC is over and you have filed the report under Section 173 of the Code, the courts have the power to disagree with you while taking cognizance of the said report and the offences mentioned therein in accordance with the provisions of Section 190 CrPC. Court may add or delete accused or any offence and form its own opinion after judicial application of mind.

One factor which may disturb a proper investigation is the public pressure. You cannot avoid it in a sensitive case or a big scam. One should not be carried away by it. In a society in which we live, various kinds of pressure, criticisms etc., are bound to come up. It should be taken into account and kept in mind but investigation should be based on correct facts and reliable evidence which comes on record during the course of such impartial investigation. You should not be carried away by criticisms whether in the Nithari cases, Anti-Sikh riot cases, Dera Sachcha Sauda cases, or any other cases or in handling the trial of a sensitive case, or any case if you are legally on the right track. One thing is that you should be sure of your findings based on admissible and or convincing evidence. Check your conscience. One should appreciate public outcry for proper investigation. It is not sufficient to do your job properly but it should be shown to have been done properly. If there is an outcry that some person is not at all investigated or properly investigated, the CBI should show by its actions that it has covered everybody involved in the case or those who had handled the matter. If I am being investigated for submitting a proposal, then all others who had approved the same on the basis of which I took further action on it should also be investigated.

Investigation by media is another factor which may disturb you sometimes. They also have a job to perform. There is competition. They have to struggle hard for commercial existence whether it is print media or electronic media. They serve a public cause. Many a time they try to take you away from your considered line of investigation. They bring out so many information either positive or negative and one may find them to be useful and helpful. They have wide operating resources and network and one has got the opportunity of getting so much of information from them or from their news and debates. Take and consider whatever is proper and correct with reference to the field investigation outputs and keep in mind all other inputs they bring out because at the end of investigation you have to form your opinion on facts before you file your report in the court. Their never ending efforts would be, appreciated in bringing out facts and all information in the matter.

Thus, the role of the Investigating Officer is to do his job honestly without fear and according to law and collect all possible legally admissible evidence, in public interest.

Chapter 2

Role of Supervisory Officers

Having been an Investigating Officer and then a Supervising Officer myself, I feel that the Supervising Officers should possess practical knowledge and first hand experience in investigation and procedures of court trials otherwise it would prove to be practically impossible for them to provide a relevant, logical, and purposeful guidance to the subordinate Investigating Officers. Directly recruited officers in the CBI who perform the task as Investigating Officers—whether in the rank of Sub-Inspectors, Inspectors or Deputy Superintendents—are highly educated, intelligent with a good grasping power. After investigating a number of cases, gradually they attain perfection. In view of this there is no point in bringing officers from outside, on deputation and put them as Supervising Officers to oversee the investigation and trial proceedings and also run a branch of the CBI, where various type of cases are under investigation, unless that very officer has adequate exposure in the field of investigation and subsequent process of trial in the court. In fact, in the interest of the organisation, it is advisable to select such officers, who are capable of significantly contributing to the field of investigation. The officers who have over the years supervised the investigation of a large number of sensitive crimes, vigilance cases and have also followed up the trial process in the courts, would prove to be beneficial to the CBI. There is no point in dumping officers on deputation just for the purpose of making it a deputation oriented department. It can not be denied that vested interests could spoil the organisation itself. Truly, the organisation needs capable officers for guidance during the investigation and taking on the spot decisions. And that needs adequate experience. This norm applies to officers in the rank of Superintendent of Police and above. As far as CBI officers are concerned, they have exposure to down to earth realities and practical experience of the job and therefore are better in handling different tasks. Supervising Officers should have thorough knowledge of the procedure of arrest, preparation of arrest memo, of search and preparation of records, recording of all other legal reports, memos etc., and of ways and means for collecting legally admissible evidence.

Let's remember that CBI is a specialised investigating agency. In any sensitive case, the Investigating Officer is immensely under pressure, as he has to handle a lot of things. Besides investigating and supervising the work of assisting Officers, he has to appear in the court and satisfy the judicial officer, besides filing the reports. Further, he has to maintain the day-to-day case diaries. He has also to prepare internal reports to be submitted to senior officers. Besides tackling the accused in custody, he has to wind up the investigation in a proper and effective manner, within the stipulated period of 60 or 90 days, as the case may be, in connection with which he would again be under tremendous pressure. Hence, he needs support and not mere supervision.

I have observed that many Supervising Officers at the lower level usually ask the Investigating Officers to draft the report or comments for them, which they have to submit to senior officers. Actually, the CBI needs such officers who understand the facts well and are able to make their own notes, giving their opinion and put them up. It would be unfair to presume that only the officer knows everything and the intelligent, capable Investigating Officers do not and are supposed to carry out the orders only. As a Supervising Officer one should provide leadership to his team while being a part of the team. He may sit with them and assist them. His job is to provide infrastructural facilities, human resource assistance, like stenographers and logistics like, vehicles and so on. In spite of having such facilities, it would be a failure on one's part if he or she doesn't check, whether the officers in the field are getting these facilities or not. The Investigating Officers and the prosecutors are the personnel, who actually need vehicles. This requires serious consideration for providing them with vehicles and other required facilities. The senior officer should check with them, to ensure that they are not suffering for want of any of the basic facilities.

While in the field, the investigating officers have to spend a lot of time, away from their families. In many cases, they do not have the facilities of accommodation, transport, etc. In today's context, each of them should have gadgets like laptop and mobile phone etc. Although, things are improving now, yet there is need to do more to improve the working conditions. The irony is that in many cases, the officers even do not have a constable to provide drinking water and tea from the canteen. Particularly, it becomes quite difficult, when witnesses are being examined by them. One more thing. It is high time that the misuse of constables at the residences of the officers, under the pretext of security etc., is done away with. They should be used for the official work only. We have to maintain the dignity of service. Here, I must say that sometimes, we had to face such type of officers who always abused and treated their subordinates like slaves. In my opinion the CBI can acquire officers from outside, with managerial and administrative qualities, experience and attitude, and who are capable of adjusting to a different type of working atmosphere and culture. I am also of the firm opinion that there is no justification in making the CBI, a dumping ground. Recently, number of officers were taken from SSB as Investigating Officers. The process is on. There is also an attempt to get the deputationists absorbed over looking the claims of large number of professionally competent and experienced Investigating Officers/Inspectors, for promotion to the rank of Deputy Superintendent of Police. It is high time to wake up!!!

Chapter 3

Role of Investigating Officers and Problems faced by them

I recollect that as Investigating Officers, we used to go on tour, often without getting reservations in trains, spending nights at railway platforms and searching for cheaper hotels at various places as the travelling allowances were meagre. But, nobody bothered about such difficulties faced by the Investigating Officers. The funds under the head "TE" for re-imbursing the expenditures incurred by the officers on tour, exhausted within six months or so and then we had to spend from our pocket and wait for months for further funds to come. We used to get orders to perform journeys in lower classes, because of the lack of funds. These problems are not new, they have been there for decades now. Even today, the Investigating Officers have to go on tours, most of the time without reservation, arguing with the ticket collectors in trains and then wait for months to get their TA bills re-imbursed, because funds are not usually available. Adequate funds, in this category or head have not been and are not being made available by the Government. Nobody sees to it that if a task is assigned to the officers, they should not be made to suffer on account of non-availability of funds or facilities. The officers and Investigating Officers remain on tour for months together and on return again proceed on another tour within a week and so their bills should be paid immediately. What is needed is to check whether the funds made available are inadequate or there is mis-management in disbursement of funds, internally. Notably, there are branches engaged in local work only and on the other side there are those who take up national level assignments, involving lot of touring and long stays outside, in various states.

Plainly speaking, the Investigating Officers play vital role in any investigating organisation. Once the investigation is over, the Prosecutor comes on the scene. Even during investigation, the Investigating Officer and the Prosecutor, in many cases, have to work in collaboration and it is this close co-ordination which results in a successful investigation. In fact, even after investigation, it is this team work, which results in successful prosecution of a case. But they live in the same society, from which they get the informer, complainant, witnesses and also the accused. Therefore the society should help these officers. I was talking about the Investigating Officers and the prosecutors. There is a sort of identity crisis. It is high time that we try to understand this and regard, respect their contribution to the society and make their life easy, comfortable and happy so that the out put could be better. They are the back-bone of the organisation.

A major problem is that there are number of competent officers, working in the same rank for more than fifteen years. There is stagnation with no scope for promotion. Obviously, promotion is one factor, which motivates an officer to work with dedication. It should be given in time, otherwise they end up in frustration. Those who work hard should be encouraged and rewarded. But, unfortunately, the Investigating Officers, who worked very hard for a long time, got gifts in the form of all type of diseases, like hypertension, heart problem, diabetes, eye ailments, liver and kidney problems etc. while, their families also suffered. Out of the total strength of Investigating Officers, about 25 per cent to 30 per cent have always remained vacant, which is the case even now. There is also a need to relax the eligibility conditions, as a one time measure, if necessary and promote all deserving officers and fill up these vacancies. More officers should be recruited in the rank of Sub-inspectors and they should subsequently be trained, they should be provided with facilities and with an atmosphere conducive to independent functioning within the framework of law. Further, their career must be made more fruitful as well as field of operation be expanded. Those who are fit for the job should be promoted, every five years, upto the rank of SSP. Then promotions should be considered after every eight years of service upto the rank of Joint Directors, in accordance with merit. Thereafter, according to merit and seniority and in view of vacancies. In the rank of DIG there should be 50 per cent CBI officers and in the rank of Joint Directors and Additional Directors/Special Directors there should be a 25 per cent quota for CBI officers. If that much is done, I am sure, the organisation will shine. Officers are taken on deputation from CISF, CRPF, BSF, ITBP, RPF, Railways, Customs, Central Excise etc. From state police forces, officers in rank of senior sub-inspectors and Inspectors do not come. Most of the stuff is absorbed. In such a situation, how can you expect any specialised agency like CBI, to function, effectively. There has been no positive approach in recruiting about eighty or more sub-inspectors, directly every year and if this would have been done, then the department would not have needed to beg from any other organisation to send officers on deputation. I do agree that such directly recruited officers, who are highly educated, intelligent and hardworking, may not be 'yes' men. Well, technical persons can be taken on deputation for the Technical Cell in the CBI. Besides that, there is no need to take outside staff as Investigating Officers. CBI cadre should be built up, now.

It is high time that the organisation looks after the health and well-being of the investigating and prosecuting officers and all the officers and personnel, down the line. Because a healthy worker will produce more result oriented output, which will in turn be in the interest of the organisation. Having a gym in the office is not the only answer. Regular yoga classes, periodical medical check ups and facilities for appropriate treatment appear to be the right efforts to solve, this problem. Coming back to the problem of stagnation in promotions, it may be added that instead of solving this serious matter, separate posts of Additional SP and also that of Senior SP were created, which could not solve the problem. In any Central Government Department, the Central Government employees, who are competent and deserving should be given promotions. This would result in better outcomes. Investigation and prosecution are inter-connected and supplementary to each other and so, there is an absolute need to concentrate on both these fields of work for getting effective results. Thus, all the above opportunities should be provided to the prosecutors also. There is need to have departmental prosecutors for ensuring better results in lower courts. Although for handling cases in superior courts the organisation engages senior counsels yet depending on private lawyers to handle CBI cases in lower courts is not a good idea.

Thank God, the conditions have somehow improved. Earlier, we had seen very bad days when the life was very tough as there was no sense of welfare measures and nobody bothered about the family of an Investigating Officer, when he was on a long tour. There was no communication facility available like now and the family problems came to be known, only when the officer returned home from tour. Earlier, getting accommodation was also a great problem but now a CBI colony is there and DDA flats were also allotted to the CBI and as far as I recollect these steps were taken during the tenure of Shri R.D. Singh as Director. Then promotions were very rare and we lost several years in the process. Besides working against all odds, non-availability of facilities like accommodation, transportation and food etc., we were expected to arrange for these things on our own. It was the case with the Supervising Officers, who might visit a place for supervision of the case. Forgetting about his own facilities, the Investigating Officer had to see that the boss gets good accommodation, proper transport and good, hygienic food and timely reservation in trains etc. Earlier, the facilities were either not there at all or were limited. Now, guest houses etc., are available but still the system continues.

Inder Dev, Advocate, a practitioner at the High Court Bench at Lucknow was killed while on his way back home, in May 2002, outside the High Court complex. The investigation was entrusted to the CBI. Investigation revealed that there were disputes regarding property. A thorough investigation brought to light the involvement of one Manna Lal, an Advocate. The murder had been carried out by the gang of Vikram Yadav at the instance of the aforesaid advocate Manna Lal. The gang of Vikram Yadav, Brijesh, Chotu and Ved Prakash was traced. The team was camping at Lucknow. One day in May 2003, I received a call from DIG, Loknath Behera, who was on leave, that the team had met with an accident and a Head Constable had died on the spot and other team members had been wounded badly. The DIG had called me, as an injured ASP had somehow managed to inform him. Soon after, the local Sub-inspector of Police on duty, and the SHO of the concerned Police Station of the area informed me that the dead body of the Head Constable was lying at the Police Station and they were trying to retrieve the badly damaged Maruti van, which had got stuck in between two trees and the Inspector, who was sitting on the front seat was seriously injured and the ASP, whose left leg had been fractured due to the accident, had managed to jump down from the van and the Sub Inspector's right leg was badly affected. He also told me that the left hand of the Inspector had got stuck up and it was difficult to save it. In the given situation, I requested him to do his best to save the officers and take steps to move the officers to the nearest hospital for proper treatment. He also told me that the nearby villagers were helping him in the rescue operation. He did an excellent job and later informed me that he had managed to move all the officers to King George Hospital in Lucknow. I immediately instructed the other members of the team to rush to King George Hospital and handle the situation. Senior officers directed DIG, CBI, Lucknow to make all required arrangements. The Investigating Officer Vijay Kumar, then DSP (now retired as SSP) alongwith one Inspector, one Sub Inspector and one Head Constable were chasing the gang to nab them. It was early in the morning and the driver lost control of the vehicle and rammed the van in between two adjacent trees. The Inspector, who was from Sikkim police on deputation in the CBI died in hospital. Necessary assistance was provided to affected families. The dead bodies were brought to Delhi and taken to their respective places by officers. The injured DSP and the Sub Inspector were treated at the hospital. They had suffered badly. They had to undergo long treatment, on their own. It may be mentioned here that there was no arrangement to look after and provide proper treatment to the officers in such cases. We would make a show for few days and forget about it soon. They had to suffer themselves. The investigation of the case required to be continued. Inspector M.S. Phartyal, Inspector Kailash Sahu and Sub Inspector Naresh Indora faced the trauma of the incident, as they were members of the team, but, fortunately, were not in the van and therefore it was pretty difficult for them to forget the sufferings undergone by their team. I recollect them telling me that the Inspector while struggling for his life, in the hospital, was urging them not to leave the gang. The brave officers were ready for their duty within two days and they tracked down the gang, arrested all the gangsters and subsequently, we charge sheeted them along with others involved in the crime. I salute these officers. The case was under trial in a Lucknow court. The officers, injured there suffered throughout and are still suffering. The question is: are we not bound to pay attention to such problems? There are so many instances. Even at present, Inspector Ramesh Kumar, a good and sincere investigating officer, who suddenly had a stroke, is in the hospital in a completely paralysed state. How many senior officers know about it or have visited him in the hospital and are helping his family. Recently, a DIG rank IPS officer suddenly fell sick and died due to cancer. So much of care and assistance was given to him and the family was and is being looked after. It is a good gesture. We should take care of our men. But how many CBI cadre officers, who are sick, are being taken care of?

Chapter 4

Years under various Directors

When I joined CBI, late Shri F.V. Arul was the Director till 06.05.1971. He was a great and sincere officer. He was followed by D. Sen (late), a true professional and every body was scared of him. I was posted to the General Offences Wing of CBI, at Madras (now Chennai) and handled anti-corruption cases including cheating, forgery etc. Then I was transferred to the Economic Offences Wing in Madras where we investigated economic frauds including crimes related to imports and exports. It was then that Director D. Sen inspected that branch and observed that I should work in a Central Branch and I was transferred to the Central Investigation Unit (Crimes) in Delhi in 1976 and then worked in the Special Investigation Unit-1 where we handled fraud cases. After Mr. Sen, Mr. S.N. Mathur held charge for about 2 months. With the change of the Government in 1977, a new Cell was created to investigate cases against Indira Gandhi, Sanjay Gandhi and other cases related to or crimes committed during the Emergency. I was posted to that Cell called the Special Investigation Cell. Shri C.V. Narasimhan became the Director and remained so from May 1977 to November 1977. He said we are, in a way, at war and should not ask for facilities. We investigated Jeep scandal case relating to misuse of official position and obtaining favour in the form of vehicles during the election by the then Prime Minister. Former Prime Minister was arrested in that case but there was no specific instructions regarding the prayer to be made in the Court and therefore the Court released her. We also investigated the Road Roller scam and cases connected with Maruti Company of Sanjay Gandhi. We also investigated the Congress Souvenir case, which was against some ministers relating to fund collection for the Souvenir of the Congress Party from Corporate bodies by putting pressure. After him, John Lobo was the Director from November 1977 to June 1979. He had also worked in the CBI earlier and was thorough in his work. The above cases continued besides other cases. There was change in the political set-up. Then RD Singh (late) became the Director and remained so till January 1980, for a short period. He was a good officer and during his period, the CBI got many facilities. Then JS Bawa became the Director, with the change of Government at the Centre. Congress Government had come to power. The cell was dismantled and all officers were transferred except for 2-3 including me and we were asked to handle all those cases as we were connected with their investigation etc. New special public prosecutors were appointed in place of earlier ones. I recollect the scenes created in the CBI Special Court in Dehradun, whenever Sanjay Gandhi appeared there in the Road Roller case. The cases ended up in closure and or discharged as the special prosecutors did not argue for proceeding with the cases. Then, we investigated different type of cases and some against the earlier set-up. Some murder cases were also investigated by me and others. I investigated 2 murder cases of Hyderabad and one Nurse missing case of Kerala on the orders of the Supreme Court of India. Mr. Bawa remained as Director from January 1980 to February 1985. He was an efficient and able administrator.

Terrorist Crimes

It was in 1984 that the CBI was exposed to terrorist crime investigation after the Blue Star Operation. It was a new field. Shri Bawa was the Director. A new unit then called, Punjab Unit was created. As many cases came up, a full–fledged Cell named as Special Investigation Cell-II was created in 1985 for dealing with terrorist cases. I was posted to that cell. It was also called Punjab

Cell. The earlier cell became Special Investigation Cell-I. Number of terrorist cases of Punjab were taken up and large number of hardcore terrorists were arrested by us. We filed charge sheets against number of terrorists. M.G. Katre was the Director from February 1985 to October 1989. A dynamic officer and it was a tough time for the CBI. Some weapons were purchased for the officers in the Cell. We were trained in handling weapons. We used to go and operate openly in Punjab. At the initial stage the local police were not co-operative and did not have the firing power whereas the terrorists were using AK-47 rifles. The .303 rifles had become out-dated. Besides the Blue Star operation case, we also investigated the case against hardcore terrorist Sarabjit Singh of Jammu who was trained in Pakistan for terrorist activities in India. On return to India, he alongwith Mithbain Singh of Jammu committed a number of terrorist crimes in Jammu. He also prepared a note in Gurmukhi, provoking the Sikh jawans to revolt against the Government for the Blue Star operation and distributed copies of the said seditious note in the Sikh Regiment of the Army resulting in a revolt by some Sikh soldiers in Jammu who marched to the Pakistan border in Jammu. Sarabjit Singh was also chargesheeted for this. The Cell also used to hold co-ordination meetings regularly which were attended by Director Generals of Police of terrorist crime affected states and other senior officers and information about terrorist activities, details of gang members, hide-outs, details of associates etc., were shared with the affected and participating states. It was quite useful for the concerned states. We also shared the information received from one state with the other state which needed such information. The co-ordinated activities resulted in a consolidated effort to handle the menace. We investigated General Vaidya murder case and also the Punjab National Bank, Ludhiana, Punjab dacoity case. Hardcore terrorists Harjinder Singh alias Jinda and others had looted about 6 crores from that bank. They used to loot from the public, banks etc., and procure latest weapons and terrorise the people. When Harjinder Singh alias Jinda was arrested in an encounter, from CBI side I and Shri A.K. Ohri interrogated him in the Army Hospital. For security reasons, he was admitted in the Army Hospital. He told us that they have tracked the residential addresses of the CBI terrorist cell officers and also told us where the children of these officers are studying etc. When we asked him as to why they did not harm or kill the CBI officers investigating those cases, he told us that Bhindranwale had instructed them that CBI officers are not their enemies at that time. When we asked him as to when the CBI officers became their enemies, he replied that Bhindranwale had told them that if any of their cases investigated by the CBI ends in conviction or if any of their men dies in CBI custody, then CBI will become their enemy and they should not hesitate to kill the CBI officers in question. While we were investigating the Bank dacoity case, one terrorist was killed in an encounter and he was reportedly involved in that case. They felt that he was in CBI custody and he went on asking us about it when we told him that he was not in CBI custody. Then he told us that thinking that CBI had killed him, they had tracked and followed a CBI vehicle to attack it at a secluded place and the vehicle turned and moved towards Chandigarh on which they overtook the vehicle and found that CBI Chandigarh co-ordination cell officers were in it and therefore they left it and came back. He said that if we had been there they would have pumped the vehicle with bullets from AK-47 rifles. We had a local co-ordination office in Chandigarh headed by a DIG there and they also used to coordinate with the Punjab police and interrogate the terrorists arrested by the Punjab Police, etc. The attempt to attack us is not strange because when I arrested Bhai Mohkam Singh, right hand man of Bhindranwale and kept him in custody in Jammu as the case was in Jammu, Manbir Singh of Khalistan Commando Force and his men attacked the Jammu CBI office at 01.15 AM covering themselves with blankets armed with AK - 47 rifles and on seeing them, the J&K Police armed guards who were guarding the office with .303 rifles left their rifles and ran away. They had searched the office but I alongwith M.K. Bhat, the then Inspector had left the office just 15 minutes before that through the backside exit. On a complaint from the guards, the J&K police had enquired into this incident and found it to be correct. There were other attempts also. Coming back to Jinda, he told us that CBI officers do not have weapons but only identity cards and they were not scared of CBI. After this, I recollect, some imported weapons were procured and we were trained at the BSF centre. Some Bullet Proof jackets were also purchased. The Government permitted the officers to take official journies by air etc. I recollect Jinda having told us that we go with security, but they can take position at a distance and fire from AK - 47 rifles and one bullet will definitely hit us. Security was not of any help. He also told us to place two guards with AK - 47 rifles in front of his bed and he will escape through the gap between them though he was on a stretcher with bullets inside both his thighs due to the encounter. That was their mental make up and they were ready to die. I recollect that in the Gen. Vaidya murder case, two terrorists were traced and detained in New Arc, New Jersey, USA and extradition proceedings started there and the Courts ordered for extradition but the accused were not extradited. It was in 1987-89. Later on when Mr. Bill Clinton, the President of America visited India in March 2000, some victims of terrorist crimes put pressure and on his return to US, the US Government ordered extradition and asked the Indian Government to send the team immediately. Team of officers went and brought the two accused. It took years for them to understand the problem of terrorism. We also investigated the case of attempt on the life of Shri Rajiv Gandhi at Rajghat, Delhi and chargesheeted the accused. A case of funding of terrorists in Punjab by Mrs. Kuldeep Kaur of London was also investigated.

In the meantime, in 1990 we were asked to investigate the terrorist cases of Jammu & Kashmir. We investigated a number of cases of Srinagar and arrested a number of terrorists and charge sheets were filed in the Courts. Some such cases of North-East were also investigated. Air Force personnel murder case, HMT General Manager's murder case, All India Radio, Srinagar Director's murder case, Vice Chancellor Mushir-ul-Haq murder case etc., were some of the cases of Srinagar which were investigated. A case of ambush by ULFA activists in Assam killing police officers was one of the important cases of North-East to be investigated. The Minister was the target but they missed him. About 57 terrorist cases including two POTA cases were investigated by the CBI. Many cases are still pending in various courts. When Ashwani Kumar became Director, he reviewed these cases. On account of blasts and terrorist crimes at that time, these cases were also frequently reviewed by the Ministry of Home Affairs and I recollect having attended number of such meetings alongwith the Director and effective action was taken in those cases.

We had an effective information sharing system with the terrorist crime affected states which yielded good results in tracking, arresting and prosecuting the terrorists. CBI was the Nodal agency in this regard.There used to be a terrorist crime monitoring system. The same and or similar system of collection of intelligence and exchange or sharing of the same with the concerned state police agencies for effective handling of terrorist activities and curtailing them should be introduced in the CBI itself by creating a separate Zone in the CBI for this purpose rather than creating NCTC which is in controversy. Since CBI is an investigating and prosecuting agency as well as an intelligence collecting agency, the states should come forward to participate in it which would be in the interest of the country and such system or arrangement should only be used to handle terrorist activities on a national level network without playing any politics. We had such an arrangement and CBI interacts with all such state police agencies in many matters and also co-ordinates the Interpol channel network system. Therefore, this will be a good idea and it will also not disturb the Federal policing system.

Terrorists used to get funds from sympathisers and or sympathisers abroad or other persons in Pakistan in person and or through Hawala transactions and there was lot of information on this. We used to receive good and relevant information about terrorist activities, hide outs from Royal Canadian Mounted Police (RCMP) of Canada through their officers in Delhi which helped in handling terrorist activities, movements, network and cases. The information was shared with the concerned states and also presented in the meetings held. Canada was being used by the terrorists as one of their bases. A case of funding of terrorist activities was registered in 1991 and investigated. I recollect having arrested Moolchand Shah, the kingpin of Hawala transactions in Bombay. He was brought to Delhi and interrogated. Many things came out. During searches in that case a diary was seized from the house of Jains which later on became famous. In the meantime, after Katre, Dr. A.P. Mukherjee became the Director in October 1989 and remained so till January 1990, for a short period. He had vast experience of CBI functioning as he had worked in CBI. Then R. Shekhar was the Director till December 1990. He had also served in the CBI. Vijay Karan was the Director thereafter till June 1992.

It was during his tenure that we investigated the Rajiv Gandhi assassination case. A Special Investigation Team (SIT) was constituted for investigation, which was headed by D.R. Karthikeyan and consisted of a number of other officers of various ranks. I was also transferred to the SIT. It functioned under the control and supervision of S.K. Datta, the then Additional Director and Vijay Karan, Director. Both of them camped continuously in Chennai and contributed significantly to the successful detection of the case. Everybody contributed, individually and collectively. It was a good investigation. But there were clues indicating involvement of LTTE, within few days of taking up the investigation. The photographs taken by accused Hari Babu pin pointed the accused, when these were published and information started to pour in. We received good information from Sri Lankan police. Much information about the movement of the accused was received. Unfortunately, the two important accused Sivarasan and Subha could not be arrested as they committed suicide before they could be arrested. We should also remember the police officers including the SP who lost their lives while providing security to Rajiv Gandhi. The DIG and the IG who were also on duty were at a distance. A very sad incident. The case ended in conviction. Chief Minister of Punjab Beant Singh's murder case was another important case of similar nature professionally investigated by the CBI, by a team of very few officers. This case also ended in conviction. I may explain here that there were and are large number of important or sensitive cases which were detected or are being detected by a team of 3 or 4 officers. There has been shortage of officers. All important cases need a good team for effective output. Since everybody cries for CBI investigation, people may be thinking that the CBI has thousands of investigating officers. We always go on shifting officers from one team to another to keep up with the pressures. Quality of execution of any assignment depends on the continuity of the team. This applies to prosecution work also. In the meantime, S.K. Datta became Director in June 1992 and remained so till July 1993.

Ramjanam Bhumi-Babri Masjid Case

On 6th December 1992, Ramjanam Bhumi-Babri Masjid disputed structure in Ayodhya was demolished, during a *karseva*.

The case relating to the demolition, registered at the police station of the area against lacs of *karsevaks* name and addresses not known was transferred to the CBI on 13.12.92. A Special Investigation Cell was created for investigation of the case. It was called as Special Investigation Cell-IV or Ayodhya Cell. I was transferred to that cell and nominated as the Chief Investigating Officer of the case. S.K. Datta had worked in the CBI for long and was familiar with the process of investigation and had handled terrorist cases also. When he retired, Vijaya Rama Rao became the Director on 31.07.1993 and remained so till 31.07.1996.

In August 1993, 48 more cases related to the demolition case or connected with the incident were also taken up for investigation and were marked to me for investigation. To explain it, immediately after the demolition of the Ramjanam Bhumi-Babri Masjid structure at Ayodhya on 6.12.1992, Crime No. 197/92 was registered at Police Station Ramjanam Bhumi at 17:15 hours against lacs of *karsevaks* name and adresses unknown, on a complaint given by Priyamvada Nath Shukla, Station Officer of the jurisdictional Police Station. After 10 minutes, at 1725 hours, another case Crime No. 198/92 was registered at the same police station against 8 named accused persons namely L.K. Advani, Dr. M.M. Joshi, Vinay Katiyar, Ashok Singhal, V.H. Dalmia, Giriraj Kishore, Ms. Uma Bharti, Sadhvi Rithambara, on the complaint given by Ganga Prasad Tiwari, the then Station Officer-in-charge of Ramjanam Bhumi Police Chowki, regarding shouting of provocative slogans from the stage nearby over the public address system resulting in rioting and storming of the structure by the *karsevaks* and demolition of the same and therefore for creating communal disharmony, affecting national integration and creating enmity between the two communities, causing fear etc., as covered under Sections 153–A, 153–B and 505 of the Indian Penal Code. During the course of demolition, the media persons who were taking photographs of what was going on or videographing the same were assaulted and their cameras, reels etc were destroyed. With regard to this, 47 media persons had filed complaints in the police stations.The main case of demolition Crime No. 197/92 was entrusted to the CBI on 13.12.1992 whereas Crime No. 198/92 was investigated by the Crime Branch, Uttar Pradesh who filed a charge sheet/report under Section 173 of the Code of Criminal Procedure on 27.2.1993, against the same 8 accused persons for offences under Sections 153 A, 153 B, 505, 147, 149 Indian Penal Code, in the Special Court so created for that case at Lalitpur. This was pending in the Court, sitting of which was shifted to Rae Bareli in July, 1993. During the course of investigation of Crime No. 197/92, the CBI came across evidence of conspiracy to demolish the structure, planning, training of selected *karsevaks*, statements, assertions, speeches and shouting of such provocative slogans by the leaders etc., before 6th December and thereafter on 6th December from the dais or otherwise, assault on media persons to prevent them from recording what was going on, etc. etc. The video cassettes so collected contained extra-judicial confessions of some accused about the conspiracy to demolish the structure and therefore CBI added offence under section 120-B IPC to the FIR of Crime No.197/92 (CBI case No. 8(S)/1992) and continued investigation. Subsequently, on 25.8.1993, the State Government *vide* notifications transferred investigation of Crime No. 198/92 and the other 47 media assault cases to the CBI. After investigation in all the 49 cases mentioned above, the CBI filed a consolidated charge-sheet on 5.10.1993 against 40 accused persons in the Special Court at Lucknow, for commission of offences under Sections 120-B, 153 A, 153 B, 505, 295, 295 A, 147 Indian Penal Code and some of the accused identified, to be the demolishers were also charged for offences under Sections 332, 338, 395 Indian Penal Code also, as all the offences were found to have been committed in the course of same transaction considering the continuity of acts, proximity of time and unity of purpose and they could not have been separated from one another. A Special Court of Magistrate and another that of a Additional Sessions Judge were created at Lucknow for inquiring into and disposing of all cases relating to demolition of the structure, so investigated or charge sheeted by the CBI. On this, the Rae Bareli Court transferred all the records of Crime No. 198/92 to the Lucknow Court. Subsequently, after further investigation, a supplementary charge sheet was filed against 9 more accused making the total number of accused as 49. The Special Judge at Lucknow ordered on 9.9.1997 for framing of charges against all the accused for all the offences. This was challenged by 33 accused persons in the High Court and the High Court *vide* judgement dated 12.2.2001, found technical defect in transfer of Crime No. 198/92 to the Lucknow Special Court and struck down all proceedings in that case. The High Court, however, observed that this defect could be rectified by the State Government by issuing a fresh notification. This judgement was not challenged by the CBI as per the decision taken at that time. One Mohd. Aslam Bhure filed SLP in the Supreme Court against the above said order dated 12.2.2001 of the High Court stating that there was consultation with the High Court for establishing a Special Court for inquiring into and disposing of all the cases relating to demolition of the disputed structure at Ayodhya, so investigated by the CBI and, therefore, there was no need to have consultation for entrusting each and every case belonging to that class of cases to the Special Court so created at Lucknow for the purpose, and therefore, the High Court judgement was erroneous. The CBI requested the Government of Uttar Pradesh to rectify the defect by issuing a fresh notification but this request was declined by the State Government stating that it was a conscious decision by the State Government to keep Crime No. 198/1992 separate. While this SLP was being heard in the Supreme Court, the State Government of Uttar Pradesh and the High Court appointed a Presiding Officer to the Special Court at Rae Bareli for Crime No. 198/92. On this, the Supreme Court on 29.11. 2002 ordered that there is a Special Court for this case at Rae Bareli and Mohd. Aslam cannot have any grievance on this point and dismissed the SLP. In view of these developments, the CBI filed a petition in the Rae Bareli Court requesting the Court to take appropriate steps to comply with the Supreme Court order. The Court directed the CBI to obtain the Court files relating to the case and thereafter ordered to file the report of further investigation in the case as the CBI had obtained permission for further investigation from the said Court in this case. Therefore, the CBI had to file a supplementary charge sheet in Crime No. 198/92 in the Rae Bareli Court against the 8 named accused persons as already charge-sheeted by the CB–CID. This was done because at that time the Revision petition filed by the CBI against the order of the trial Court not framing charges of criminal conspiracy against the 8 accused specially named in the FIR of Crime No. 198/92 and dropping of proceedings against the 13 more VIPs stating that they are the abettors and conspirators who provoked the demolishers from the dais, was pending for decision in the High Court and it was found not possible to separate the demolishers and the conspirators in the cases and to that extent in any case and try them at two different places and the CBI's case was that there was a single general conspiracy to demolish the structure that day. Subsequently, one of the accused was discharged by the Court but it was challenged by two witnesses and not by the CBI and the High Court ordered for framing of charges against all the 8 accused persons and the trial is going on there. 27 accused are facing trial at Lucknow and the 13 more are not being tried anywhere. The case of criminal conspiracy was broken into two. So many things happened in these cases. A final legal solution will come up in course of time to conclude the cases logically. When the Justice Liberhan Commission submitted its report, the Ministry of Home Affairs and the Home Minister wanted to know whether on the information mentioned in the Report anymore person could be charge-sheeted by the CBI out of those listed out in the Report. Possibility of making one person from the list as accused was to be explored. Examination of the report indicated that there is no material to bring in anymore person as accused in the case already pending in the Court. Symbolic *karseva* was allowed by the Hon'ble Supreme Court *vide* order dated 28.11.1992 and therefore making arrangement for the same was not an offence. Now, these cases are pending in various Courts and therefore no more comments are made about them.

Shri Vijaya Rama Rao was a true professional police officer and knew his job well. I recollect the late night sittings for days together that he had in the cell going through each and every document, cassettes etc., and giving points for investigation. He was welfare minded. He fought for and got government orders raising the pay of CBI cadre Superintendents of Police and increasing the quota in respect of CBI cadre officers in promotion. Perhaps, he was the only one Director who could sense and understand the contributions of the CBI cadre officers and wanted to give them what they really deserved.

Goa Child Sex Abuse Case

Another case of very sensitive nature investigated at that time related to sexual assault of children of an Orphanage for destitute children run by Dr. Freddy Peats of Goa, in Goa by himself and some foreign tourists who used to visit Goa. Investigation disclosed that certain type of injection was given to the children and they were sodomised and or forced to indulge in indecent acts. Syringes seized from the orphanage contained narcotic drug traces on examination by the Laboratory. One New Zealander and one Australian were extradited and they as well as Dr. Freddy Peats were convicted and sentenced to life imprisonment. Dominique Sebire, a French national involved in the crime was also arrested, but he managed to escape from India, while on bail on medical grounds, by procuring forged passport. Request for extradition was not agreed to by France.They said that there is no provision in their laws/legal system to extradite their citizens to another country. They refused to extradite him. They were requested to try him in that country according to their law. But nothing happened so far. Similarly, Yorgen Yogi, a German was also not extradited. He was traced and examined and he admitted having committed the crime but they did not take any action. We requested them to extradite Yorgen but they refused. We requested them to try him in that country but nothing happened. One Swedish was also traced but he was not extradited to India. We sent all the evidence to them, as requested by them but no action was taken by them. It came to light that such things are not offences there. One from Thailand involved in the case was once detained in London but he was released by them. Now, again he has been arrested by the British police and the request for his extradition is being considered and processed. This case was considered to be very serious by the international community and specially by the international police.

Uttarakhand Agitation Cases

We also investigated about 64 cases related to atrocities on Uttarakhand agitationists. Arun Bhagat was the Special Director during this time. He was a seasoned officer and guided us properly and effectively. We had to convince the High Court of Allahabad that it will not be possible for the CBI to take up hundreds of cases related to the incidents but only important and sensitive cases could be taken up without disturbing other cases under investigation by the CBI. After investigation, chargesheets were filed in the cases of molestation, rape, murder, police firing etc.

After Vijay Rama Rao, Joginder Singh became the Director on 31.07.1996 and remained so till 30.06.1997. There was change of Government at the Centre and he and both the Additional Directors, at that time, were from Karnataka cadre.

Cochin Spying Case

I recollect an important case of spying by some French national accused off the shores of Cochin (Kochi), Kerala which was transferred to the CBI. Using sophisticated equipments and *Vessel*, they mapped the sea bed in front of Southern Naval Command and collected details of magnetic anomalies at different points. According to experts it affected our Naval operations. They stated that they were collecting data for Aqua culture possibilities at that place for breeding King Fish and Mackeral. According to experts it was false, keeping in mind the high current and high waves at that place and that such fish were not available there. They were chargesheeted for various offences. One of them stated that they were searching for the *Vessel of Vascodagama* which had sunk in that area with diamonds etc., worth thousands of crores. Analysis of the data collected by them indicated that they had traced a ship with a flag on it. If they were not spotted and checked, they might have taken away the said national resources from there. On the request of the French Government and on furnishing of undertaking by the French Ambassador in India and the assurance of Government of India, the High Court permitted them to go to France for four months which was extended by another two months. They wanted to meet their families.The French Ambassador had given an undertaking that the French government will make them available for the trial on expiry of that period. But they never turned up. The French Government refused to extradite them. So the case has been pending. It is strange that foreigners could come and conduct survey within our waters and we did not know about that. But for the interception by a Navy helicopter, they would have taken away the diamonds etc. I recollect that we wrote to the Indian Institute of Oceanography and also to the Navy, through proper channel, asking them whether the national assets could be retrieved from the sea but they expressed that they will not be able to sustain a long stay at that depth for checking and retrieving the assets as it required the divers to stay for long down the water at so much of depth. Well, this national asset worth crores were still there, which could not be retrieved.

We did not put pressure on the French Government to send the two accused to India to face trial, as promised by them. It is nothing but a fraud. I recollect that the French President was to visit India and before he arrived, the French Government wanted that the two accused be taken out of the country as there was hue and cry in that country. Indian Government agreed and on the assurance given by the French Government, we moved the High Court of Kerala for releasing them for four months and the High Court agreed. But later on, they said that they cannot extradite their nationals. Very sad. If an Indian is involved, we would have immediately put him on the next available flight and sent him. We are very poor in such policy decisions. We are taken for granted for such lenient considerations. We should be strong and fight to save our commitments and reputation. Here, I recollect that Mrs. Kuldeep Kaur, a Kenyan National of Indian origin, married to a popular Indian leader in Southall in London was arrested at Indira Gandhi International Airport at New Delhi, on the allegation of funding terrorist activities in India. The case was transferred to CBI and I investigated the case. It was found that she had been visiting India frequently. She had met a terrorist, who was a British national, lodged in Jammu jail in a terrorist case in disguise as junior advocate of Shri Bhim Singh, senior advocate. She acquired a false name and along with Shri Bhim Singh went to the jail and met the terrorist. She stayed in a hotel as an Indian national. Offences under the Foreigners Act, impersonation etc., were made out. At that time, Mrs. Margaret Thatcher, the then Prime Minister of United Kingdom wrote to Shri Rajiv Gandhi, the then Prime Minister of India to free Mrs. Kuldeep Kaur and allow her to go back to London. There were several meetings. Shri Katre was the Director. We told the government that there is a criminal case. Shri Chidambaram was the Minister of State in-charge of CBI. There was a meeting with him and the Prime Minister and the Government wanted the case to be withdrawn and we told that a written order is required because a report is to be filed in the Court for its consent to withdraw the case in public interest. As per Section 321 CrPC, cases can be withdrawn in public interest.

The Government decided to withdraw the case and as decided, the Home Secretary gave an order in writing that the Government of India has accepted the unconditional apology given by Mrs. Kuldeep Kaur and decided to allow her to go back to UK and necessary action to withdraw the case be taken. We filed a detailed report in the Court, enclosing the order of the Government and requested the Court to allow withdrawal of the case. The Court felt that even if there is no evidence that she was funding terrorist activities, there is evidence of commission of other offences and therefore it will direct the Chief Judicial Magistrate to take further legal action according to law. Finally, on our request, the Special Judge under the TADA Act accepted the report and allowed to withdraw the case. Immediately she was released from the Jammu jail, brought to Delhi and put on the next flight to London. Tickets were arranged by a former Indian High Commissioner to UK. Will any Indian citizen get such a treatment in a foreign country?

I had become Superintendent of Police in 1993 and supervised investigation and trial of many sensitive cases. I recollect that the facilities that Shri Vijay Rama Rao got for CBI cadre officers were withdrawn, subsequently by his successor.

Uphar Cinema Tragedy Case, Rungta Kidnapping Case and Ajit Sarkar Murder Case

After Joginder Singh, R.C. Sharma became the Director on 30.06.1997 and continued till January 1998. One of the cases investigated during this period was the Uphar Cinema fire tragedy case. Though it sounds to be a small case, practically it was a tough case as it had many angles to be probed into to reach at the main cause of fire and deaths. Many agencies were involved in granting a licence to a cinema hall. Therefore the role of each of such agencies for the structural deviations and lapses in fire safety measures in the building were to be investigated. Thereafter, D.R. Karthikeyan became the Director for a short duration from 31.01.98 to 31.03.98 and thereafter Dr. T.N. Mishra was the Director till 04.01.1999. Number of cases remained with the CBI in different branches over the years, at different times both sensitive or otherwise. In 1998, N.R. Rungta kidnapping case was effectively and efficiently investigated by the branch where I was posted. He was a businessman and Vishwa Hindu Parishad leader from Varanasi. He was called from his office down and kidnapped by Mukhtar Ansari, MLA, Uttar Pradesh and his gang. There were ransom calls and some of them were tape–recorded. Even after receiving the ransom amount, the gang did not release him. The family paid the ransom money without informing the police. Neither the dead body of Rungta was recovered nor his whereabouts were known. The accused arrested disclosed that the body of Rungta was thrown into the Ganges. Accused were chargesheeted. Another important case related to murder of Ajit Sarkar, MLA (CPM), Purnia, Bihar by Rajesh Ranjan alias Pappu Yadav (ex-MP) and his gang. Pappu Yadav was defeated in the election and he felt that Ajit Sarkar was responsible for it. Accused were chargesheeted and convicted after a lengthy trial. The Investigating Officers and the *pairvi* officer did a good job in this case. All these cases are very serious in nature and it is tough to investigate and detect these type of cases. The Investigating Officers remain under tension throughout the investigation struggling to collect evidence to detect the case.

Ranchi Teacher's Murder Case

From 04.01.1999 to 30.04.2001, Dr. R.K. Raghavan was the Director. NDA government was in power. Dr. Mishra remained just for 9 months and was transferred out. The most important case during this period was the IC 814 hijacking case. Mostly, Supervising Officers do not investigate cases. As SP, SSP and DIG, I had investigated 54 cases. This hijacking case was my 50th case as Supervising Officer and was an important case and therefore explained in detail in chapter 5. There were other cases as usual entrusted by the Constitutional Courts etc., There was a case of murder of Ranjana Palith, a teacher of Ranchi. On the face of it, it looked like a case of burning. There was hue and cry and the case was given to the CBI. On going through the post mortem report, we found that the cause of death was 50 percent due to burning and 50 percent due to bullet injury. In otherwords she was shot at and burnt. Therefore, the scene of crime was scanned and the dust, stone particles etc., around that were sent to the laboratory. On examination, the experts found a piece of damaged jacket of a bullet. The ballistic expert opined that it was part of a

.38 bore bullet. Such bullets belong to service weapons and therefore a police officer or so was involved. On further investigation, it was found that the local Police Station Sub Inspector was found with her in hotels etc., and he had an affair with her. On that day, she received a phone call and then she dressed nicely, wore jewellery like a bride and left the house. Then her body was found. The service revolver of the Sub-inspector in question was seized and sent to the Ballistic expert but the recovered bullet piece did not match with that. Then all the .38 bore revolvers of the Police Station and adjoining Police Stations were seized and sent to the Ballistic expert who matched the piece of bullet jacket with the weapon of another Sub Inspector of the same police station. That officer could not explain how his weapon was used. Finally, on arrest and interrogation, it was found that the other Sub-inspector who was a suspect had used the revolver of this Sub-inspector to commit the crime, by interchanging the revolvers without the knowledge of the innocent Sub-inspector. He was identified to be the person found with the victim in the hotel. He was chargesheeted and later on sentenced to life imprisonment by the Trial Court.

Madhumita Murder Case

During the period from 30.04.2001 to 06.12.2003 when P.C. Sharma was the Director, there was emphasis on disposal of cases pending investigation for more than two years. In the process, due to the drive many cases were disposed of and many of them ended in filing of chargesheet. The Director had vast experience of CBI investigation process and working as he had worked as SP and in above ranks including as Special Director. In the Special Investigation Cell-IV we handled large number of sensitive cases. Madhumita murder case involving ex-Minister of Uttar Pradesh Amarmani Tripathi was one of those cases. A professional investigation was carried out by the Investigating Officers Rajah Balaji and Hari Singh, who also efficiently and dedicatedly pursued the trial work in the court resulting in conviction of the accused.

DFO Murder Case

Sanjay Singh, Divisional Forest Officer, Bihar was murdered by the MCC Naxalites as he did not allow them to run a parallel government in that area. When he protested to the pasting of posters by them, he was forcibly taken to a nearby forest and shot dead. Two Naxalites were apprehended and later on convicted. The commander was also arrested, later on and chargesheeted. This was the first case under POTA, handled by the CBI.

I was promoted as Deputy Inspector General of Police in October 2003 and given charge of Special Crimes Region, Delhi. In this Region we handled so many important cases. All credit goes to the Investigating Officers and prosecutors who worked hard to detect the cases and carried out the trial work effectively leading to convictions.

To continue with the life in the organisation, under the leadership of various officers, I add that U.S. Misra became the Director on 06.12.2003 and continued to be so till 06.12.2005. He was a seasoned officer who knew his job and functioning of the CBI as he had worked with the CBI in various capacities. He was Special Director before becoming Director. He was a professional. We never felt any tension during his tenure. Discussions were all professional. A number of sensitive cases were handled in my Region during his time. Gohana, Haryana rioting case and a murder case which caused the rioting were investigated, the accused arrested and chargesheeted. One Highway robbery and double murder case in Gurgaon was also successfully detected. Garbeta, Midnapore (West Bengal) lynching case was investigated, finalised and charge sheeted. Andaman Arms Haul case was finalised and accused were charge sheeted.

Cash for MLAs Case of Chhattisgarh

We investigated the cash for MLAs case of Chhattisgarh in which ₹ 45 lakh were paid for purchasing six BJP MLAs for forming the Government and not to allow the BJP—which got the maximum seats—to form the Government. A letter was also given by the party which was defeated in the election expressing its support to such a Government to be formed and the conversation was tape–recorded by the other party. The letter was proved and the voice in the tape–recorded conversation was also proved and the amount was also seized. The facts which came out during investigation were as follows:

Assembly Elections were held in the State of Chhattisgarh and the results were declared on 5.12.2003, but as on 4.12.2003 the results in respect of the 90 seats had come up and the Congress (I) Party headed by Ajit Jogi had won 37 seats, BJP-50 seats, NCP–1 seat and BSP-2 seats. Immediately on seeing the result of the election Ajit Jogi tendered his resignation as Chief Minister on 4.12.2003 and the Governor Krishan Mohan Seth while accepting the resignation of Ajit Jogi asked him to continue as the Chief Minister till the formation of a new Government. Therefore, as on 4.12.2003, 5.12.2003 and 6.12.2003, there were hectic activities within the political parties for formation of a Government. There was possibility of an attempt to cause defection. Investigation disclosed that P.R. Khunte, BJP MP had shifted to Ajit Jogi's side during the election campaign in November 2003 and had taken part in various meetings in favour of Congress candidates. When questioned during investigation, P.R. Khunte explained that he was forcefully taken by Ajit Jogi and his men and made to campaign for them. However, according to Virendra Pandey, complainant, P.R. Khunte was on the side of Ajit Jogi.

According to the complainant Virendra Pandey, all the elected BJP MLAs were called to Raipur on 4.12.2003 for electing the leader/Chief Minister. On 5.12.2003 at about 4 PM, he received a telephone call from P.R. Khunte, MP who was with the Congress, who told Pandey that he (Pandey) can play a historic role in the formation of Government in the State. When he asked P.R. Khunte as to how, Khunte told him that if they try, Baliram Kashyap, MP, a Adivasi can become Chief Minister with the help of Ajit Jogi who has 37 MLAs including himself and Jogi was sure of getting support of two BSP MLAs and one NCP MLA. He told Pandey that if they managed to break and get defected six BJP MLAs, then it is possible to form a Government by Baliram Kashyap. Khunte also told him that Ajit Jogi had told him that he had already arranged with Ms Mayawati and it will be done. Pandey did not show more interest and told him to ring up after one and half hour. At that time, Pandey was sitting in a room in Piccadilly Hotel alongwith Kamleshwar Aggarwal, Ramesh Modi, Sunil Soni and Kailash Murarka. Khunte asked Pandey, before talking, whether there was anybody with him and he had told him that there was nobody and Pandey had come out of the room as the mobile signal was not clear. When Pandey came inside the room after the talk, he asked the above four persons whether they had any instrument for recording the telephone conversations and they said that they did not have the same.

About two hours thereafter, Pandey again received a call from Khunte who told the same thing and asked, whether Pandey had talked to anybody. Pandey told him that he did not talk to anybody and asked him to give a ring in the night at about 8 PM. Then it was decided that Khunte will talk to Pandey, the next morning. According to Pandey, he suspected some conspiracy by P.R. Khunte, Ajit Jogi and some others to cause defection in the BJP to get a Government of their choice formed in Chhattisgarh. Therefore, he wanted to tape record further conversations and the activities of P.R. Khunte and Ajit Jogi. He checked up and obtained such type of instrument from his friend and fixed it to his landline telephone no. 2442766 but there was no call from Khunte till 9 AM and Pandey suspected whether Khunte and Ajit Jogi had smelt something and therefore, made a call to Khunte and asked him to contact on the landline. Few minutes thereafter, he received a call on the landline phone from Khunte and he tape recorded the conversation which is in the audio cassette and he proved the same. Khunte told him that if necessary Ajit Jogi will talk to him and therefore, Pandey told Khunte to give his landline number to Ajit Jogi. About 5-6 minutes thereafter, Ajit Jogi telephoned to him. According to Pandey his suspicion about the conspiracy got strengthened. The conversation between him and Ajit Jogi is in the tape. Ajit Jogi promised support and that he will not ditch the Government to be formed. Pandey also asked whether Smt. Sonia ji has given green signal/*Hari jhandi* to which Ajit Jogi answered in the affirmative (I remember, some telephone calls were found to have been made to Delhi leaders including 10 Janpath number by Ajit Jogi from his telephone during that time and a slip of paper with telephone number of Ms. Mayawati was found and seized from the official residence of Ajit Jogi during search in this case). It was then that Pandey told Ajit Jogi that for persuading the MLAs, money was required. According to Pandey, he wanted to have a full picture of the conspiracy being hatched. Pandey was convinced that without clearance from the high command and the party president Smt. Sonia Gandhi, Ajit Jogi would not have taken such a decision at his end to give Congress (I) MLAs support. When Ajit Jogi asked as to how much money will be required, he told him that initially it may be about 15-20 lakhs and Ajit Jogi immediately agreed that he will arrange the same. Then Pandey told Ajit Jogi to send the money through P.R. Khunte as he felt that he could have some physical evidence of the conspiracy being hatched. Two hours thereafter, Khunte rang him up and told him that 20 lakhs have been received and asked him to go to Khanij Bhawan and from there make a call so that he can send the same through his son. Accordingly, Pandey arranged the vehicle of his friend Dr. Suresh Aggarwal and went in the said Maruti Zen car. On reaching Khanij Bhawan, he made a call to Khunte and Bunty. Om Prakash Khunte, s/o P.R. Khunte came in their car and brought two bags which were transferred to his car. Virendra Pandey brought the two bags and kept them in his house and sent back the vehicle to Dr. Suresh Aggarwal.

Immediately, Pandey telephoned to Dr Rajan Dubey, Member of State Working Committee on his mobile and requested him to come immediately with his car and he came within half an hour or so. Pandey explained the sequence of events to Dr. Dubey. Then Pandey and Dr. Dubey went to latter's house. On the way Pandey telephoned to Sanjay Joshi, All India General Secretary (Org) of BJP who was available in Raipur and requested him to come to Dr. Dubey's house and accordingly, he reached there. Pandey explained the situation to them and handed over the audio-tape to Sanjay Joshi. Since there was no light, Sanjay Joshi went to the house of Lakhiram Aggarwal, BJP leader for meals and took the tape with him. They discussed whether they should expose the conspiracy. Two hours thereafter, Sanjay Joshi telephoned to him and told him to go ahead to expose the conspiracy. Pandey kept in touch with Khunte and told him that he had talked to Baliram Kashyap and 5-6 other MLAs whereas he did not do so. But he wanted to convince Khunte, in order to unearth the conspiracy. He also told Khunte that if the MLAs are won over, they are to be segregated and kept in separate places and whether he had talked to Ajit Jogi. He also told him that it is necessary to meet Ajit Jogi to obtain a letter from Ajit Jogi confirming the support of Congress (I) to the rebel government to be formed and also the balance money. In the meantime, the complainant Pandey also talked to Baliram Kashyap, who had gone to his native place, from the mobile phone of Dr. Rajan Dubey and asked him to come to Raipur and also told him that if Khunte or Ajit Jogi telephone, he may tell them that Pandey had talked to him and on reaching Raipur further action will be taken. On the way Baliram Kashyap received a call from Ajit Jogi and he told him the same. Therefore, when Baliram Kashyap reached Pandey's house at about 7 PM, he told him that Ajit Jogi had contacted him promising support to make him Chief Minister. The complainant, on checking, found that there was a call on Baliram Kashyap's mobile from mobile phone no. 9425205048. Immediately he called that number which was received by Som Prakash Giri who promised to call back after half an hour after checking with Ajit Jogi. Thereafter, Baliram Kashyap and Virendra Pandey went to Dr. Rajan Dubey where, as decided, Baliram Kashyap talked to Ajit Jogi and asked about the place of meeting. Ajit Jogi said that after half an hour Som Prakash Giri will tell the place. Pandey explained that this talk was not taped as the instrument was kept at his house only. After sometime Giri informed them to go to Radiant School on the Uparwara Road and Ajit Jogi will come with the letter and money. Giri told Baliram Kashyap to come in his own car and Giri will accompany them from Bhagat Singh Chowk. Accordingly, they picked up Giri from the Chowk and informed Sanjay Joshi that they were going ahead. As fixed, Ajit Jogi came along with Amit Jogi. Pandey and Baliram Kashyap sat in Jogi's car and they discussed at length in the vehicle which kept on moving, being driven by Amit Jogi and Ajit Jogi gave a letter confirming support of Congress (I) to the Government to be formed under Baliram Kashyap. Amit Jogi said that the rebel MLAs will be taken and kept in Bangalore, secretly. Then Pandey and Kashyap were dropped at a place. The vehicle of Kashyap was following their vehicle. Amit Jogi then instructed his man to give the money and the said man made a call to somebody with his mobile and then came and sat in the vehicle of Kashyap, with them and at near Radiant School from a vehicle they were given ₹ 25 lacs. Both Pandey and Baliram Kashyap stated in detail the various promises made by Ajit Jogi and Amit Jogi and role of Som Prakash Giri. The driver and bodyguard of

Baliram Kashyap also proved the facts. Therefore, the incident stood proved by the complainant, Baliram Kashyap, Ghanaram Kaushik (bodyguard of Baliram Kashyap) and Lalit Mandavi (driver of Baliram Kashyap) and the role of P.R. Khunte, Ajit Jogi, Amit Jogi and Som Prakash Giri were established. Bureau Chief of Zee TV, Raipur who had tracked the activities has also proved the movement of the vehicles on Uparwara Road and also the presence of Surya Kant Tiwari and Som Prakash Giri at that place.

After receiving the money of ₹ 25 lakhs, Pandey made a call to Sanjay Joshi who asked them to go to BJP office for the press conference and in the press conference the audiotape was played in open to the media and the public and it was heard by the public and therefore, according to Pandey, there is no secret or fraudulent method used in the operation as they wanted to expose the illegal activities of Ajit Jogi. He explained that since the Government was in power at that time, the police would not have taken any action in the matter, and therefore, they decided to do it themselves and expose it before their government came to power. The money was also shown in the press conference and therefore, the transaction was proved to be genuine. As decided by the leaders and on legal advice, Pandey and Baliram Kashyap went to Anti Corruption Bureau, Raipur in the morning of 7.12.2003, after their Government was formed and filed a joint complaint and handed over the money of ₹ 45 lakhs and letter given by Ajit Jogi as well as copy of the cassette given to him at the BJP office. The ACB officers on registration of the case made transcription of the cassette and sealed it along with other items and it remained in sealed condition. During the course of investigation, the said copy of the cassette was found to be an edited copy and not the original cassette. One copy given to the Governor by Shri Arun Jaitley was also collected and after making enquiries, another copy could also be traced but these were copies only but the conversation related to the allegations in question and the voices have been proved, scientifically. According to Pandey, he had handed over the cassette to Sanjay Joshi and they had got about 50 or so copies of the cassette made from a shop in the market which were distributed and therefore the original cassette got mixed up and might have gone to one of the leaders or activists and is not traceable as subsequently many copies of the same might have been got prepared and circulated. The facts disclosed by the investigation are to be subjected to judicial pronouncements on facts and legally admissible evidence and therefore no more comments are made. Opinion of legal experts was also obtained but it was not so clear and the case remained under scrutiny. Till I retired, the case was pending for a decision.

Ram Avtar Jaggi Murder Case

Another important case was the one relating to the murder of Ram Avtar Jaggi, NCP leader in Raipur in which Amit Jogi and a large number of other accused were arrested and chargesheeted. The judgement delivered by the trial court in this case is under appeal and therefore no comments are made on the merit of the case. This is a sample case to show how initial investigation can be manipulated to charge-sheet innocent people who volunteered to become accused for money and therefore without commenting on the merit of the case against others, the story is that under pressure, the police facilitated projection of four persons arranged and hired from Varanasi and one from Raipur as the accused who had allegedly committed the murder. They were paid in lacs and the two persons who managed to get them were also paid by an influential person who was interested in making out a false story to shield some persons in connivance with some police officers. As per the plan they purchased an old vehicle, took it and set it on fire near Ambikapur to project that the accused while escaping to Varanasi, after the murder, had burnt the vehicle used by them in committing the murder. On getting information, the local police seized the burning vehicle. Therefore, on the advice of the concerned police officers, another old vehicle was purchased by the two agents who took it to the same area and burnt it. The police officers investigating the case went and took it on record. The plan was that these fake accused will confess and go to jail for three-four months and using influence they will be released through discharge from the case. However, this did not happen. They would have been convicted if the case was not transferred to the CBI. During CBI investigation, the two agents became approvers and unfolded the story and the five accused confessed before the court that they were innocent. CBI proved the story to be false. CBI chargesheeted 31 accused in the case including the five who volunteered to become accused for money and the two agents who later on became approvers and gave evidence as witnesses. Twenty–nine accused were convicted including the five who after taking money became fake accused. Nineteen of the accused were sentenced to life imprisonment. The case is pending in the higher courts and therefore no further details can be given.

Krishna Nand Rai Murder Case

Besides this, another important case was the case of murder of Shri Krishna Nand Rai, MLA (BJP), Ghazipur, UP by a criminal gang of Mukhtar Ansari, MLA. There was rivalry between the two groups and Mukhtar Ansari's gang waylaid Krishna Nand Rai's vehicle and pumped bullets on the inmates including Krishna Nand Rai. Dreaded criminal Bajrangi and his men did the job for Mukhtar Ansari and the gang. The question is from where they got AK-47 rifles and why the intelligence collection is so poor specially when you know that the gang is prominent and dangerous. What we needed is a determination to eliminate any such type of dreaded gang and if that is there then everything will fall in place. Accused were arrested and chargesheeted. Again the problem is that the witnesses will not speak in the Court due to the threat resulting in acquittal of the accused. The victim's wife had moved the Supreme Court for transfer of the case out of Uttar Pradesh. Recently, the Supreme Court transferred the case from Ghazipur Court to a Delhi court and the trial will start soon. As I said earlier, it is difficult to collect evidence in such cases as people are afraid of speaking the truth. We camped in Ghazipur. Our team raided the house of MLA Mukhtar Ansari there but some wanted criminals had already escaped from there at that time. We were told by the police that they were instructed not to look towards that area while passing through as it was treated as Mecca and they were surprised how the CBI raided the area and the house of Mukhtar Ansari. Mukhtar Ansari, MLA, his brother who is also a Member of Parliament and other hardcore criminals involved in the crime are in jail. They will face the trial, now, in Delhi.

The Director stressed on disposal of cases pending investigation for more than two years. The cases were pending for various reasons. Priority was given to this so that more attention could be given to fresh cases. Similarly, cases pending trial for more than 20 years were continuously reviewed besides thousands of other cases pending trial. Here, I may mention that there is a target fixed for each branch of the CBI for disposal of cases under investigation and under trial every year. The progress made in this regard is reviewed regularly. All these years, besides what has been stated above, investigation and trial of many other cases were on.

Housing Scam

During December 2005 to July 2008 when Vijay Shanker was the Director, there were a number of cases that we handled. There were large number of Co-operative Group Housing Society cases entrusted by the Delhi High Court. This included the cases against 100 Housing Societies which were allotted with land by the DDA. Besides this there were more than 100 such societies wherein land was to be allotted. The investigation took lot of time as each case involved examination of thousands of documents by the experts also. The charge–sheets pending in the courts will take years to be processed keeping the voluminous documents in question besides large number of accused etc. There is need to have more Fast Track Courts for these cases.

Patribal Fake Encounter Case

Anantnag, J&K fake encounter case in which five civilians were killed by an Army Unit claiming that they were Pakistani militants, involved in the massacre of 36 Sikhs in Chittisinghpora was another important case, so investigated. There was hue and cry and therefore, the case was handed over to the CBI. Investigation revealed that the civilians were abducted first and subsequently their dead bodies were handed over to the Police Station by the Army unit stating that they were killed in an encounter. It was established that the victims were not Pakistani militants. Army officers involved were chargesheeted. It is pending trial. On the question of requirement of sanction to prosecute, in this case, the Supreme Court of India has passed an order. In case the Army holds Court Martial proceedings, witnesses will have to be examined there.

Computer Teacher Murder Case

A case of murder of a computer teacher in Hoshiarpur, Punjab by a peon of the said Computer Institute is another case. Sanjay Singh, the peon wanted to have sex with the teacher. To make her unconscious and then to do what he wanted, the peon went to the nearby medical shop and obtained three pills telling them that his mother had not been getting sleep. Next day which was a Saturday, after the students left at 1 PM, he mixed one pill in tea and gave it to her. After half an hour, he gave another cup of tea with 2 pills in it. After drinking that cup of tea, she fell asleep within few minutes, on the table itself. He brought his blanket and spread it on the floor, dragged her down on to the blanket and tried to rape her. When she tried to wake up and threatened him, he strangulated her and killed her. He bundled the body with his blanket and dumped it in his room at the back of the institute. In the night, he carried the bundle to a distant building under construction and dumped it at the back side. It had rained just before and therefore his foot–prints were found there. Next day the dead body was recovered. But by that time, the peon had reached his village in Meerut, UP to attend the marriage of his brother. He was to go the previous day but because of the incident he could not go. On Sunday morning he left that place. There was hue and cry as no evidence of rape was found from examination of the clothes of the victim and vaginal swab taken by the doctors during post mortem examination. Therefore the case was transferred to the CBI. There was allegation by her parents that the clothes and the swab were manipulated or changed. The first suspect was the peon as the three students who left at 1 PM stated that when they left the Institute, the teacher and the peon were only present. Thereafter, her dead body was found. During investigation of the peon, on his disclosures, the sandal, bag, purse of the teacher were recovered from the nearby places. The empty strip of sleeping pills was also recovered. CBI sent the clothes of the victim to CDFD Laboratory in Hyderabad but no semen was found in them and neither in the swab. No DNA could be generated from them. Then the blanket was sent to CDFD Laboratory for examination. In the blanket, body fluids of the peon and that of the victim teacher were found. When strangulated, the victim had passed urine in the blanket. The blanket connected the victim and the accused with the crime. The owner identified the blanket to be that of the peon. In the Court, after the charge–sheet, the peon admitted his guilt during the trial and was convicted and sentenced to life imprisonment by the court, keeping his prayer and other factors like his age etc., in mind.

ACP Rajbir Singh Murder Case

Delhi Police ACP Rajbir Singh's murder case is another important case. An alert police officer of Delhi Police who was a terror to the militants, was killed by a small property dealer in Gurgaon. He was a friend of the ACP. Rajbir Singh had invested money in real estate business in Gurgaon and wanted to earn easy and quick money to meet his various requirements. He had asked the property dealer to give him the money on that fateful Monday and the property dealer had told him that he had talked to somebody in Hissar but it was difficult to bring the money by road. On this Rajbir Singh had given him a weapon for safety and for bringing the money. On that Monday Rajbir Singh went to the shop of the property dealer in Gurgaon and asked him for the money. He was in need of the money that day itself. When the property dealer said that he could not get the money, Rajbir Singh shouted at him and threatened to kill him if he did not give it that day itself. He made a call to somebody and from the talk, the property dealer felt that Rajbir Singh was planning to kill him and decided to shoot at Rajbir Singh as there was no other way out. At that time the electricity connection went off in the area. Taking benefit of that, the property dealer moved to the opposite side to switch on the inverter and from the back shot at Rajbir Singh. He fired two bullets. A bullet does not recognise the status or identity of a person. It simply passes through. The accused who was in judicial custody when the case was taken up by the CBI made a voluntary confession before a Magistrate narrating the sequence of events which forced him to shoot at and kill Rajbir Singh that day in his shop and that he had no other option but to kill Rajbir Singh. The case is under trial.

Dera Sachcha Sauda Cases

There were three cases pending investigation against Chief of Dera Sachcha Sauda, Sirsa, Haryana, in the region. On an order from the High Court that a senior officer should investigate these cases and a report be submitted on the fixed date, the Director ordered me to investigate them. One was a rape case and the other two were murder cases.The cases were under investigation for sometime but witnesses were not coming forward to speak the truth, may be because they were afraid. Accordingly, I investigated these cases, with the assistance of a very active DSP Satish Dagar who had been investigating these cases and also DSP K.S. Negi. Investigation disclosed that the Chief of the Dera was involved in these cases. After investigation chargesheets were filed in these cases. The cases are pending trial.

Vijay Shanker had a vision for the CBI in mind. With this in mind, he hired Management experts for re-modelling the CBI to make it ready for 2020. The experts studied the functioning of the CBI and suggested measures to improve its effectiveness. Accordingly some action was taken to spread it geographically by opening branches in some places where there were no branches.

Nithari Killing Cases

The most important cases of the time were the **Nithari killing cases**. There were serial killings. These cases were first of their kind in the country and perhaps in the world where a person having necrophilia allured women and girls, killed them, raped them, cut the bodies into pieces, ate the flesh and disposed of the bodies just around the house. Out of 16 cases, one case has already been decided by the Supreme Court of India with death penalty to accused Surender Koli. Some more cases have also been disposed off with death penalty to the accused. The details (in chapter 7) will be of interest to the reader as such cases are very very rare.

Ashwani Kumar, the then Director General of Police, Himachal Pradesh took over as Director, CBI on 02.08.2008. He had worked as Joint Director and subsequently as Additional Director in the CBI, earlier. A very gentle and honest officer mingled with all officers and interacted freely with the Investigating Officers encouraging them, motivating them, telling them not to be under tension and do their duties without pressure. I found him taking quick decisions in various cases. Immediately on joining, he asked me why I have not been promoted. He told me that he knew my ability when he worked as Joint Director (Policy) in the CBI and looked after the performance of the CBI, being in that post. I recollect his comments that I should have been promoted as Joint Director 2-3 years back. I appreciated this gesture as I never heard or felt any officer in that position expressing so. It was a genuine concern for CBI cadre officers. In fact, I had lost about eight years, with reference to the eligibility requirement under the Recruitment Rules, as there was no regular schedule for holding Departmental Promotion Committee meetings, in time, for promotions, earlier. The Administration Division used to sleep over it. Otherwise I would have become eligible for another promotion.

I recollect being told by U.S. Misra, the then Special Director that since the then Director was away, he had attended the DPC meeting for promotion of CBI Superintendents of Police to the rank of Deputy Inspector General of Police, in the UPSC office and on scrutiny of the records including Annual Reports, there was an impression amongst the members of the Committee as to why I was not promoted earlier. I also recollect that when I was moving in the corridors of North Block for some official work, sometime, in the end of 1992, S.K. Datta, the then Director, who was going out of his office, told me that he had sent the file for my promotion and is pursuing it with the Ministry and the UPSC. I do remember that when I was promoted as Superintendent of Police in February 1993, Alexander Daniel, the then DIG in CBI expressed so much of happiness. Other officers who showed concern about my promotion were M.L. Sharma, who was AD and then Special Director and Loknath Behera, who was DIG at that time. Coming back to Ashwani Kumar, Director, he had enquired with the Administration Division and found that a proposal was sent few months back for my *ad hoc* promotion as Joint Director and therefore, he, immediately issued an order on 5.08.2008 posting me as in-charge Joint Director alongwith two other IPS officers. I recollect his instructions to function as full - fledged Joint Director and take decisions, accordingly. The proposal sent earlier was not pursued by anybody forcing me to send queries under the RTI Act to the PMO, DOPT, UPSC and the CBI as I had become eligible otherwise in September 2008 for regular promotion. The *ad hoc* order came in January 2009, the month in which I was to retire. But for the query under the RTI Act no such order would have come. Moreover, but for Ashwani Kumar, others who never wished CBI cadre officers to be at that level would have played mischief to see that the order was not issued. The administration never pursued the proposal. In case of IPS officers, the order is issued at least a day before the due date. Regarding my regular promotion, the matter was lying there. UPSC and the DOPT put the blame on the CBI. It is necessary that these institutions take the responsibility because such steps are very important in the interest of the officers working in the cadre. Since promotions, as per rules, are the right of the deserving public servants, it is necessary that the concerned people take prompt and timely action to see that it is given to the officers. There should be a mechanism to fix the accountability for the failure and punish the guilty. In the history of the CBI, I was the only cadre officer recruited by the CBI as Sub Inspector of Police in the department to reach this post, so far. Many appeared to be not happy. It is the considered opinion and feeling of CBI cadre officers that those who join on deputation do not appreciate CBI officers coming up in the cadre. They do not bother that the CBI cadre officers who are eligible and fit, require to be promoted.

As Joint Director, Special Crimes Zone-I, I monitored the investigation of large number of sensitive cases besides running after the progress in the trial of large number of cases under the Zone. I roughly recollect having completed and disposed of 74 cases in the Zone which were under investigation, between August 2008 and January 2009, when I retired. I also got disposed of some cases under TADA pending in the Courts. I recollect, the case of dacoity and looting of ₹ 6 crores from Punjab National Bank, Ludhiana by terrorists which was investigated by us in 1987 was pending trial. I called the special public prosecutor handling the case in the Court and asked him about the delay. He told me that the case at that stage was pending for want of production of the cash book of the bank for the day of dacoity and examination of the concerned bank witnesses. Immediately, I talked to the Chief Vigilance Officer of Punjab National Bank and wrote a letter to him with the result, on the next date in the case, the document was produced and the concerned bank officers were identified and were present in the Court. The case was got completed. The prosecutor said that nobody bothered and took interest in the matter, earlier. Number of terrorists of North-East India were shown as absconders and therefore the cases were pending. I pursued with the DG concerned and many of those absconders were caught. I recollect that few days after, since the Joint Director of the other Zone went on leave, I held charge of that Zone, also. The Director wanted to discuss the Mecca Masjid case and some other cases. Then while reviewing the case, I felt that there were reasons to believe that Mecca Masjid blast, Ajmer Dargah blast etc., could have been caused by Hindu fanatics also, and gave reasons while suggesting for looking into this angle. Subsequently, this was found to be correct. Perhaps the police had some information about such possibilities but no effort appeared to have been made to probe in that direction, for reasons known to them.

Anti-Sikh Riot Cases

The anti-Sikh rioting and other cases were under investigation at that time. The investigation was going on since receipt of the order from the Ministry of Home Affairs on examination of the Nanavati Commission Report in that matter. There were many commissions so appointed since 1984 and finally, the Nanavati Commission, after consolidating all the material received by the commissions namely the Marwah Commission, Mishra Commission, Dhillon Committee, Kapur-Mittal Committee, Jain-Banerjee Committee, Ahooja Committee, Potti-Rosha Committee, Narula Committee and the affidavits and other material received by it, had submitted a report recommending that at least in ten FIRs there is need to conduct further investigation. After verification about the FIRs, about eight cases were registered. Some were in my region and some in other regions. As usual, I guided the officers in the cases. We requested the victims to come out with truth. It was found that they were scared to tell the truth as they were helpless and were still under the same type of shock which they faced in 1984 and were trembling with fear whenever our officers contacted them. There were indications that Sajjan Kumar and others were involved. We approached the concerned Sikh authorities, Gurdwara Management Committee and the advocates fighting the cases. Finally, a dynamic and young Inspector R.K. Jha could manage to convince them to muster courage and speak the truth. Since the evidence came up after so many years, to be sure on our side about the veracity of the statement given, we produced the witnesses before the Magistrate and their true statements were recorded by the Magistrate which established the involvement of Sajjan Kumar and others. When I became Joint Director, I found that in the other Region (which also came under me), the cases were pending as such. The cases were expedited resulting in collection of true and solid evidence. The witnesses expressed that they wanted to speak the truth earlier but nobody listened to them. They were threatened not to give evidence in the court. The atmosphere outside was not favourable. It appeared that proper attention was not being paid to work out these cases and therefore, I instructed the Investigating Officers to make sincere efforts to detect the cases and identify the culprits. They also told me that Jagdish Tytler had visited the branch and that after investigation, a closure report has been filed in his case. However, two witnesses Jasbir Singh and Surinder Singh claimed to be eye-witnesses, were reported to have gone to USA. They were contacted but they refused to come to India as they were scared of their safety. Therefore, we contacted them and asked them whether they would be able to give a true statement if the officers visit New York and California and they assured that they would make a statement. In a discussion, Ashwani Kumar ordered that the team should go to USA to record the statement of these two witnesses. Accordingly, one SP and one ASP were sent to these places in USA after getting the approval of the Central Government and the team, with the assistance of the Indian Mission in USA examined these two witnesses and recorded their statements in the Indian Missions there. I recollect that we had got the assistance of the Sikh leaders in Delhi for this work. This was in December 2008 or so. Then the team had reported that a large number of Sikhs were found assembled outside the Indian Missions at those places as it was known that the CBI team would be visiting these places. Then the teams were asked to verify the facts stated by these witnesses and collect more evidence. Witnesses named Jagdish Tytler with regard to the incident at Gurdwara Pul Bangash in which 3 Sikhs were killed. Closure Report had been filed in the court before that branch came under my charge. Two officers were sent to USA to record the statements of 2 witnesses who did name Jagdish Tytler. Even in 1984, role and names of H.K.L. Bhagat and others were being reported. H.K.L. Bhagat died. The new government headed by Rajiv Gandhi was silent. It was free for criminals to act. A very few Sikhs conspired and killed Smt. Indira Gandhi. It was unfortunate and a crime to think and consider all and innocent Sikhs as involved and or responsible and massacre them. All responsible should be held as accountable and punished. In January, I retired. On the basis of evidence collected, afterwords, reports were reportedly filed in the Courts. It is necessary that in all the cases victims get justice. The cases are under trial.

Here I may point out that Ashwani Kumar was very straightforward and when he reviewed some pending cases including the MLA cash case, anti-Sikh rioting cases, Mecca Masjid case, case of death of a foreign girl in Goa Beach etc., he had told me that we should be fair in our investigation and should not leave out anybody involved in the cases. He was clear in his mind and passed very clear orders in the cases. I had the opportunity of working with him only for about six months but it was a different experience, all together.

The life in the CBI was full of memories. There were so many cases of different nature. Every case was an experience. All the above Directors were active leaders and handled the organisation in their own way, style and individual leadership qualities. When we were doing MBA from IGNOU, we were told that each leader has his own characteristic style of getting the work done and running the organisation. Each of us respond differently to the surroundings and face or compromise with the situations, according to our inbuilt personality. In the process, one may go by the wind to protect himself but the other against it to protect the institution. Insulating the institution from external interferences and spreading confidence down the line by and through bold and impartial decisions are the two important requisites that the CBI expects from its chiefs. Some cases might have been diluted or not effectively handled and/or allowed to be handled, but that cannot be generalised. Well, such things should not be done and also should not be allowed to be done. It will only be a satisfaction to feel or respond that there are courts to review them.

Unfortunately, many times, this organisation was headed by officers who never headed the police of the state, to which they were allotted. Some never handled a tough posting in their state or headed the Vigilance set-up or Crime Investigation set-up. Besides them, I enjoyed working with all other senior officers. It was an opportunity to work with so many dedicated Investigating Officers and I learnt many things from them. It is not possible to explain each and every case so handled. It is also not possible in view of some sensitivity involved and or judicial trials going on. Some cases disposed of by the trial court or otherwise can be referred to or explained to share and or exchange experience. Let me start with IC–814 hijacking case which was the 50th case investigated by me as a Supervising Officer.

Chapter 5

IC-814 Hijacking Case (Kandahar Case)

The Kandahar Hijacking case was a significant and serious case, by all means. Those days, the Indian Airlines had been operating an International Flight from Delhi to Kathmandu, Nepal, daily. The Flight IC–813 from Delhi to Kathmandu used to take off at 11:30 AM and reach Kathmandu at 1:00 PM. The return flight IC–814 used to take off from Tribhuvan Airport at 1:50 PM Nepal time (1:35 PM IST) and reach Delhi at 3:20 PM IST. The crew members used to operate IC–939 from Hyderabad to Delhi in the morning and the same aircraft thereafter operated as IC–813/814.

On 24.12.1999 as there was some technical snag in the aircraft IC–939 from Hyderabad to Delhi, it was decided that aircraft operating as Flight IC 263 Calcutta- Delhi sector will also operate as IC–813/814. The scheduled time of departure of IC 263 from Calcutta was 07:00 hours. However, on that day due to poor visibility, it departed from Calcutta at 08:40 hours and landed at Indira Gandhi International Airport, Delhi, Domestic Terminal at 11:15 hours. After the due procedure the aircraft was moved and parked at the International Terminal at Delhi at 12:55 hours. However, the flight IC–813 could take off from International Terminal only at 14:00 hours on account of an 'engineering-delay' of 40 minutes due to some problem faced in closing the cargo door hydraulically. The aircraft IC–813 landed at Tribhuvan Airport on 24.12.1999 at 15:45 hours Nepal time (15:30 IST).

The following were the crew members of the said flight:

- Capt. Devi Saran, Pilot;
- Capt. Rajender Kumar, Co-pilot;
- Flight Engineer Anil Jaggia;
- Ms. Sabita Khalka, Air Hostess;
- Ms. Tapa Debnath, Air Hostess;
- Ms. Rajni Shekar, Air Hostess;
- Ms. Sapna Menon, Air Hostess;
- Ms. Kobita Mukherjee, Air Hostess;
- Mr. M. Satheesh;
- Mr. Anil Sharma, Flight Purser.

As per the Passenger Manifest of flight IC-814 of 24-12-1999 from Kathmandu to Delhi there were total 179 passengers besides the above said 11 crew. Out of them 24 were foreign nationals as mentioned below:

Nepalese : 8

Japanese : 1

American : 1

Canadian : 1

Italian : 1

Spanish : 4

Guinea Bissauian : 1

French : 2

Swiss : 3

Australian : 1

Belgian : 1

There were 155 Indian passengers on board including five hijackers (who hijacked the aircraft declaring themselves as Indians). The 11 crew members were also Indians and thus there were 166 Indians on board. When drawn, the seating arrangement on board, as per the manifest, boarding card etc., was as explained below:

Seating Arrangement

2B - S A QAZI
(Burger)
3A - A.A.SHAIKH
(Chief)
8C - Z.I.MISTRY
(Bhola)
19G - S.A. SAYEED
(Doctor)
23G - R.G. VERMA
(Shankar)

Note :

■ = Occupied by the Hijackers

░ = Occupied by the Passengers

□ = Vacant

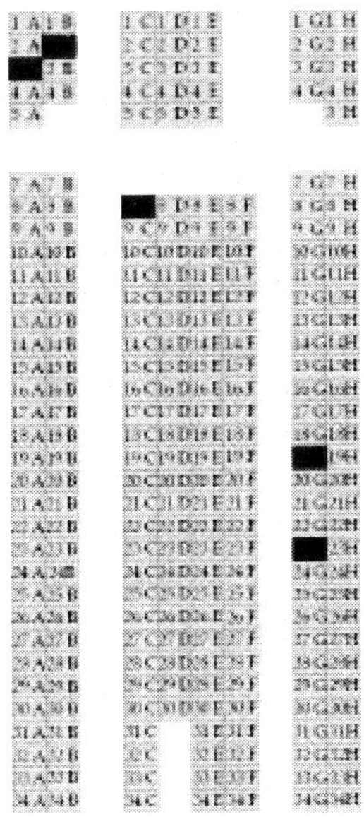

The aircraft took off from Tribhuvan Airport at 16:27 hours Nepal time or 16:12 hours IST. While starting the engine and preparing for take off, the pilot Capt. Devi Saran had told the flight purser Anil Sharma to serve tea to them in the flight. Before the take off, the pilot locked the cockpit door as per the procedure. When the aircraft was cruising at 26,000 feet and was near Lucknow under the control of Air Traffic Control (ATC), Varanasi, Anil Sharma informed the pilot on intercom that tea was ready and on clearance being given by the pilot, Anil Sharma came to the cockpit with tea. At that time the aircraft was in contact with ATC Varanasi. When Anil Sharma left the cockpit after serving tea, one person wearing a red monkey cap entered the cockpit with a revolver in his right hand and a hand grenade in his left hand. He was wearing a grey colour suit. On entering the cockpit, that person told the pilot and co-pilot *"Koi Harkat Nahi Hona Chahiye – Mere Is Hath Mein Grenade Hai, Agar Koi Gadbad Hui to Uda Diya Jayega, Iski Pin Nikli Hui Hai"*. He asked Capt. Devi Saran *"Aap Ke Paas Kitna Tel Hai"*. The pilot and the co-pilot told him that they had fuel upto Delhi only. He then directed the pilot *"Isko Aap Lahore Le Chalo"*. The pilot told him that the aircraft cannot go to Lahore as there was no fuel. On this the said person threatened the pilot that if the aircraft was not taken to Lahore *"Is Tayyare Ko Brust Kar Denge"*. The pilot asked him whether he could inform the passengers that the aircraft had been hijacked and on being permitted by the said hijacker, the pilot informed the passengers on the PA system, requesting them to be calm and be seated. The hijacker warned the pilot that whatever he had told to the passengers on the RT system, he should explain the same in Hindi to him. He also warned that before speaking to anybody, he should explain the details of the conversation in Hindi to him and get his permission. On this, the pilot asked for permission to inform ATC, Varanasi that the aircraft had been hijacked. On being permitted the pilot informed ATC Varanasi at 11:23:38 GMT (16:53:38 hours IST) that they had been hijacked.

Sampath Kumar, Controller and YK Rohilla, Watch and Supervisory Officer in the ATC, Varanasi as well as UN Singh, Aerodrome Director handled the aircraft. At 16:54 they asked IC–814 about endurance on board. The pilot informed the ATC that the aircraft had endurance of 3 hours and that the aircraft was 11 knots away from Lucknow. Then the ATC asked IC 814 to contact Lucknow. At 16:56, the pilot informed that the hijackers had everything on board *i.e.* pistols, bombs and everything. At 16:57 the ATC instructed IC–814 to contact ATC Delhi on Frequency 120.9 and 132.4 MHz for assistance. Then the pilot informed that they were heading West. The ATC asked whether the aircraft was heading West from Lucknow. The pilot informed ATC that they were heading on radial to Jalalabad and they had been instructed by the hijackers to head towards West only. At 16:57 the ATC informed J.S. Ahuja, WSO and Raj Kumar, ATC Controller who were on duty in the ATC, Delhi about the hijacking. The aircraft crossed Lucknow at 16:57 and then changed over to ATC Delhi.

At 17:00 and 17:04 Member (Operations), Airport Authority of India at New Delhi was informed about the hijacking. At 17:10 ATC Varanasi informed the Cabinet Secretary (Prem Singh, PA) about the hijacking. At 17:14 hours they informed PA to Director General Civil Aviation (DGCA).

The pilot had contacted ATC Delhi on frequency 120.9 at 16:57 hours and informed "we have been hijacked and squaking 7700" and that the aircraft was 17-18 miles out of Lucknow. At 17:00 hours the pilot had told ATC Delhi that "They want us to go to Lahore only." Himanshu Joshi, Senior Manager and Jyothi Prasad, DGM, on duty in the ATC Delhi handled the aircraft. At 17:03, Delhi Radar identified IC 814 and took control of the aircraft. The pilot asked the ATC about weather condition in Lahore. ATC asked the pilot about total passengers on board and the endurance to which the pilot replied that there were 189 passengers on board and 2 hours 20 minutes of endurance. Then the ATC passed on the weather at Lahore airport. At 17:11, the pilot had told the ATC that the aircraft was 58 miles short of Sikanderabad in Uttar Pradesh and requested the ATC to obtain landing permission from Lahore. The ATC told the pilot that they were trying for it and gave the routing and then asked him to contact on frequency 124.2 MHz. Mr Joshi, on instructions, contacted ATC Lahore at 1718 and talked to Mr Khurram who was on duty in the ATC and passed on the details of the hijacked aircraft and requested for permission for landing at Lahore as the hijackers wanted the aircraft to land in Lahore only. Mr Khurram informed Mr Joshi that the aircraft was not permitted to land in Lahore. By this time all concerned officers were informed, who started monitoring the situation.

At 17:24 ATC Delhi informed IC–814 that Lahore had refused to accept the flight for landing. IC–814 informed ATC Delhi that the hijackers were insisting that the aircraft would go to Lahore only and nowhere else. ATC Delhi wanted to know the number of hijackers and therefore asked the pilot in a code form as "Number of Hotel India Juliet". This was because the hijackers were controlling the cockpit. The pilot replied "1...2...3...4...5". At 17:25 he informed the ATC that there were 189 passengers and also "they have got everything on board, everybody has got pistol, revolver, everything". Then the chief hijacker in the cockpit told the pilot that they had 'Dynamite' also and therefore the pilot informed the ATC that they had "dynamite and hand grenades". At 17:32, IC–814 was overhead Delhi and informed that the aircraft had 1½ hours of endurance only and wanted information about routing to ASARI via Butop which were the en-route contact controls and the information was provided. At 17:34 Mr Joshi again contacted ATC Lahore but got the same reply. At 17:36, the pilot obtained the frequency of ATC Lahore as 132.2 from ATC Delhi. The pilot informed that the hijackers had told him as *"Kisi Tarike Se Unko Manaeye Lahore Walon Ko"* and added "That they wanted to go to Lahore only……*Hamare pass fuel nahin hai aur unki manzil kuch aur hi hai"*. At 17:43, the pilot informed *"vo keh rahe hai ki agar koi bhi hamare sath gadbad hui to sara jahaz hum uda denge….unke paas sab kuch hai….*Everything they have on board". Then the pilot contacted ATC Lahore and requested permission to land which was refused. ATC Lahore also told the pilot that they are blocking the runway. ATC Lahore warned the pilot not to enter Pakistan airspace. At 17:49 Mr. Joshi contacted ATC Lahore and spoke to Mr. Najib who informed that IC–814 was in contact with them. All these developments were duly informed to HS Khola, Director General, Civil Aviation who was the Chairman of the Central Committee.

At 17:56 Mr Joshi contacted Mr. Dobriyal, Duty Officer, Raja Sansi Airport, Amritsar and informed him about the hijacked aircraft and advised him to take all necessary action. At 17:57 the pilot informed Delhi that they were 81 miles from Lahore and the hijackers were not allowing them to go anywhere but wanted to land in Lahore only otherwise they would kill the passengers one by one. The hijackers insisted to land on the blocked runway. The pilot informed ATC Delhi about this and that the hijackers were telling "if you are not going to land in Lahore, we will kill one passenger on board".

At 18:00, the pilot informed the ATC that "Pakistan is not letting us to enter their airspace, now you tell us what to do….we are coming up position ASARI….can we proceed overhead Lahore or proceed to Amritsar". Delhi advised the pilot to proceed to Amritsar. The pilot asked for the frequency of Amritsar at 18:02

and Delhi gave the same as 118.3 MHz. Thereafter Delhi ATC could not contact the aircraft. The aircraft had switched over to Amritsar frequency. At 18:06 Delhi again contacted Lahore ATC for Delhi- Lahore PIA (Pakistan International Airlines) flight No. 815 but Lahore did not allow saying that Lahore air field had been closed.

Delhi ATC allowed IC–814 to go to Amritsar. Pilot thereafter informed that the hijackers are not permitting to land at Amritsar. The pilot wanted the frequency on which ATC Amritsar was operating and Delhi ATC gave it as 118.3 and 119.7. The pilot also asked ATC Delhi whether they had talked to Lahore to which the latter replied that they were in contact with Lahore and instructed to hold at East of Amritsar. At 18:05, Delhi ATC informed IC–814 that Lahore was not available on DSC and they were not permitting other aircraft, even their PIA aircraft also, for landing and departure. Thereafter the aircraft came in contact with ATC Amritsar.

Aircraft at Amritsar

The hijackers refused to allow the aircraft to land in India. The pilot, co-pilot and the flight engineer continued to plead with the chief hijacker in the cockpit to allow landing of the aircraft for refuelling and finally succeeded. ATC Amritsar had received intimation at 17:20 IST from Cpl P.P. Singh of Indian Airforce that IC–814 was hijacked and the aircraft was 100 NM from Delhi and the pilot was telling that the hijackers wanted the aircraft to be taken to Lahore. Pradeep Dobriyal, Dinesh Kumar, D.S. Mann, Sr. Manager Aerodrome and Trilok Singh, Sr. Aerodrome Officer were on duty. The information was passed on to the Airport Director Mr Mulekar who instructed D.S. Mann to contact the DM, SSP, the Airforce Commander and other members of the Aerodrome committee to come to the ATC. Hospitals, fire station etc., were also alerted. At 18:44 the pilot informed that he was coming for landing at Amritsar. At 18:45, the pilot informed that the hijackers wanted the aircraft to be refuelled and therefore asked for the oil tanker and that the hijackers had instructed him to park the aircraft on the runway. The aircraft landed at Amritsar airport at 19:00 hours.

The ATC told the pilot to park the aircraft at Dumble 16 *i.e.,* at the end of runway 34 but the pilot told them that he would park on the runway itself as directed by the hijackers. Mr Mulekar told Mr. Dobriyal to ask the pilot to put any of the hijackers on the RT transmission and also inform the demands of the hijackers. The pilot informed that the hijackers did not want to talk to the ATC. The pilot went on asking for the bouzer. As instructed by the hijackers, the pilot informed the ATC at 19:05 hours that if the bouzer did not come within five minutes they would blow up one of the cockpit crew. Member (Operations), AAI, Mr. Robey Lal and the Cabinet Secretary had instructed ATC over phone to delay the refuelling at 18:53 hours and at 19:02 hours Mr Robey Lal had checked up with Mr. DS Mann about the landing of the aircraft. Before landing of the aircraft, Mr Narenderjeet Singh, DM, Mr Parampal Singh Siddhu, SSP; Mr Jaswinder Singh, DIG, Border Range and the Airforce Commander had reached the ATC. On the instructions of the Director General of Police, Mr. J P Birdi, IG (Commando), Punjab Police also reached the ATC. The Punjab Police did not have the expertise to conduct any possible commando operation, in the situation, at that time. It could have been done by the NSG only on a decision by the Crisis Management Group. The officers discussed about the situation and interacted with the Central Committee and the CMG.

As it was not a scheduled flight and it was late, the Indian Oil Depot was closed and it took time to get the oil tanker. When it came, they wanted security to move towards the aircraft. It was decided to send two policemen in civil dress with revolvers in the drivers cabin. Mr. Dobriyal was also sent with a walkie- talkie in the bouzer. The aircraft was surrounded by the police at a distance as it was their duty, to see that no unwanted person reaches the aircraft. The bouzer was instructed to park at a distance of 200-300 metres so that the pilot could see it. At 19:07 (13:37 GMT) the pilot informed the ATC that the hijackers have said *"Kisi ne ustadi dikhane ki koshish ki to sabko bhoon ke rakh denge"* and they had everything including AK-47 with them. At that time Mr Mulekar told the pilot that *"No ustadi–only flight delay because fuelling station was closed–* we have already taken action- your aircraft will be refuelled". The pilot said *'AGAR 5 MINUTES SE JYADA LAGE*

THO HUM ME SE EK NAHI HOGA" and they would shoot the passengers. The pilot and the crew had a great responsibility on board to save the aircraft and the passengers. The officers on the ground on the other hand had to delay the flight to enable a proper decision by the CMG for a commando operation. Any commando operation was to be decided keeping the magnitude of casualty and that the aircraft was on the middle of the runway as the hijackers had perhaps decided to pre-empt any such operation. The hijackers had a binocular through which they were watching the movement of people outside.

Just before the landing of the aircraft, one "J Lal" identifying himself as Joint Secretary in the Ministry of Home Affairs, New Delhi contacted the Tower and asked about the position of the aircraft. He spoke to Mr Mulekar in English with authority and Mr Mulekar told that person that the aircraft would be landing within a minute or two. He asked about the intention of the pilot and Mr Mulekar told him that the pilot was asking for refuelling. Then that person asked Mr Mulekar whether he had talked to Delhi and obtained permission for refuelling on which Mr Mulekar had told him that he did not need any permission to refuel the aircraft. Then the telephone was disconnected. After about 15 minutes, J. Lal again telephoned and asked Mr Mulekar about the position and the intention of the pilot. Mr Mulekar told him that the aircraft had landed and the pilot wanted refuelling. J. Lal disconnected the telephone.

Mr Mulekar went on talking to the pilot and the pilot went on asking for the bouzer. According to the Indian Oil Depot Manager and the staff they could not go near the aircraft because the engines were on. According to the pilot, after landing at Amritsar airport, the hijacker code named as Burger (whose name was disclosed as Sunny Ahmed Qazi later on) instructed him not to switch off the engines till the bouzer comes. The hijackers saw one or two scooters going on the parallel road and panicked and threatened that they would kill the passengers if the fuel bouzer did not come immediately. The chief hijacker (whose name was disclosed as Ibrahim Athar) kept the revolver on the head of Capt. Devi Saran and the hijacker Burger kept a revolver on the head of flight engineer Jaggia and they threatened to kill both of them if the refuelling was not done immediately. In the meantime, the pilot saw the bouzer coming to the runway but it stopped 400 metres away from the aircraft and did not come near the aircraft. The pilot turned the aircraft 180 degrees at 19:21 hours. He informed Mr Mulekar that the guns were on their head. At 19:25 hours, he told Mr. Mulekar that the hijackers had already killed one passenger. The pilot went on asking the ATC to send the bouzer near the aircraft. Hijacker Burger (Sunny Ahmed Qazi) was very active and often coming to the cockpit and going back to the cabin. Hijacker Doctor (Shahid Sayeed Akhtar) was having a knife in his hand.

While this was going on in the cockpit, on board, the Executive class or 'J' class passengers namely Arvind Grover and wife Smt Vaishali Grover; Ramesh Grover, Abhinav Khandelwal, Daman Kumar Soni, Anil Kumar Khurana, Rajender Singh and his wife Smt Satvinder Kaur of New Delhi, Saibal Chander Kar of Noida, Prashant Kharwadkar of Mumbai, Ullal Balakrishna Bhatt of Bangalore etc., were moved out of the J class by the hijackers Burger and Doctor to the Economy class. All the passengers were threatened with revolvers and knife and were tied to the seats. They were blind folded by the hijackers Burger, Doctor, Bhola alias Zahoor Ibrahim Mistri and hijacker Shanker alias Shakir alias Rajesh Gopal Verma with the seat covers with the help of the Air Hostesses who were forced to do so under threat. The passengers were asked to bend down and not to look up. Some of the passengers who tried to look up were beaten up. The hijackers then selected young and well-built passengers namely Pawan Garg of New Delhi, Daman Kumar Soni, Rajinder Dogra, Abhinav Khandelwal, Satnam Singh, Rupin Katyal, Chandra Prakash Chabra and took them to J class, tied their hands at the back and then tied them to the seats. According to Pawan Garg, hijacker Burger pulled him and took him forcefully to the J class and six more passengers were also brought there and tied. Rupin Katyal was sitting on his right side. The hijackers were instructing the pilot but it appeared that the pilot was not agreeing and therefore the hijackers threatened that all the seven passengers will be killed. When the pilot refused to take off, the chief hijacker in the cockpit ordered hijacker Doctor to kill on which the latter caught hold of Satnam Singh and stabbed him with the knife 7–8 times on the neck. Satnam Singh started bleeding. In the meantime the chief hijacker again shouted 'kill' on which hijacker Doctor caught hold of the hair of Rupin Katyal and stabbed him with the knife on the neck and chest several times as a result of which Rupin Katyal was seriously injured and was bleeding. He was lying on his seat and was crying with pain. Hijacker Burger brought flight engineer by dragging him from the cockpit and showed injured Rupin Katyal and Satnam Singh and thereafter, the Flight Engineer was taken back. Rupin Katyal was asking for water. However no water was given to him. Thereafter, hijacker Doctor covered Satnam Singh and Rupin Katyal with a blanket. After 2-3 hours Pawan Garg and others except Rupin Katyal and Satnam Singh were taken to the Economy class and threatened not to tell other passengers about the stabbing.

Daman Kumar Soni stated that when they were taken back, he heard Rupin Katyal saying *"papa pani- papa pani'* in a faint voice. Satnam Singh stated that on being stabbed he became unconscious. Rajinder Dogra stated that when Rupin Katyal was crying and asking for water, hijacker Doctor put a pillow on the mouth of Katyal and pressed it. Other passengers who were also there said the same thing. After this, hijacker Doctor came enquiring about doctors and took Dr (Mrs) Anita Joshi of Nainital who was on board the flight, to the J class where she treated both Rupin Katyal and Satnam Singh with the available medical facility on board. When asked, hijacker Doctor told her that they are doing this because some of their associates are in Indian jails and they wanted to get them freed.

Hijacker Burger told the pilot that they had killed three passengers. Burger kept the revolver on the head of the pilot and instructed him to tell the ATC that they had killed four passengers. Accordingly, the pilot informed the ATC that the hijackers had killed four passengers and requested the ATC to send the bouzer. At that time hijacker Burger hit on the head of Mr Jaggia with the butt of the revolver saying *"Ye bahuth boltha hai'*. Hijacker Burger kept the revolver on the head of Jaggia and started reverse counting from 30. When he came to number 16, Mr Jaggia covered the mouth of Burger with his hand and the pilot touched the feet of the chief hijacker Ibrahim Athar and told him that the bouzer has come and was parked at a distance and would be coming near for refuelling. It was at this time that Burger pulled Jaggia to the J class to show him that they had killed some passengers.

When Jaggia was dragged back, the pilot saw one spot of blood on the shirt on the left shoulder portion of Jaggia and Jaggia by shaking his head indicated to the pilot that the hijackers have stabbed some passengers. At that time, the chief hijacker pressed the revolver on the head of the pilot and threatened him to move the aircraft and take off without refuelling. According to the pilot he requested the chief hijacker to wait for some time as the bouzer would be coming near. The pilot did not want to take off from Amritsar or Indian territory. Then the chief hijacker started counting from 16 downwards and when he came to number 2, the pilot had no option but to take off from Amritsar for Lahore. According to the pilot he knew that he had fuel upto Lahore. The hijackers did not allow the pilot to take the full length for take off. They told him to take off from the place where the aircraft was parked. Since there was no fuel weight, the cockpit crew took precaution so that they could take off without taking the benefit of full length of the runway.

According to the pilot he took off with great risk as there was no response from the ATC for sending the bouzer near the Aircraft. According to the pilot the ATC man said *"aap apna duty kar rahe hain, hum apna duty kar rahe hain"*. On taking off, hijacker Burger told the pilot to go to Lahore. Accordingly the pilot contacted ATC Lahore for permission to land and also informed the ATC that they had been hijacked and did not have fuel and therefore, they had to land at Lahore. ATC Lahore told the pilot that the airport was closed for the aircraft, ATC Lahore switched off all navigation aids. They also switched off high intensive light on the Apron.

When the pilot could not see the runway of the airport anywhere and there was already reserve light on both the fuel indicators, the pilot thought that he might have to opt for force landing at some place. Therefore, he talked to the hijackers that he would crash on which the chief hijacker asked him whether they were on Pakistan territory. The pilot told the chief hijacker and Burger that they were on Lahore and then both the hijackers told the pilot that if they were in Pakistan territory he might crash and they were ready to die.They also told them that they were government servants and would get insurance money and they should crash. The pilot then came down to take a chance to see whether he would be able to see the runway since on the GPS he and the co-pilot could make out that they were overhead Lahore. When he came down he saw a busy market and he pulled up again as he thought that it would not be proper to kill so many innocent people. He saw a black spot and when he turned he heard a few noises on the ATC line which appeared to be some conversation between ATC and somebody on the ground that the aircraft was going to crash. According to the pilot when he was coming down, ATC Lahore might have watched on the radar and thought that the aircraft was going to crash and that was why immediately ATC told the pilot that the runway lights were on. Immediately the pilot managed to land on the runway and stopped the aircraft in the middle of the runway as forced by the hijackers.

On landing at Lahore airport, the pilot requested ATC to provide fuel as desired by the hijackers. The hijackers wanted to confirm whether it was Lahore or not. Accordingly, the pilot requested the ATC to send a person down the runway so that the hijackers could see for themselves. Immediately, ATC Lahore sent a jeep from which a man got down from the jeep at a distance and came towards the aircraft by walk. He was wearing a white Salwar Kameez and a black jacket. The hijackers were not convinced and said that the man could not be a Pakistani and they wanted some vehicle to be sent so that the registration number could be checked by them. Accordingly, the pilot requested the ATC to send a vehicle with registration number.

A jeep came near the aircraft and the hijackers saw the Lahore registration number on it. They agreed that they were in Lahore. By then, the bouzer came and the ground staff connected the bouzer. On seeing some security personnel near the aircraft, the chief hijacker directed the pilot to move the aircraft. It appeared that the hijackers were scared. On pressure, the pilot moved the aircraft little and because of this the bouzer got disconnected and its nozzle got broken. The hijackers told the pilot to tell the ATC to move the security personnel away otherwise they (hijackers) would start killing the passengers. The pilot, accordingly, requested ATC Lahore to move the guards away. ATC informed that these security people were for the security of the aircraft and not for any other action and they were the routine security persons available at the airport. The bouzer people confirmed to the ATC over walkie-talkie that nozzle of the bouzer had been broken. The pilot requested the ATC to send another bouzer. The pilot told the chief hijacker and Burger that on account of pressure from them, he had to move the aircraft which resulted in the breaking of the nozzle and therefore, another bouzer was to be called for. The hijackers told the pilot that they did not know anything, they wanted refuelling. After about 20 minutes, the ATC sent another bouzer and refuelling was done. They picked up about 33 tonnes of fuel. The pilot and co-pilot requested the chief hijacker to off load few injured passengers, ladies and children and the chief hijacker and hijacker Burger agreed.

Therefore, the pilot requested the ATC to off load some passengers but ATC Lahore did not agree. ATC Lahore told the pilot "You wanted fuel, now you go off from here". The chief hijacker also told the ATC and asked to allow off loading of injured persons, ladies and children but ATC Lahore did not agree. Therefore, chief hijacker told the pilot and co-pilot to take off. The hijackers allowed the pilot to use full length of the runway because of the weight. They were threatening the pilot with revolver. The aircraft took off from Lahore at 22:32 IST (17:02 GMT). SK Handa, Additional General Manager, ATC, Delhi had received intimation at 22:38 IST from Karachi that IC–814 had taken off from Lahore at 22:32 and headed towards Kabul but the destination was not known.

As soon as they took off from Lahore, the pilot asked the chief hijacker as to where they wanted to go. The chief hijacker told them to go to Kabul. Therefore, the pilot asked ATC for Kabul routing. Lahore told the pilot to steer to the left and wait for further instructions. After few minutes, Lahore gave them the routing and frequency etc. The aircraft headed for Kabul and contacted Kabul. They told HF Kabul that they had been hijacked and the hijackers wanted to land at Kabul. Kabul told the pilot that there was no night landing facility in Kabul. The pilot informed the chief hijacker and Burger accordingly. Hijacker Burger then talked to ATC Kabul and asked for some persons. Thereafter hijacker Burger told the co-pilot to ask about Kandahar and co-pilot asked ATC Kabul about Kandahar. ATC Kabul told the co-pilot that even Kandahar was not available as there was no staff. The chief hijacker and Burger instructed the pilots to go to Dubai. The pilot told ATC Lahore that the hijackers were forcing them to go to Dubai and asked for Dubai routing. The pilot told ATC Lahore that Kabul and Kandahar were not available for landing and they were heading for Dubai. ATC Lahore gave Dubai routing.

While passing through Karachi, they contacted ATC Karachi and informed about the hijacking and their destination as Dubai and also the routing. En route they received a message from ATC Lahore that Kabul had given them a message that Kandahar was open for them and they could land at Kandahar. According to the pilot, he had managed to see that the hijackers did not hear this message. He did not want to go to Afghanistan territory and worsen the situation further. Karachi told them they could not over fly Iran and Tehran as they had instructed Karachi to tell them not to enter their territory. Therefore, they had to take a longer route. En route, they contacted Muscat and UAE. ATC UAE informed them that Dubai and Sharjah were closed for them. The Pilot told Dubai radar that they had no other choice because they had less fuel and they had to land in Dubai as per the instructions of the hijackers. The CMG, the Ministry of External Affairs got into action to put pressure on the UAE Government to allow the hijacked aircraft to land. After some time, Dubai ATC told them that they could land at Minhad air base which was about 20 nautical miles from Dubai. The hijackers agreed and the aircraft landed at Minhad air base at 01:34 IST.

As soon as they landed, hijacker Burger shouted at the pilot to stop the aircraft on the runway itself and they applied sudden brake. Burger told the pilot to keep the aircraft in motion. Accordingly, they kept on moving. Burger watched outside with night vision binoculars. The hijackers were instructing the pilots to stop the aircraft suddenly and they told them that they could not do so as it was not a bus. Then, they agreed. They told the pilots to move on the runway itself.

Aircraft at Minhad

On landing at Minhad base, the pilot asked ATC for fuel. ATC told them that they did not have fuel facility there and they had passed on the message to Dubai which was about 40 kms and it would take about 45 minutes. The hijackers kept on threatening the pilot that if refuelling is not done immediately they would start killing more passengers. The ATC sent a small bouzer and therefore, it was sent back. They were asked to send a big bouzer. The pilot also asked the ATC for food, water and fruits.

The hijackers also wanted food and so ATC told them that it would take time. The bouzer came after about two and half hours. The pilots requested the chief hijacker to off load some passengers. ATC bargained for release of passengers against fuel and asked to release injured, old, women and children. They asked that against every tonne fuel, one passenger should be released. The hijackers did not agree first. They told that after refueling only they would off load the passengers. The hijackers told the co-

Satnam Singh

pilot to tell the ATC that they wanted to off load some passengers in Lahore but Lahore did not accept and the hijackers promised to off load some passengers after refuelling. The ATC was firm. Accordingly, 30 tonnes of fuel was taken. The hijackers off-loaded 27 passengers mostly ladies and children, injured passenger Satnam Singh and the dead body of Rupin Katyal.

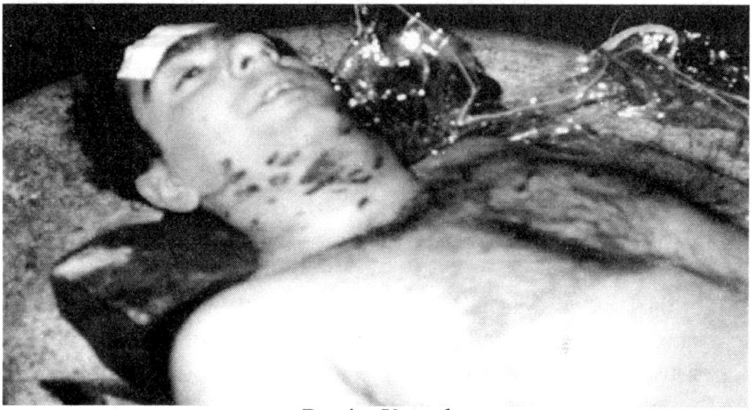

Rupin Katyal

ATC told them that they had arranged food for the passengers from the city and the same was being sent to the aircraft. The pilot informed the chief hijacker that food was coming to the aircraft. Immediately 2 or 3 catering vans came near the aircraft. The hijackers became panic. They apprehended some danger of some commando operation. Immediately, the chief hijacker told the pilot that they did not want food and threatened them to take off. In the meantime, ATC Minhad asked the pilot to clarify the demands of the hijackers. The pilot asked the chief hijacker but the chief hijacker told him *"Hum baad me bathayenge"*. The hijackers refused to allow food inside.

At Minhad when chief hijacker also went near the door as the passengers were being released, the pilot told the ATC that he was going to crash on the runway and asked emergency facilities like fire engine etc. The co-pilot advised the pilot not to do that as it might cause more damage as they had full fuel. The pilot asked the ATC to remove the vehicles on the runway but the hijackers told the pilot to take off as such. The pilot and the flight engineer agreed to crash the aircraft after take off from Dubai. However, the co-pilot did not agree for the same because of the danger to the passengers. They took off from Minhad at 00:50 GMT = 06:20 IST in the morning of 25.12.99.

The hijackers told them to go to Kabul. ATC UAE gave them routing to Kabul. The co-pilot asked the chief hijacker about their demands. The chief hijacker told him "later". At this time, the hijackers were behaving properly with the pilot. They also took tea with them. The chief hijacker lifted his monkey cap up to mouth and took tea, thus, the pilot, co-pilot had seen his face at that time itself. Co-pilot asked the chief hijacker about his name and native place but the chief hijacker just smiled. When the flight was in air, the hijackers collected five life jackets and kept them separately with them. When asked about their plan by the flight engineer Jaggia, the chief hijacker and hijacker Burger told that they would make them to swim. The flight engineer told them that there was no water on the way to Kabul. But the chief hijacker and hijacker Burger told them that when they were coming to Dubai they had seen ocean and how it was that there was no sea/ocean on way back. The cockpit crew explained to the hijackers that they were going through the other route where there was only desert and confused them. According to the cockpit crew the hijackers had some idea of jumping out of the aircraft. When they came in touch with Radio Kabul, Kabul informed that there was a message from their headquarters that Kandahar was open for them. This was informed to the chief hijacker and Burger, and they agreed. Accordingly, they headed for Kandahar and Kandahar welcomed them.

Aircraft at Kandahar

The aircraft landed at Kandahar at about 08:33 AM IST on 25.12.99. As soon as they landed, the hijackers shouted "stop, stop". Therefore, the pilot stopped the aircraft on the runway itself. Pilot saw one open jeep or van with six people sitting on the backside with rocket launcher and they waved towards cockpit and the chief hijacker and hijacker Burger also waved towards them. According to the co-pilot, Afghanistan authorities put some blockade with fire engines. Some security persons with arms surrounded the aircraft.

The pilot switched off the engine. Hijacker Burger called one Taliban man through signal. Taliban people came near to the cockpit in a car and climbed on to the top of the car. Then the chief hijacker told the pilot and the flight engineer to go to the cabin. Accordingly, the pilot, co-pilot and flight engineer went to the cabin. In the 'J' class, they saw baggages and in the 'Y' class they saw the passengers blind folded. They were made to sit in the 'Y' class in the front. There were two hijackers. According to the Captain, when they were moving out of the cockpit, hijacker Burger was opening the window in the cockpit and had put his head out to talk to the Taliban security people. For about 15 minutes, hijacker Burger and the

security persons on the jeep discussed something. After about half an hour, one hijacker came to the cabin and called them. They went to the cockpit. The chief hijacker told them to talk to ATC Kandahar. ATC instructed them to follow one white jeep. Accordingly, they followed the jeep and parked the aircraft at a place so pointed out by the Taliban people. The Taliban blocked the aircraft with a fire engine and posted security guards. Hijacker Burger told the pilot, co-pilot and flight engineer to go back to 'Y' class. Accordingly, they went to the 'Y' class and sat in front of the passengers.

On 26.12.99, the hijackers called the pilots and flight engineer on and often for technical help like increase of volume, decrease the volume of RT, adjusting the temperature, changing the frequency on the VHF etc. They returned back after attending to the work. The pilot saw a hijacker who was called, Shankar sitting at the back. Another hijacker called Bhola was sitting near them. Another hijacker called Doctor was in the cabin here and there and also used to go to the cockpit. The co-pilot used the rear toilet, hijacker Bhola was sitting with a revolver and a knife in his hand. According to the co-pilot Bhola was young. Shankar was well built and had a grenade in his right hand, he had thick eye brows, a little darkish. Hijacker Doctor was wearing specs. Shankar had moustaches. Burger was normally built and all of them had black monkey caps. The chief hijacker was sitting in the cockpit. He was of 5'5" height, with little darkish colour and had rectangle specs. He was wearing a red mask.

On 26.12.99, on the request of the pilot, the chief hijacker allowed removal of blindfolding. In the night the chief hijacker told the pilot that they had checked in baggage in the cargo hold and they wanted it to be taken out. The pilot told him that only the ground staff knew how to open the cargo hold. That night, again the hijackers wanted to open the cargo. The pilot did not agree at all. The hijackers threatened the pilot and flight engineer Jaggia with the revolver and took Jaggia down. It was very cold outside and was about -10 degrees. Mr Jaggia started shivering and hijacker Burger thought perhaps the old man would die and opened the nearby Jeep, put him inside and started the heater. Later on Jaggia was brought in. In the night, the pilot and co-pilot heard the voice of hammering the cargo hold.

On the morning of 27.12.99, flight engineer Jaggia told the co-pilot that the hijackers had two bags in the cargo and they brought one bag inside the aircraft and they had more weapons. The pilot and co-pilot also saw more sophisticated pistols and different coloured and types of hand grenades with the hijackers. When the pilot went to the cockpit, he also saw about hundred bullets lying on the pedestal.

On 27.12.99 morning, the hijackers threatened the passengers and crew that they would kill them if their demands were not met and that nobody had come from India. After some time, hijacker Burger announced that the United Nations team had come and they were talking to them. The cockpit crew wanted to talk to UN delegate. Capt. Devi Saran obtained permission of the chief hijacker and spoke to the UN delegate and requested him to inform the world leaders about the problem and telecast the same through CNN, BBC and Star TV and requested the representatives of the countries, whose nationals were on board to take immediate and necessary action to negotiate with the hijackers. The pilot told the UN representatives about the condition on board. The UN representatives wanted three hours time to inform the concerned authorities. The hijackers agreed. After some time, hijacker Burger informed that the diplomats of the concerned nations had come to Kandahar. He also then informed that Indian delegation had come. The passengers and crew members were little relaxed. The cockpit crew asked hijacker Burger about their demands. Burger told them that they wanted the release of 36 militants from the Indian jails and they had made other demands which he did not tell the pilots.

On 28.12.99, the negotiations were on. The chief hijacker called Capt. Devi Saran to the cockpit and told him that the Indian negotiators were not accepting their demands. The pilot asked the chief hijacker about their demands. The chief hijacker told the pilot that they wanted release of one person against which they would release 15 ladies and children and patients. The pilot sat down and requested the chief hijacker to spell out their full demands for release of all the passengers and the crew and that the Indian negotiators wanted the same. The chief hijacker told the pilot that he would think over. The pilot came back to the cabin.

After about half an hour the chief hijacker came to pilot Capt Devi Saran and told *"Captain Sahab Hamne Aap Ki Baat Maan Li Hai Aur Poori Mange Bata Di Hain"*. The hijackers were very rude to the passengers that day and they even did not allow the food to come in and no water was supplied to the passengers. The situation inside the aircraft was getting worse. The toilets were not cleaned, water was not available.

On 29.12.99, chief hijacker came to the cabin and the pilots talked to him and requested him to relax their demands. The chief told them that the situation had completely changed and they had become the hostages and the Indian Government had become the hijacker. The chief hijacker just smiled and told the pilots that they will see and negotiate and he went back. That day at about 11' Clock food came and at about 12' Clock water was also supplied. However, in the morning time the APU failed and therefore, they opened the window shutters. The chief hijacker told the pilot to get the refuelling and accordingly Bouzer came and refuelling was done. At the time of refuelling, pilot Capt Saran and flight engineer Jaggia also went down to monitor the refuelling on permission given by the chief hijacker. The pilot saw two Walkie-Talkies with the chief hijacker and on one of the Walkie-Talkies he could see 'Kandahar ATC' written on it.

That was of a different make with LC Display. On that Walkie-Talkie the chief hijacker was talking to someone and the person at the other end was telling him that he had brought napkin papers. The chief hijacker told the pilot to go out of the cockpit to the cabin. Accordingly, the pilot went to the cabin but till evening he could not see any toilet napkin in the aircraft anywhere. That day the chief hijacker told the pilot to take rest because they had to take off any time. In the night on 29.12.99 active hijacker Burger announced that ladies, children and patients should sit in the 'J' Class.

He wanted 15 people in the 'J' Class. On the request of the pilot he added 15 more in the list. Five more persons were added by Mr. Jaggia. Accordingly about 35 ladies, children and patients were shifted to the 'J' Class. However, suddenly in the night of that day the said persons were sent back to their seats in the cabin and it appeared that the talks had failed.

On 30th morning at about 8.00 AM the chief hijacker came and announced that their demands had not been met and they would start killing one by one and all the passengers and crew members would be killed. He asked everybody to remember God. Hijacker Burger also announced that the talks had failed and he also threatened to kill all the passengers and crew members on board and instructed all to bow their heads. The pilot Capt. Saran went to hijacker Burger and asked him as to what was the matter.

Burger told the pilot that their demands had not been agreed to by the Indian team and they would start sending *'Tohfa'* to the Indian team. The pilot accordingly came back and sat on his seat. Immediately the Taliban commandos surrounded the aircraft.

Hijacker Burger told the co-pilot that the guards were likely to attack and the hijackers would fight with them. However, after about an hour the commandos moved out. This happened twice that day. Then the chief hijacker came and announced that the talks had been resumed again as the Foreign Minister of Afghanistan had intervened. After about two hours hijacker Burger told the pilot that their demands had been met and Government of India had agreed to release three persons and the modalities of release were being worked out. So everybody was happy but some passengers were still in doubt and therefore, the pilot went to the cockpit and talked to the Indian negotiators with the permission of the chief hijacker and they confirmed the news to be correct. Accordingly the pilot came back and announced the same to the passengers.

At about 12.00 hours hijacker Burger informed that 50 percent of the demands had been met. Two hours later he informed that 80 percent of the demands had been met. At about 3.00 PM hijacker Doctor came to the front and told that 100 percent of the demands had been met. That night the passengers and crew got very good food. All of them were waiting for release.

On 31.12.99 the passengers and the crew waited for their release. The situation inside the aircraft was very bad and it was stinking. At about 5-5.30 PM that day one aircraft landed. Before landing of the said aircraft the hijackers were trying to open the cargo hold but they did not succeed. Hijacker Burger told the passengers and the crew to take their hand baggages, luggages from the 'J' class. He made sitting arrangements by putting the sick people in the front, ladies with children thereafter and then husband and wife, then family and then other people and the crew at the last. He instructed them to get down from the aircraft through the second gate *i.e.,* cabin entry gate. One van came near the aircraft and immediately all the hijackers got down and got into the van. They took one Taliban officer forcibly as a cover for their safety.

While leaving hijacker Burger said *"Insha Allah, Phir Milenge"*. Burger was searching for his binocular but he could not find it. During the detention in Kandahar, hijacker Burger had freely interacted with the passengers whenever the situation was positive and given autographs which were collected during investigation. After the hijackers left, the crew found the binocular in the cockpit and the same was handed over to the negotiating team.

According to the pilot, the Binocular was given to Mr. Jaswant Singh, External Affairs Minister. During investigation, the Minister was requested to hand over the same to the CBI as it is a case property also used in the commission of the crime. The OSD and other staff of the Minister said that it was a gift to the Minister by the hijackers and kept in a room in the Ministry. There were correspondences, I recollect. Finally, a reply was received that it is available and will be produced as and when requisitioned by the court. Hope the Ministry preserves this case property. Then one Indian delegate came on to the aircraft and announced that they were safe and would be taken to Delhi. The Taliban authorities checked the passengers who were getting down. They also checked the hand baggages. There were two special flights. One flight left at 6 PM and the other at about 6.30 PM and landed at Delhi Airport at about 21.00 hours and 21.30 hours.

Indian Negotiating Team and Negotiations with the Hijackers

Immediately on coming to know of hijacking of IC-814, the Indian High Commission at Islamabad became active. At 17.25 hours. *Zee News Channel* flashed the news of hijacking. A control room was set-up in the Mission to monitor the situation minute by minute. At 18:10 hours – Foreign Secretary contacted the High Commissioner and informed him about the hijacking and asked him to approach the Pakistan authorities and request them to let the plane land at Lahore Airport. Indian High Commissioner spoke to the Chief of Protocol Farooq Ubaid since the Foreign Secretary of Pakistan was not available but the latter informed that they would not let the plane land at Lahore Airport under any circumstances. Contacts with the Pakistan Government continued by which time the plane landed at Lahore. When the plane took off for Kabul, the Indian Government got in touch with the Taliban authorities. They wanted clear instructions from the Indian authorities regarding handling of the matter. Finally, Indian negotiating team consisting of three high level officers reached Kandahar on 27.12.99 evening. Before that an officer of Indian High Commission at Islamabad was sent to Kandahar who interacted with Taliban Foreign Minister Mr Muttawakkil and Gen. Usmani, Area Corps Commander and requested them for help. On arrival, the Indian team started negotiations with the hijackers. The hijackers demanded the release of Maulana Masood Azhar but did not give their full demand. This was informed to the Taliban authorities, who asked the hijackers to give their full demands whereupon on 28.12.99, the next day a full list of demands including the release of 36 terrorists in custody in India, the coffin of Sajjad Afghani and a sum of 20 crore dollars written on a sheet of paper by the hijackers was sent to the Taliban. The following were the full demands of the hijackers:

Release of:

- Maulana Masood Azhar;
- Mohammad Arif. S/o Aleemuddin Khan;
- Saif-ullah Khalid S/o Shear Khan;
- Mohammad Saeed Khan S/o Suleman Khan;
- Mohammad Shafeque (Abu Jundal);

- Mohammad Yosuf Khawja S/o Mohammad Ayub;
- Nisar Ahmed S/o Mohammad Zaman;
- Sultan Ahmed Miana S/o Gulam Jillani;
- Naveed Iqbal S/o Mohammad Iqbal;
- Nasir Ikram S/o Qazi Ikram-ul-Haq;
- Abdul Haji S/o Malik Mohammad Ajmal;
- Mohammad Ishfaq S/o Mohammad Shafi;
- Shahid Latif;
- Sohail Ahmed Kataria S/o Shahbaz Khan;
- Mohammad Nazir;
- Nasir Aftab;
- Umer Sheikh (England);
- Muzamil Ahmed Dar S/o Ghulam Ahmed Dar;
- Farooq Ahmed Raja S/o Mohammad Shear Khan;
- Nasar-ullah-Langrial;
- Syed Sajid Ali S/o Shahpal Shah;
- Salah-ud-Din Qasmi;
- Mushtaq Zargar;
- Aamar;
- Basharat Ali S/o Ali Ashgar;
- Alam Khan S/o Behram Khan;
- Raheel Ahmed Hashmi S/o Mohammad Mushtaq Hashmi;
- Shahid Mohammad S/o Ali Afsar;
- Mohammad Khalid Bukhari S/o Khadam Hussain Bukhari;
- Naseer Ahmed S/o Mohammad Bashir;
- Syed Waqar Shah S/o Imam Shah;
- Mohammad Ikram Balooch;
- Mohammad Sakhi Zaman S/o Buland Khan;
- Ghulam Mohammad Butt S/o Haqa Butt;
- Nashi Ullah S/o Nazir Ahmed;
- Jaffar Ali S/o Sabir Ali;
- [We want the coffin of "Sajjad Afghani Shaheed"];
- [And we also want $ 20,00,00,000 (Twenty Crore Dollars)]".

On receipt of the demands, the Indian team conveyed these demands to Delhi. On the evening of 28th, Gen. Usmani told the hijackers that the demands had been seen by the Taliban leadership and they had found that the demands for money and for coffin of Sajjad Afghani were un-Islamic. He told the hijackers to delete these demands. Mr Muttawakkil, Foreign Minister of Taliban also told the hijacker to delete these demands. Finally the hijackers told Gen. Usmani that in view of their respect and regard for the Taliban they would drop these demands. With the demands for money and the coffin of Sajjad Afghani were withdrawn, negotiations regarding release of other terrorists continued. After continued negotiations, it was agreed on 30.12.99 for release of Maulana Masood Azhar, Umar Sheikh and Mustaq Zargar. This was communicated to Delhi. On approval by the Govt. of India, the cases pending against these three militants were withdrawn and all the three militants were released and taken to Kandahar on 31st afternoon. Minister of External Affairs Jaswant Singh also went to Kandahar in the flight to see that the passengers were safely released. On arrival of the three militants the hijackers left the aircraft and escaped in a Taliban van. There was no attempt to seize the weapons and hand grenades from the hijackers.

Breakthrough in the Case

The Mumbai Police had received a tip off from Intelligence agencies about a mobile phone no. 9820110945 which was in constant touch with some Pakistan numbers and on 25.12.99 they started monitoring it. The Mumbai Police monitored the calls and found that calls were being made to Pakistan from the mobile phone. In the meantime the Mumbai Police Crime Branch received information that the accused wanted in the Borivalli Police Station case relating to the bank dacoity at Maharashtra Cooperative Bank were hiding in a particular place. In October 1999, a dacoity took place in the Co-operative Bank, Borivalli and a case in Crime No. 338/99 was registered at Borivalli Police Station under Sections 342, 452, 394, 397, 34 IPC and Section 3, 25 Arms Act.

On 30.12.99, the Crime Branch, Mumbai Police, after careful verification, searched Room No. 2, Anwar Chawl, Sampai Nagar, Behram Bagh, Jogeshwari where they found Abdul Latif Adam

Momin alias Patel and Mohd. Rafiq. On search of the flat, the police seized mobile phone no. 9820110945, two AK-56 rifles, two loaded magazines of AK-56 rifles, 4 anti–Tank rifle grenades, one 'Gupti', one dagger, passport of Abdul Latif No. A-446947, MDL No. MH01-98-24131 of Mohd. Salim (accused Yusuf Azhar brother-in-law of Maulana Masood Azhar), another mobile phone no. 9820277112 (of accused Abdul Latif) and a sum of ₹ 1,05,000/-. Abdul Latif and Mohd. Rafiq were arrested from there.

On questioning them and getting the address of another hide-out, police also searched the Patanwadi flat from where they arrested Mohd. Asif alias Babloo, Pakistani national and seized one imported pistol from him alongwith ₹ 1,72,000/- in Indian currency. On interrogation and getting information about further hide outs, they also searched flat 707, B Wing, Golden Soil Apartment, Jogeshwari and arrested Yusuf Nepali alias Bhupal Man Damai, Nepali citizen (accused in the hijacking case) and his family. From the said flat they seized one black colour pistol with a loaded magazine, Indian passport no. 0646697 in the name of Ansari Tariq Mohd., Indian passport no. A–1862893 in the name of Josaf David Peter, Indian passport no. B-0723176 in the name of Farooq Abdul Aziz Siddiqui (hijacker Shankar), Indian passport no. B-0646681 in the name of Siddiqui Javed Amjad (chief hijacker), Indian passport no. B-0093147 in the name of Ahmed Ali Mohd. Ali Sheikh (chief hijacker).

From the personal search of Yusuf Nepali the police seized one railway ticket no. 31191460 dt. 25.12.99 for journey from Gorakhpur to Mumbai by five passengers by Kushi Nagar Express of 25.12.99 as well as one chit of paper containing the address of Golden Soil Apartment flat and mobile phone number of Abdul Latif.

Investigation carried out by Mumbai Police Crime Branch disclosed a passport racket and therefore they registered cases and took up investigation. On interrogation, Abdul Latif, so arrested, disclosed details of the hijacking and obtaining of passports and motor driving licences etc., on forged documents for the hijackers.

Registration of FIR

The Indian Airlines, the owners of the hijacked aircraft did not lodge any complaint of hijacking of their aircraft with the police. The ATC or the Airport Director in Varanasi or those in Delhi filed no complaint. The situation was being monitored and therefore it appeared that they forgot to take this important step of filing a complaint. By the time they were thinking about this, the aircraft had already left India. However on 25.12.1999 Mr Mulekar, Airport Director, Raja Sansi Airport, Amritsar sent a complaint to the SHO of the area regarding landing of the hijacked aircraft at Amritsar Airport on 24.12.1999. This was being processed. Mr Mulekar had sent a reminder to the SHO and entries were found in the general diary of the Police Station. However, no case was registered by the Amritsar police.

On 25.12.1999 at 08:30 PM, Sarad Sen, Airport Manager, IGI Airport Delhi had telephoned to the IGI Airport Police Station and informed that Indian Airlines special flight which had gone to Dubai to bring back the passengers released by the hijackers would be landing at Indira Gandhi International Airport, New Delhi at about 10:45 PM with 26 passengers and one dead body and necessary action be taken in this connection. Entry regarding this was made in the Daily Diary and copy was given to SI Sanjay Sharma for necessary action who alongwith HC Dharampal no. 248-A left for taking necessary action. SI Sanjay Sharma alongwith the head constable, went to the ceremonial lounge of the airport, on receipt of the above said DD entry where SHO, Addl SHO and other Sr Officers were present. He alongwith HC Sohan Pal and constable Mahipal Singh went to Bay no. 42 at about 11PM on 25.12.1999 where the special flight from Dubai carrying the released passengers of the hijacked aircraft IC-814 of 24.12.1999 was parked. Most of the released passengers were ladies or children and from the enquiry with the passengers, it was learnt by the sub-inspector that on 24.12.1999 the flight IC-814 which had taken off at about 4:30 PM from Kathmandu was hijacked by five youth having knife, pistol and hand grenade who created terror. The passengers were forced to bow down their heads and when some passengers attempted to lift their heads they were stabbed with knife. After sometime, the aircraft landed at Amritsar Airport and the hijackers by force and threat made the aircraft to take off to Lahore. From Lahore in the same night by use of force and threat they took the flight to Dubai. At Dubai the hijackers released some of the children, ladies and old persons including one Satnam Singh having injuries on his neck and one dead body of the person who died on account of stabbing injuries caused by the hijackers. Out of fear none of the passengers was ready to make any statement. Injured Satnam Singh was taken to a Nursing Home by the Indian airlines doctor. The sub-inspector after coming to know that the dead body had reached the cargo, went to the cargo complex where some of the relatives of the deceased met him.

He collected one coffin containing the dead body from Indian Airlines staff. On being shown the dead body, the relatives identified the dead body as that of Rupin Katyal, R/o No. 37, Sector 14, Gurgaon. On inspection of the dead body, one stab wound on abdomen, four stab wounds on chest, 21 stab wounds on neck, six stab wounds on the face and one abrasion on the nose were found which appeared to have been caused by a sharp edged weapon. The sub-inspector prepared a report and sent the same through head constable Dharampal to the police station for registration of the case. The sub-inspector mentioned that as the circumstances and enquiry revealed that the main occurrence has been found to have been committed at Amritsar in India, therefore, '0' FIR may be registered and sent to Amritsar in Punjab. He has also mentioned that special report may be sent to ACMM and Senior Officers through special messengers. The sub inspector remained busy in completing the formalities about the deceased.

On 26.12.1999 on the complaint given by sub inspector Sanjay Sharma, '0' FIR was registered in the Police Station under Sections 365,341, 342, 506, 307, 302, 147, 148, 149, IPC, Section 27 Arms Act, Section 5 of Explosive Substances Act and Section 4/5 of Anti-Hijacking Act 1982. The FIR was transferred by ACP: Palam to SSP Amritsar on 26.12.1999 stating that the offence fell under the jurisdiction of Amritsar District. On the basis of this, FIR no. 145 was registered at Police Station Raja Sansi on 29.12.1999. On the request of Government of Punjab, the investigation of this FIR was transferred to the CBI by the Government of India and accordingly, a case was registered on 11.1.2000 in the CBI and the investigation was taken up.

On the basis of information given by Abdul Latif arrested in the bank dacoity case and thereafter in the passport racket case, verifications were made at different places and also in Nepal and many facts came to light indicating his involvement in the hijacking case. However, complete story and the conspiracy angle were not clear. To get at the truth, the CBI arrested Abdul Latif in the hijacking case and interrogated him thoroughly after getting him on police custody remand.

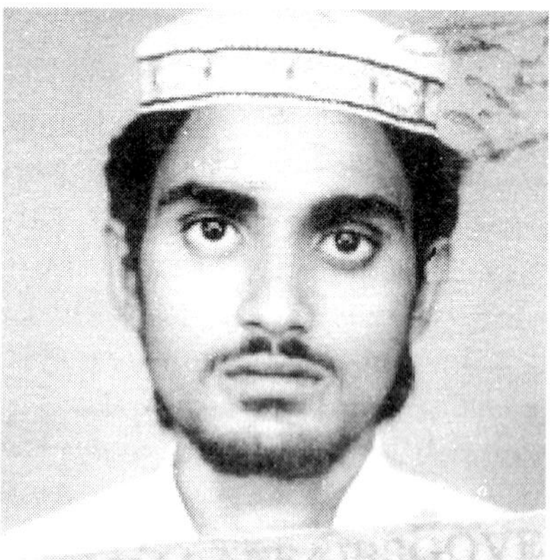

Who is Abdul Latif?

Abdul Latif Momin alias Abdul Rehman alias Patel alias Imran, R/o Flat No. 104-A Wing, Sani Shopping Centre, Opposite Jogeshwari Railway Station (W), Patel Estate Road, Mumbai – hails from District Patan, Gujarat state. He studied in Madarsas. In 1993, after the Babri Masjid demolition, he went to Saudi Arabia and worked there in a Masjid as Imam for about two years. There he came in contact with one Anwar, a Pakistani national who was a teacher there in a Madarsa. In the end of 1994, he came in contact with Zakir Kashmiri through Anwar. Anwar told him that Zakir Kashmiri was the brother of Pakistani militant Farooq Kashmiri who is fighting to liberate Kashmir. Anwar also told him that Farooq Kashmiri is the second–in–command of Harkat-ul-Ansar/ Harkat-ul-Mujahiddin (HuM). Anwar also told him that Fazal-ur-Rehman Khalil is the chief of HuM. Zakir Kashmiri talked to Abdul Latif telling him that Indians are against Muslims and provoked him to do *'Jehad'* against India. He also told him that they should take revenge against India for demolition of Babri Masjid. On being brain-washed by Zakir Kashmiri in the name of Islam, he went to Pakistan for *jehad* against India. He went to Dhaka where he was given a Pakistan passport by Pakistan militant Faizullah. In Karachi, he was received by Rashid Siddiqui and Qari Naved, Pakistani militants. Rashid Siddiqui was chief of HuM in Karachi. After about 10-15 minutes Qari Naved sent Latif alongwith a guide to Islamabad where they stayed in the building of HuM where Fazal-ur-Rehman and Farooq Kashmiri had their office and residence.

Fazal-ur-Rehman provoked Latif to fight against India and sent him to HuM training centre in Khost, Afghanistan. He alongwith others were trained in handling and operating weapons like AK-47, Pistols, HMG/LMG Rifles, Rocket launchers for 40 days. Thereafter he remained there. In April 1996, Fazal-ur Rehman, chief of HuM, sent him to India to work with Pakistan militants Rashid Siddiqui and Abu Sayeed. He came back to Mumbai and assisted in transporting Pakistani militants to Srinagar etc. In April 1998, he again went to Karachi. Rashid Siddiqui told him that Yusuf Azhar, brother-in law of Maulana Masood Azhar was trying to get Maulana released from the jail. Latif was trained in preparing explosives. Thereafter, in June 1998, Fazal-ur-Rehman sent Latif to the ISI training centre where he was trained for a month. After that Fazal-ur-Rehman instructed him to work with Yusuf Azhar, in Mumbai and help him in militant activities against India and also in getting Maulana Masood Azhar freed from the jail. Latif came to Karachi by air where he was received by Naeem alias Ali and Abdul Rauf, younger brother of Maulana Masood Azhar. As instructed, Latif also brought four Pak militants to assist Yusuf Azhar in Mumbai. Then Yusuf Azhar went to Karachi.

In February 1999 Ali alias Naeem asked Latif to talk to Yusuf Azhar in Pakistan on the number given by him. Accordingly Latif telephoned from his Mobile no. 98201-64879 to Yusuf Azhar on his Karachi Phone No. 5886697 and talked to him. Yusuf Azhar instructed Latif to arrange a flat in Mumbai as he would be coming back soon. He also told Latif that one boy named Akhtar would also be coming alongwith Amjad alias Haider. Accordingly,

Latif made efforts and got a flat in April 99 in his name as Javed Siddiqui in Madhav Building, 1st Floor, Opposite Oshwara Bus Depot, Link Road, Goregaon (W) on a rent of ₹ 2200/- pm and also paid the advance ₹ 70,000/-. However, even before he could arrange this flat, Amjad and Akhtar reached Mumbai and stayed at Ekta Chawl. This room was taken on rent by Amjad in 1998 itself and Ali, Bablu, Chaman alias Abdul Rahim, Pakistani militants were also staying there. Latif started living in the Madhav Building flat.

In the end of April' 99 Yusuf Azhar came to Mumbai alongwith Shakir alias Rajesh Gopal Verma (hijacker Shankar). Shakir alias Rajesh Gopal Verma is a resident of Shakkur in Pakistan. Both Yusuf Azhar and Shakir alias Rajesh Gopal Verma stayed with Latif in the Madhav Building flat. Yusuf Azhar gave the photograph of Ibrahim Athar alias A.A. Sheikh for preparation of Indian passport. Latif obtained the photograph of Shakir alias R.G. Verma from him and gave both these photographs to Suresh of M/s Seven Travels near Bombay Central Post Office to arrange passports for Ibrahim Athar in the name of Ahmad Ali Mohd. Ali Sheikh and for Shakir alias Rajesh Gopal Verma in the name of Farooq Abdul Aziz Siddiqui. The passports were to be obtained using forged ration cards and school certificates. Suresh agreed to arrange passport without production of the required documents for ₹ 4,500/- per passport. Suresh used to arrange the required documents for getting passport, himself, showing the persons as Indian citizens. He filled up the passport application forms on the information given by Latif. Latif gave his name as Imran to Suresh which he noted down. Latif also gave his pager no. 9628227148 and mobile phone no. 9820110317 to Suresh which he noted down in a Register which was seized during investigation.

In June, 99 Yusuf Azhar, Ashraf alias Nawab went to Jammu to arrange escape of Masood Azhar. Masood Azhar and his associate Sajjad Afghani made an attempt to escape from the jail but in this attempt Sajjad Afghani got injuries and died. Yusuf Azhar and Akhtar were picked up by the Police on suspicion when they were found roaming near the jail. However, Ashraf managed to escape and telephoned Naeem alias Ali at Mumbai. Ali telephoned Manager of the Hotel where they were staying and requested him to get Yusuf Azhar and Akhtar released. The Manager was not told the real facts but was requested to help them to get released and the Hotel Manager did the same. This attempt to escape through the tunnel from the jail also failed. Maulana could not be released.

In June 1999, on return from Jammu, Yusuf Azhar told Latif to arrange another flat on rent and that nobody should know about this. Accordingly Latif arranged flat no. 707, B Wing, Golden Soil Apartments, Raj Nagar, Jogeshwari (W) at ₹ 3500/- rent pm in the name of Javed Siddiqui and paid ₹ 40,000/- as advance. After arranging this flat Latif alongwith Yusuf Azhar started living there. In the end of June, 99, Latif alongwith Yusuf Azhar went to Dhaka via Calcutta. They stayed in a Hotel at Fakirapol. After a week, Yusuf Azhar went back to Karachi instructing Latif to stay back there in Dhaka.

In July 1999 Yusuf Azhar telephoned to Latif and told him that Abdul Rauf, younger brother of Maulana Masood Azhar would be reaching Dhaka via Kathmandu and he should receive him at the Airport. He gave the flight details to Latif. Accordingly Latif received Abdul Rauf at Dhaka Airport. Abdul Rauf told Latif that they were trying to secure release of Maulana Masood Azhar and for this purpose their brother Ibrahim Athar is arranging weapons etc., in Kathmandu. Abdul Rauf asked Latif to help them in this work and Latif agreed.

After few days Shakir alias Rajesh Gopal Verma and Akhtar came to Dhaka from Mumbai and from there they went to Pakistan. Fifteen days later Shakir alias Rajesh Gopal Verma (hijacker Shankar) and Sunny Ahmad Qazi (hijacker Burger) reached Dhaka from Karachi. Few days after Mistri Zahoor Ibrahim (hijacker Bhola) also reached Dhaka and met Abdul Rauf. A few days after Sayeed Shahid Akhtar (hijacker Doctor) and Ibrahim Athar (hijacker chief and brother of Maulana) also reached Dhaka separately. During this time Abdul Rauf hired a flat on rent in Sabzi Mandi area and they all started staying in the said flat. In the end of August 1999 or beginning of September 1999 a meeting was held in the said flat in Sabzi Mandi, Dhaka, which was attended by Abdul Rauf, Ibrahim Athar, Qazi Sunny Ahmed, Shahid Sayeed Akhtar, Shakir alias Rajesh Gopal Verma, Mistri Zahoor Ibrahim and Latif. In this meeting Ibrahim Athar told about the plan to hijack Indian Airlines flight from Kathmandu for getting his brother Maulana Masood Azhar released from the jail in exchange of passengers of the flight. In the meeting Ibrahim Athar informed that for the hijacking of Indian Airlines flight he had talked to the Minister of Taliban and they will get all support from the Taliban for this. The plan was to take the aircraft to Pakistan or Afghanistan. Ibrahim Athar also told that if their demand for releasing Masood Azhar and others is not accepted by the Government of India then they will blow up the aircraft and die. He requested for Latif's help and Latif agreed. Ibrahim Athar and Abdul Rauf were brothers of Maulana Masood Azhar, who was in jail in Jammu and they all were Pakistanis. Ibrahim Athar told Latif to take Qazi Sunny Ahmed, Shahid Sayeed Akhtar, Shakir alias Rajesh Gopal Verma and Mistri Zahoor Ibrahim to Mumbai and arrange Indian passports and Motor Driving licences for them for use in the hijacking of Indian Airlines flight from Kathmandu.

Investigation disclosed that Abdul Latif arranged forged passports, driving licences to the hijackers Qazi Sunny Ahmed alias hijacker Burger, Shahid Sayeed Akhtar alias hijacker Doctor, Rajesh Gopal Verma alias Shakir alias hijacker Shanker and Zahoor Ibrahim Mistri alias hijacker Bhola. These hijackers stayed in the hide outs arranged by Abdul Latif in Golden Soil Apartment in Mumbai. The chief hijacker did not come to India, according to Latif, but the passports on forged documents were arranged for Ibrahim Athar and hijacker Shankar whereas Latif and Seven Travels had submitted the application and other papers for issue of passports to the other three hijackers which were pending with the Passport office. As instructed by Abdul Rauf, Latif on 01.11.99 took Shahid Sayeed Akhtar by flight to Calcutta and then to Kathmandu and they stayed in Hotel Imperial, Sundhara. Latif made entry in the hotel register in his own name as Abdul Momin. After few days Shahid Sayeed Akhtar left the hotel and started staying in a room which was arranged by Yusuf Nepali, a Nepali citizen, a conspirator.

On 19.11.99, Ibrahim Athar (chief hijacker) came and stayed with Latif in Tibet Rest House till 23.11.99. On 19.11.99 Shahid

Sayeed Akhtar alias hijacker Doctor brought a bag containing three hand grenades and three revolvers with 30-40 bullets and Ibrahim Athar told him to keep them at some safe place as they will be used in the hijacking. Latif came back to Mumbai on 25.11.99 and arranged driving licence for Ibrahim Athar in the name of Ahmed Ali Mohammed Ali Sheikh in which name the passport was obtained earlier. Then Latif took hijacker Shanker to Kathmandu. Mistri Zahoor Ibrahim and Qazi Sunny Ahmed also came to Kathmandu from Mumbai. Latif stayed with the hijackers in Kathmandu wherein he made entries in the Hotel registers.

Shahid Sayeed Akhtar used to prescribe medicines whenever they got cold, fever etc and therefore he was nicknamed 'Doctor' by them. Qazi Sunny Ahmed belonged to a superior community and therefore he was nicknamed 'Burger'. Mistri Zahoor Ibrahim used to use the word "*Maine Bola Na*" while speaking always and therefore he was nicknamed as Bhola. Ibrahim Athar alias Ahmed Ali Mohammed Ali Sheikh was chief of the hijacking team.

On 13.12.99 Ibrahim Athar called for a meeting in Zoo, Kathmandu. Ibrahim Athar (the chief), Qazi Sunny Ahmed alias Burger, Shahid Sayeed Akhtar alias Doctor, Shakir alias RG Verma alias Shankar, Mistri Zahoor Ibrahim alias Bhola and Latif were present. In this meeting Ibrahim Athar explained the plan for hijacking of Indian Airlines flight from Kathmandu to Delhi. Till that time the understanding was that Latif will also be in the hijacking party on the flight. However, Ibrahim Athar told that day in the meeting that Latif will not accompany them for hijacking and he should go back to Mumbai because if the plan of hijacking fails then there will not be anybody in India to work for them, their organisation and their associates in the militancy work against India. Ibrahim Athar explained that at Kathmandu Airport the security staff are lazy and the security checking is lax and if somebody passes through the metal detector the security staff on duty do not pay any attention and it is easy to take advantage of this lax system. He also said that one of the team members would go in advance alongwith the weapons and hand grenades and if he is able to get inside the airport without being caught, he will telephone from inside the airport and the other four members will then go to the airport. He also explained that if the first member was caught or no message was received from him then other four members would immediately leave Kathmandu for India and go to Bangladesh and thereafter to Pakistan. Ibrahim Athar then prepared three slips in the name of Ibrahim Athar, Sunny Ahmed Qazi and Shahid Sayeed Akhtar and adopted a lottery system and said that whosoever's name comes he will go to the airport first with arms and grenades. In the process the name of Ibrahim Athar came.

It was decided that the hijacked aircraft will be taken to Afghanistan. Ibrahim Athar told Latif to book tickets for him in the name of A.A. Shaikh in the business class, for Qazi Sunny Ahmed in the name of S.A. Qazi in the business class and for Z.I. Mistri, S.A. Sayeed and R.G. Verma in the same names in economy class from Kathmandu to Delhi for any date between 20.12.99 and 30.12.99 and instructed that he should get confirmed tickets for all the persons as above for any of the dates mentioned above. Ibrahim Athar alias A.A. Shaikh gave Latif ₹ 35,000/- for the tickets and also instructed him to purchase air ticket for himself for the flight on 17.12.99 for Delhi. Qazi Sunny Ahmed alias Burger and other persons asked about the position of each member in the aircraft during and after hijacking and Ibrahim Athar alias A.A. Shaikh said that all these details will be discussed in another meeting.

Immediately after the meeting, Latif went to Himalayan Travels and purchased ticket for A.A. Shaikh alias Ibrahim Athar, chief of the hijacking team in business class for Indian Airlines flight from Kathmandu to Delhi on 27.12.99. Thereafter he went to Everest Express Tours nearby and checked about the tickets in the economy class for Bhola, Doctor and R.G. Verma but he was told that the tickets will be in the waiting list.

He was told that confirmed tickets are available for 24.12.99. Therefore, immediately he went back to Himalayan Travels and changed the ticket in the name of A.A. Shaikh, the chief for the business class from 27.12.99 to 24.12.99. After booking the ticket for the chief hijacker Ibrahim Athar, he went to Everest Express Tours and purchased ticket for R.G. Verma, Z.I. Mistri (Bhola) and S.A. Sayeed (Doctor) in the economy class for the flight of 24.12.99. Then he went to Gorkha Travels and purchased business class ticket for S.A. Qazi (Burger) for the same flight of 24.12.99. Then he also purchased ticket for himself for the Indian Airlines flight on 17.12.99 to Delhi.

After purchasing the tickets he went to Hotel Pishang and informed Ibrahim Athar alias A.A. Shaikh, the chief and others about the tickets for the flight on 24.12.99 and handed over them their tickets. He stayed in the hotel till 17.12.99. On 17.12.99 as per the programme he came by air to Delhi and stayed in Nizami Hotel at Hazrat Nizamuddin. On 18.12.99 he left Delhi by Golden Temple Mail in second class AC and reached Mumbai on 19.12.99. On arrival at Mumbai, he informed all the details about the plan to hijack and arrangements made to Abdul Rauf in Pakistan on his mobile phone no. 0092300248765 from his mobile phone no. 9820110317, as directed by Ibrahim Athar alias A.A. Shaikh, the chief hijacker. Latif kept in contact with Ibrahim Athar, the chief hijacker and other hijackers through his mobile phone on 21.12, 22.12 and 23.12.99 respectively. On 23.12.99 in the night S.A. Akhtar alias Doctor telephoned to Latif and told him that they are sending Yusuf Nepali and his family to Mumbai and he should receive them and take care of them. He also told Latif to arrange forged passports for them and send them to Pakistan through Dhaka.

At about 12:30 hours on 24.12.99, Latif received a telephone call on his mobile phone no. 9820110945 from Qazi Sunny Ahmed alias Burger from Kathmandu who informed that Ibrahim Athar alias A.A. Shaikh, the chief hijacker has managed to pass through the metal detector inside the Airport with the weapons and grenades and as decided they are leaving the hotel for the airport. Immediately Latif telephoned from his mobile phone to Abdul Rauf in Karachi on his mobile phone no. 0092300248765 and informed him the above message. At about 2.30 PM that day Latif received a call from Z.I. Mistri alias Bhola on his mobile phone no. 9820110317 and he informed that the Indian Airlines flight from Kathmandu to Delhi which was to be hijacked was two hours late. Immediately Latif telephoned to Abdul Rauf on the above mobile phone and informed him.

Thereafter Latif sat in front of the TV to hear the news of hijacking. At about 5.30 PM the TV telecast the news about the hijacking of Indian Airlines flight IC-814 from Kathmandu. Immediately he telephoned to Abdul Rauf on his mobile phone as above and informed him. Abdul Rauf told him that he should inform him all the developments of hijacking from time to time till the hijacking incident ends.

Accordingly Latif kept informed Abdul Rauf about the developments through his mobile phone. On 27.12.99 Latif received Yusuf Nepali and his family at the Railway station and took them to Golden Soil Apartment and kept them in the flat. On 29.12.99 night Abdul Rauf sent him ₹ 1 lakh through Hawala system for looking after Yusuf Nepali and his family and Latif received the amount at Shalimar Restaurant, Bhindi Bazar.

As directed by Abdul Rauf, Latif also telephoned to BBC in London and left a message that if the demands are not met, the aircraft will be blown up. On 30th Latif was arrested and on his information Yusuf Nepali was also arrested. Abdul Latif volunteered to tell the truth before a Magistrate. The Magistrate sent him to judicial custody and subsequently recorded his confession. It was found that Latif had told the Magistrate that he was wrongly told by the Pak militants that the Muslims in India are harassed by the police in India but after remaining in the custody of CBI, he understood that it was false and therefore he wanted to tell the truth.

He stated all the facts related to the incident before the Magistrate. Detailed investigation was carried out in Kathmandu by the police there, on the points given by the CBI, resulting in collection of good evidence. The CBI officers went and assisted them in handling the pointers given.

Evidence related to stay of the hijackers and Abdul Latif in various hotels, telephone calls made by them were collected. The calls made by Latif to Pakistan and also to the hijackers in Kathmandu and calls received by him from them are shown in a diagram format below:

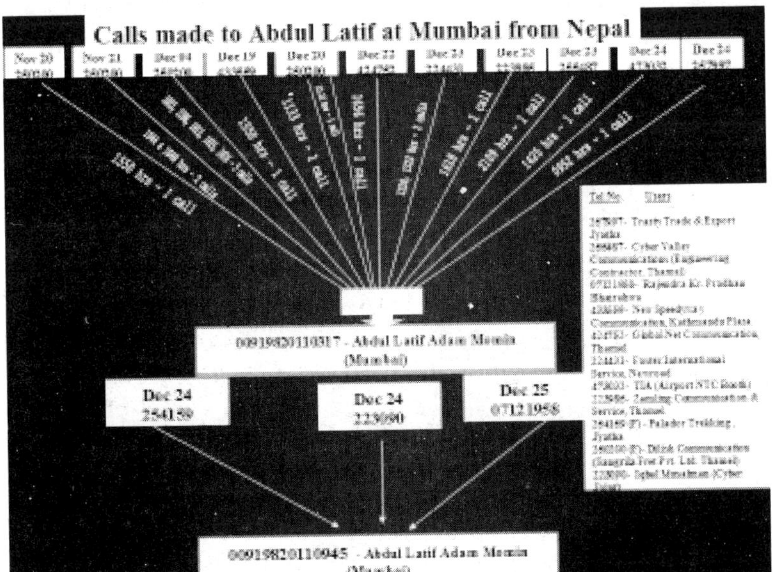

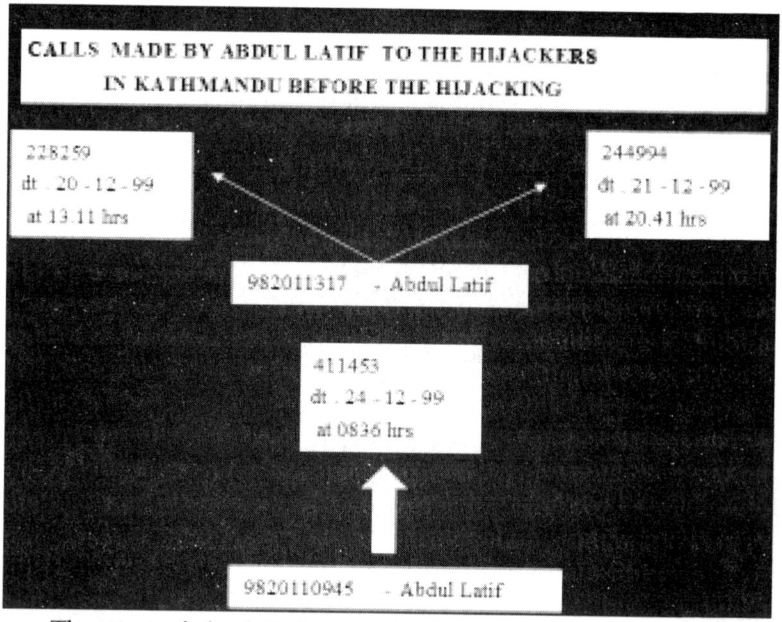

The stay of the hijackers and Abdul Latif in Kathmandu in various hotels during November and December 1999 can be projected as follows (not the actual hotel photos). This shows that they were changing hide outs regularly to avoid any detection by the police:

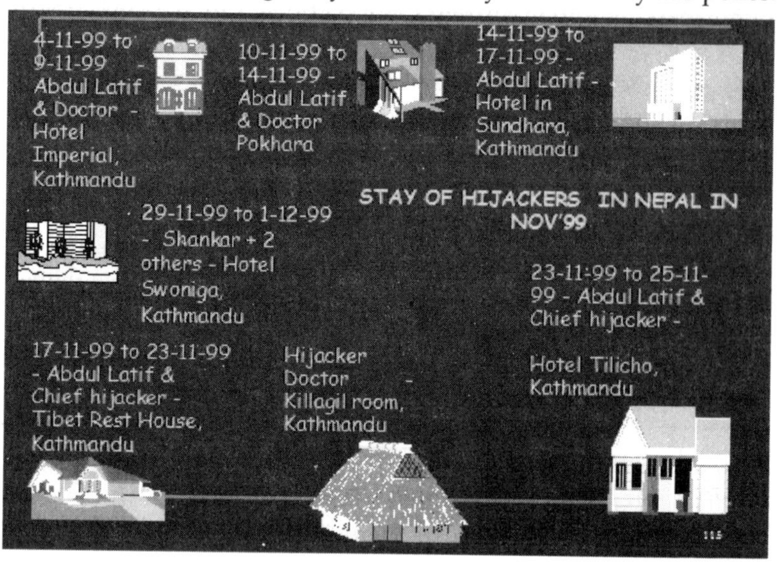

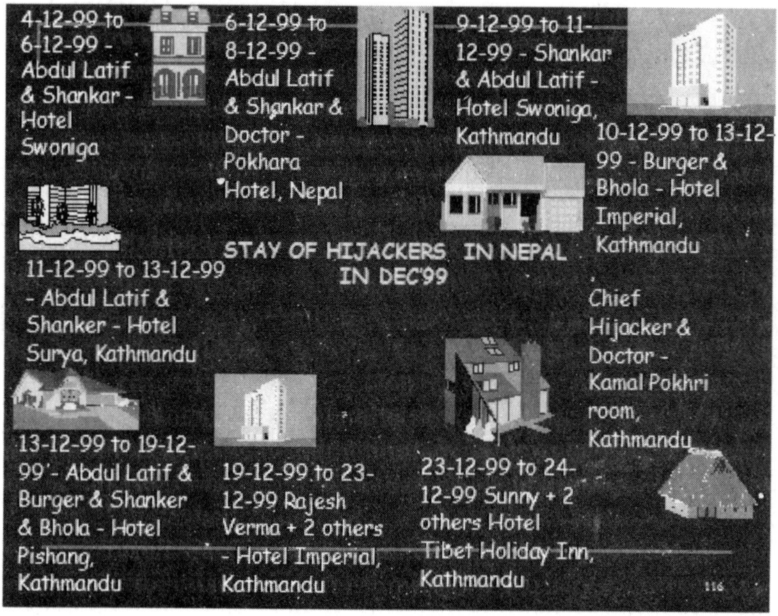

One of the passengers on board was Ms. Jeanne Moore, an American citizen who on return to USA had given a complaint that she was kidnapped by the hijackers on which a case was registered which was being investigated by the FBI. About six teams of the FBI came to India at different times and they were provided with all the relevant material.

They were requested to help the Indian investigators by getting details of the hijackers verified but there was nothing that they provided to the CBI. They informed that once they were able to indict the hijackers in the court, they would obtain arrest warrants and then they could put pressure on Pakistan to trace, arrest and hand over the hijackers. However, it appears that they could not reach that stage, for any reason.

The Indian passengers on board the aircraft were also examined by the CBI during investigation besides the crew members. They identified the photographs of the hijackers as shown in a picture format, below:

IDENTIFICATION BY PASSENGERS DURING INVESTIGATION

95 92 59 101 116

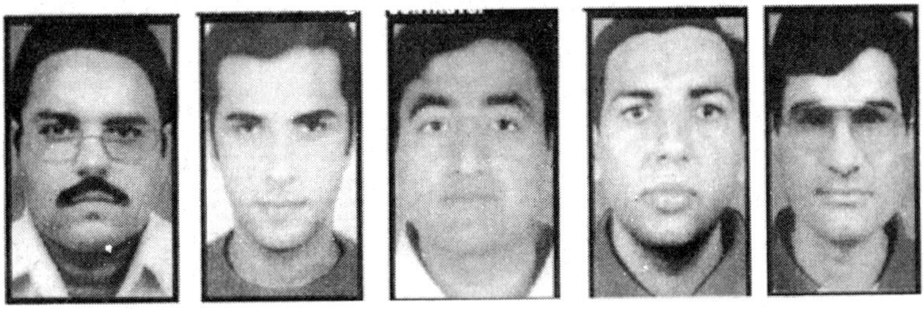

CHIEF BHOLA SHANKAR BURGER DOCTOR

IDENTIFICATION BY CREW DURING INVESTIGATION

3 2 3 2 4

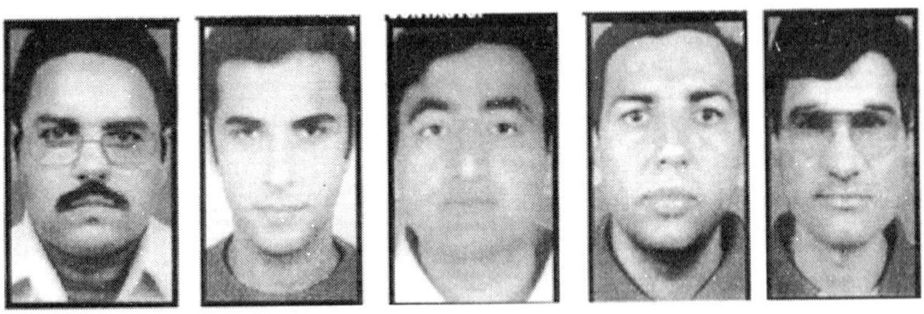

CHIEF BHOLA SHANKAR BURGER DOCTOR

Numbers above show how many witnesses identified photographs of each hijacker from number of photographs shown to them.

Result of Investigation

On completion of investigation, the CBI filed the Final Report as per the provisions of Section 173 of the Criminal Procedure Code in the court of Special Judge so appointed under the Anti-Hijacking Act at Patiala, Punjab who was also the District and Sessions Judge, Patiala, on 20.06.2000 against 10 persons which included the five hijackers and their associates involved namely

Abdul Latif, Abdul Rauf, Yusuf Azhar, Yusuf Nepali and Dilip Kumar Bhujel for the offence of conspiracy, hijacking, murder, kidnapping etc. On account of security threat to the accused and others, the trial was conducted inside the Central Jail, Patiala, as per the provisions of law. After taking cognizance of the offences, the court issued non-bailable warrants of arrest and production of the seven Pakistani nationals, accused. The accused could not be traced in India. Copies of warrants were sent to Interpol: Islamabad, Pakistan through Interpol: India with a request to trace, arrest and make available the accused for trial.

Since the validity of the arrest warrants expired, fresh non-bailable warrants of arrest were obtained and sent to Interpol Headquarters in Lyons, France for issue of Red Corner Notices to Member countries requesting them to look for, trace and arrest the hijackers and their two associates and inform the Indian authorities so that extradition request could be sent for their extradition to India for facing trial in the case. This notice was also sent to Interpol, Pakistan by the Interpol Headquarters in France for necessary action. The CBI has also sent copies of these Notices to Interpol, Pakistan with a request to trace and hand over the hijackers and their two associates.

Affidavits of the pilot of the aircraft and that of two passengers on board the said aircraft identifying the photographs of the hijackers were also submitted to the Pakistan Government through their High Commission in New Delhi requesting them to trace and hand over the accused. Pakistan Government was reminded that under the Montreal Convention for the Suppression of Unlawful Acts against the Safety of Civil Aviation 1971 (Montreal Convention), the Hague Convention for the Suppression of Unlawful Seizure of Aircraft 1970 (The Hague Convention), the SAARC Regional Convention on Suppression of Terrorism as also in accordance with the Simla Agreement and the spirit of the Lahore Declaration, they are legally obliged to arrest and hand over the seven accused to India. Such written requests were given to them on 15.01.2000, 24.04.2001 and 06.06.2001. However, there has been no response from Pakistan so far, though the matter was taken up at higher level in various meetings.

As there was no response from the Pakistan Government and the accused could not be traced in India, the trial court was requested to declare the seven Pakistani national accused as absconders and record the evidence against them as per the provisions of Section 299 CrPC. Accordingly, the trial court declared them as absconders and ordered for recording evidence against them and started the trial. The prosecution/CBI examined 120 witnesses in the court to prove the case against the accused, including the three accused present in the court.

On completion of the trial and after hearing the prosecution and the defence, the Special Judge passed the judgement convicting the three accused and sentenced them to undergo life imprisonment. This is a rarest of rare case in which the Pakistani militants hijacked Indian aircraft from a foreign country, took it by force to Afghanistan, a foreign country with which India did not have any diplomatic relations at that time and forced the Indian Government to agree to their demand and release three militants in exchange of the aircraft and the passengers. Therefore, after obtaining the approval of the Government, the CBI filed an appeal in the Punjab and Haryana High Court to enhance the punishment given to accused Abdul Latif and award death penalty to him. The remaining two accused have also filed appeals against the punishment awarded to them. The High Court has heard the appeals including the appeal filed by the CBI for awarding death penalty to accused Abdul Latif and reserved the judgement. Abdul Latif, an Indian citizen got associated with Pakistan militants for 'jehad' against India, assisted them in militant activities against India after getting training in HuM training centre and ISI training centre for militant activities against India. He was instructed to assist in getting Maulana Masood Azhar released from Indian jail by force. He assisted the hijackers and their two associates. He participated in the meeting held in Dhaka in the first week of September 1999 in which it was decided to blow up and kill all passengers of the hijacked aircraft, it necessary, to get Maulana released. In order to achieve this that passenger Rupin Katyal was brutally killed when the aircraft remained at Amritsar Airport as the pilot refused to take off from Amritsar. Katyal was tied to the seat and stabbed inside the closed aircraft. It is a rarest of rare case deserving death penalty. Any further detail regarding hijacking can only be had on arrest of the absconding hijackers and others, involved in this case.

Chapter 6

Why three Selected Militants were Important to them

The hijackers prepared a list of 36 militants in Indian jails, which was finally reduced to only three. It shows the importance of the three as far as the Pakistan based militant groups are concerned. Therefore, it is necessary, in public interest, to describe who are they.

Maulana Masood Azhar

Mohd. Masood Azhar alias Vali Adam, S/o Allah Baksh Sabir, R/o 1260/108, Kauser Colony, Model Town, District Bahawalpur, Punjab, Pakistan, arrested by Police Station CIK Srinagar in case FIR No. 1/93 under Section 3/4 TADA on 16.7.94, is a Pakistani national and Afghan trained militant of Harkat-ul-Ansar. He was holding the charge of General Secretary and was collecting funds .He was born at Bahawalpur on 10.7.1968. His father was working as a Headmaster in a Government School, Bahawalpur. He has five brothers and six sisters. His father had Deobandi (ideology) influence. After passing 8th class, he joined Jamia Islamia and passed "Almia" examination in 1989. Immediately after that he was employed as teacher in the same Jamia Islamia and he served as a teacher till April 1992.

Number of students of Jamia Islamia were under the influence of Harkat-ul-Mujahidin leader, who was an ex-student of that University. Masood Azhar was also impressed by the work of Harkat-ul-Mujahidin in Afghanistan jehad. Jamia Islamia University had on its roll the Arab nationals, Sudanese, Bangladeshis, South Africans apart from Pakistani nationals and all the nationals subscribed to the ideology of Deobandis. As such HuM was able to recruit their youth for participation in Afghan jehad. He subscribed to the cause and when in June/July 1989 he met Maulana Fazal-ur-Rehman Khalil, Amir, HuM at Karachi, the latter invited him to join the said party and to have training at Yavar in Afghanistan. Accordingly, he joined the jehadi group and went to Yavar and received training in handling of Kalashnikov rifle (AK–47) and Zokai Machine Gun (a type of Russian Machine gun). Although having sound and well- built physique and better education, he could not complete the obligatory training of 40 days to become the member of HuM but received only seven days training in handling the above said weapons and being a fatty person the remaining training period was waived. Maulana Fazal-ur-Rehman asked him to bring out a monthly Magazine for HuM. Azhar met Sajjad Afghani, a resident of Rawalkote, Pakistan Occupied Kashmir (POK) in Yavar camp of Afghanistan before he returned to Karachi.

Under the directions of Maulana Fazal-ur-Rehman, he started publishing a monthly magazine for HuM by name *"Sadai-E-Mujahid"* since September 1989 from Karachi and printed about 1000 copies per month. Most of them were distributed among the public free of cost during Friday prayers and sermon. The said magazine carried the news items of HuM, a militant organisation based at Karachi regarding its activities in Afghanistan. The magazine contained information regarding arms training given by HuM and opening of new offices of HuM all over Pakistan. The main object of the said magazine was to inform the people of Pakistan about the activities of HuM and its Jehad in Afghanistan against the Russian forces. Only Pakistani youth working in Afghanistan were affiliated with the HuM outfit and their way of working and achievements were being published in that magazine. Besides the activities of HuM in Afghanistan, religious teachings (Islamic) were also published in the magazine.

Till 1990 the HuM had opened its offices almost in all the prominent cities of Pakistan viz., Karachi, Hyderabad, Sindh, Lahore, Gujranwala and Islamabad. In the middle of 1991, he shifted the office of "*Sadai-E-Mujahid*" to Flat No. 4, Daddi Mansion, Regal Chowk, Karachi. He also used to print the bank account no. of Maulana Fazal-ur-Rehman on the last page of the magazine "*Sadai-E-Mujahid*" asking the public to contribute money. About eight lac rupees out of the contribution made by the public were spent on the activities of HuM organisation, monthly.

He used to visit Mecca in Saudi Arabia every year. In the year 1992, he alongwith Maulvi Farooq Kashmiri, Naib Amir of Central Wing of HuM and Amir of HuM Kashmir Wing visited Saudi Arabia and collected about three lac rupees in Pak currency for HuM. He alongwith Maulana Fazal-ur-Rehman Khalil visited Losaka and Chipata in Zambia to project the activities of HuM and collect funds. They delivered religious speeches in the main Mosque of Zambia. Besides this, they held Deeni Majlises in different areas in Zambia and collected about Rs. 22 lacs in Pak currency for HuM in the name of religion. After few months, he again visited Zambia and collected about Rs. 20 lacs in Pak currency for jehad in the name of religion. Then he alongwith Maulvi Farooq Kashmiri visited Abu Dhabi and collected donations of 4/5 lac rupees. They also visited Dubai and collected Rs. 3 lacs and went to Sharjah. The people of Sharjah were not interested to aid the Kashmiri militants as they felt that their relation with India was quite good. However, due to influence of Maulvi Ishaq originally R/o Pakistan Occupied Kashmir (POK) they could collect little donation from Sharjah. Few months after, he and his Assistant

Editor visited Sharjah and collected three lac rupees for the organisation. Thereafter, on the instructions of Fazal-ur-Rehman Khalil, he visited UK and made religious speeches in various Mosques in London with the help of Mufti Ismail, Maulvi of Southall Mosque in London and collected Rupees 15 lacs in Pak currency for HuM in the name of religious jehad. He met other Muslim leaders in UK including Maulana Ismail, who was engaged in construction of mosques and madarsas in recently liberated portion of Mangolia and Albania. Maulana Ismail invited him to visit Mangolia and Albania and promised to get him a passport of EEC country as it was difficult for a Pakistani to visit these countries. Then Maulana Ismail and his friend Hafiz Sahib got a Portuguese passport in the name of Adam Issa for him. Hafiz also got visas for India, Bangladesh, Pakistan on this passport.

In 1993 International pressure mounted on Pakistan for keeping the militants of different countries in Pakistan after the end of Afghanistan jehad. As a result, about 400/500 militants were arrested by the Pakistan Government. But due to pressure exerted by the people of Pakistan, the Government freed them from custody and asked the militants to leave the country and go to their respective countries. But most of the militants refused to go to their countries due to fear of prosecution. UAE Governments refused to take back the militants of their countries expecting trouble from them.

Majority of the militants went to Sudan from where they entered Somalia and joined ranks of Ittehad-E-Islami. Militants continued to correspond with them from Somalia. They remained in contact with Fazal-ur-Rehman Khalil, Amir of HuM and requested him to help that Pakistani army working under UNO in Somalia do not fight against Ittehad-e-Islami group. Most of the top ranking leaders of Ittehad-e-Islami were in Kenya from where they sent letters to HuM in Pakistan and requested for sending a team of Journalists for assessing the situation. On the directions of Amir of HuM, Azhar visited Kenya in 1993 and met the leaders of Ittehad-e-Islami where he was told that Pakistani army was working in favour of America and America was trying to establish its rule in Somalia. Azhar was asked to request the journalists of Pakistan to visit Kenya for on-the-spot assessment. Azhar stayed in Kenya for one week and returned to Pakistan. On reaching Pakistan he narrated the whole situation of Somalia to Amir of HuM, who directed him to contact the leading journalists of Pakistan. Accordingly, Azhar along with leading journalists of Pakistan and Amir of HuM Fazal-ur-Rehman visited Kenya and assessed the ground situation in Somalia and discussed with the leaders of Ittehad-e-Islami in Kenya. They assured the leaders of Ittehad-e-Islami that they all will publish the real situation of Somalia in the leading papers of Pakistan and try to compel the Government of Pakistan for withdrawal of Pak army from Somalia.

On their return, they wrote in the newspapers. The people of Pakistan were impressed on reading the publication and mounted pressure on Pakistani Government for withdrawal of Pak troops from Somalia. In this regard meetings and processions were organised, as a result of which Government of Pakistan agreed to withdraw the Pakistani troops from Somalia but till the arrest of Azhar, Pak troops had not been withdrawn from Somalia.

On the instructions of Fazal-ur-Rehman, Azhar and Maulvi Farooq Kashmiri visited Baghs, Abbasspora, Mirpora and Kotli in Pakistan Occupied Kashmir (POK) and delivered religious speeches in public meetings to inform the people about launching of jehad for liberating Kashmir from Indian occupation. They met the families of their militants, who had died in Kashmir. Sajjad Afghani had also accompanied them in this trip. In this tour Sajjad Afghani was told to take up the command and control of jehad operations in Kashmir and the route of his entry to India was via Bangladesh due to snowfall along the Indo-Pak border. Thereafter, Azhar alongwith Sajjad Afghani travelled by Emirates flight to Dhaka and were received by Maulvi Kalimullah at Dhaka Airport. From Airport they were brought to Hotel Pritan. They stayed in that hotel for two days and thereafter they were taken to Jassore by air, where Maulvi Kalimullah contacted his friend Maulana Khaliq who was a resident of Jassore. They requested Maulana Khaliq for safe journey of Sajjad Afghani to India. He escorted Sajjad Afghani and handed him over to his contact at Indo-Bangladesh border from where Sajjad Afghani crossed over to India. Azhar stayed 2/3 days in the hotel and visited Madarsas. After that he returned to Karachi by Emirates flight.

According to Masood Azhar Harkat-ul-Jehad was formed in 1980 when some youth belonging to Jamait-ul-Ulama-e-Islami and Tablig-ul-Jamat following Deobandi Ulemas wanted to participate in jehad in Afghanistan. Prominent in this were Maulana Fazal-ur-Rehman Khalil, Irshad Ahmed, Maulana Masood Kashmiri and Qari Saifullah Akhtar. Over the years, Harkat-ul-Jehad al-Islami gained momentum and also strength. The said organisation was mainly recruiting the youth from Jamia Islamia, Karachi and other Deobandi Madarsas of Karachi. Harkat-ul-Jehad al-Islami faced its first split when Maulana Fazal-ur-Rehman Khalil, the then commander-in-chief of HuJI and Qari Saifullah Akhtar who had become its Amir in 1985 following the death of Irshad Ahmed who was chief commander of HuJI and some other leaders in Afghanistan developed differences.

This compelled Maulana Fazal-ul-Rehman to form a new organisation named as Harkat-ul-Mujahidin with himself as its Amir. In this split Maulana Masood Kashmiri had joined Harkat-ul-Mujahidin only to form his own new outfit named as Jamait-ul-Mujahidin in 1990. In 1991 Harkat-ul-Jehad al-Islami changed its Amir. This prompted the Ulemas of Deobandi to work for unity. Maulana Kalimullah Khan, Chancellor Jamia Farooque, Mufti Rafi Usman, Chancellor Dar-ul-Ifta-wal Irshad, Karachi alongwith other Deobandi Ulemas initiated a dialogue with the three split up groups, asking them to unite.

Their main argument was that there should be no difference of ideology of the three organisations and if they clubbed their resources, mainly finance and arms-power, they could make their presence felt. The drain on resources from having separate office, telephone, vehicles and airing of differences to confuse the public would be stopped. Due to these efforts, in October/November 1993, HuJI and HuM decided to merge and rename the new organisation as Harkat-ul-Ansar. They wanted that Harkat-ul-Ansar should take some initiative in Bosnia but till 1994 they did not find a way to enter Bosnia.

After the formation of Harkat-ul-Ansar by merger of HuJI and HuM, a number of messages were sent to the Chief Commanders of the two outfits in Kashmir valley to merge, but they did not get any confirmation till January, 1994. Then it was decided that

Azhar should visit the Valley to confirm whether HuJI and HuM had merged with Harkat-ul-Ansar in the Valley or not and to ascertain the ground realities and to boost the morale of the militants fighting with the Indian forces in the Valley.

Masood Azhar had already obtained a Portuguese passport with Bangladeshi and Indian visas in the name of Wali Adam Issa. He started from Karachi on January 26, 1994 and arrived at Dhaka. He spent two days in Dhaka and thereafter travelled to Delhi by Bangladesh Airlines and reached Indira Gandhi International Airport in the early hours of January 29,1994. The immigration officials at IGI Airport told him that he did not look like a Portuguese but when he told them that he is a Gujarati by birth then they put the entry stamp on the passport and visa (landing documents). Azhar hired a taxi and asked for a good hotel. The taxi driver took him to Ashoka Hotel, Delhi where he stayed. Alongwith some militants, he visited Deobandi schools and famous Madarsas in Saharanpur, Lucknow etc. His ticket for Srinagar was booked for 9th of February. Abu-Mehmood, Amir of Harkat-ul-Ansar in Jammu told him that some Pakistani militants, who were fighting in Kashmir have come to Delhi for getting treatment for their injuries etc., and they are staying in Hotel Usman near Jama Masjid and he should meet them. Accordingly Azhar met Farooq, Mehboob and Qari Abu-Ubeda, militants of Harkat-ul-Ansar in Usman Hotel and encouraged them to continue the jehad. Then Azhar visited Nizamuddin dargah. He purchased 12 compasses from there to give to the militants in Kashmir valley as gift so that they could easily trace out the direction of Mecca.

On 9th February, 1994, Azhar alongwith Ashraf Dar reached Srinagar. Ashraf Dar escorted him to Madarsa Qasmian in Lal Bazar, Srinagar and arranged a room for him. Ashraf told Azhar that Sajjad Afghani would contact him in the Madarsa itself. After that Ashraf Dar went away and Azhar did not meet him thereafter. In the evening Sajjad Afghani came to him in the Madarsa alongwith his Deputy Chief Commander Amjad Bilal, R/o Pakistan Occupied Kashmir (POK) who was armed. Sajjad Afghani was from HuM organisation whereas Amjad Bilal was leading Harkat-ul-Jehad al-Islami organisation in Kashmir. Azhar told them that he has been sent by the Amir of Harkat-ul-Ansar and there should be no difference of opinion between the two organizations for getting upper hand because the main object of both the organisations was the same. For the time being both had been merged and formed Harkat-ul-Ansar and was working under the command of Sajjad Afghani. Harkat-ul-Ansar in Pakistan was not aware about the merger of both the organisations in Kashmir and therefore he was sent to check it personally.

The main objective of Harkat-ul-Ansar was to liberate Kashmir from Indian domination and to establish Islamic rule in Kashmir. Azhar enquired from them about the latest situation, then Amjad Bilal told him that he should meet the leaders of the Hurriat Conference to know the actual position of Kashmir and what Hurriat was doing in Kashmir and what their views are. Azhar assured both of them that he will try to meet the Hurriat leaders at appropriate time. They all stayed in the Madarsa for the night. Amjad Bilal told him that Ashraf would contact the Hurriat leaders on Azhar's behalf. Bilal told him that he should meet the Pak mercenaries operating in Kashmir under the banner of Harkat-ul-Ansar. Bilal decided that next morning Azhar would be escorted by Sajjad Afghani to the militants hideout in his car.

The car was driven by Sajjad himself. Azhar did not know the area or route but when they reached at their destination he was told that they have reached Matigund area, Anantnag. They hid themselves in the house of somebody not known to them. En route Farooq Ahmed met them, who was armed and had a wireless set with him and he accompanied them upto Matigund. The Pak militants were camping in the jungle. Farooq contacted them on wireless and asked them to come to Matigund. In the night about 18/19 militants (Pakistan mercenaries) including (1) Abu Qazi S/o NK R/o Gujranwala, Punjab (Pakistan), Group Commander (HuA), (2) Mohd. Zubair, R/o Jung, Punjab (Pakistan), (3) Walied, R/o Karachi came. The details of remaining Pakistan mercenaries were not known to Azhar. Masood Azhar enquired about their welfare. He found that they were happy on his visit to them and merger of HuJI/HuM to form one group called Harkat-ul-Ansar. Azhar advised them to remain united and work with dedication to achieve the object for which they had been sent to the Valley.

Azhar noted down their addresses in Pak and collected letters from them to their relatives so that he could communicate their welfare to their families on his return to Pakistan. After that the Pak mercenaries/militants left the place for their camp in the forest in the early hours of 11th February, 1994. These militants told Azhar that they are living in difficult situation and due to shortage of arms/ammunition they could not undertake any action. They demanded more arms/ammunition and told Azhar that about 50/60 mostly Pakistani mercenaries and some Kashmiri militants are camping in the said jungle.

On 11.02.1994, at about 9 AM Azhar alongwith Sajjad Afghani and Farooq left towards Srinagar in the same car. On their way back to Srinagar, the car developed some problem and stopped. Then they stopped a three wheeler whose driver checked the car and said that there is no petrol in the car. They then boarded the same three wheeler to fetch petrol from petrol pump but on the way they were intercepted by the Army patrol there who checked them and detained him and Sajjad Afghani whereas Farooq R/o Anantnag area managed his escape from the spot after firing on the Army personnel. On search, some 1200 dollars, Azhar's passport, identity card and air ticket of Indian Airlines for 13.02.1994 were recovered from his possession. They were arrested. There were many Pak militants in the jail in Jammu where Azhar was kept.

In the second week of November 1994 Bilal Ahmed Gagloo alias Altaf Alamgir, Shafatullah Shah alias Gazi Shefat, S/o Assadullah and Mohd. Muzaffar Shah held a meeting in Barrack no. 11 of Kotbhalwal Jail, wherein Sajjad Afghani and Nasarullah Mansoor (Pakistani militant) were called. In that meeting it was decided by Bilal Ahmed Gagloo that it was very difficult as well as impossible to get the release of Pak mercenaries/militants lodged in this jail. Bilal chalked out a plan for digging out a tunnel in the jail complex for managing the safe escape of Pak militants and other Kashmiri militants. Azhar, when asked, told him that he has no knowledge about the place from where the tunnel could be dug out. Bilal Ahmed told that it was his responsibility to select the place for digging out the tunnel. After some days of the meeting Sajjad Afghani met Bilal Ahmed and others and came to know that digging of tunnel inside the jail complex had been started in the back side of barrack no. 6 and one tent of blankets had been put out at the opening side of the tunnel. Sajjad was detailed for removing the debris/clay and stones of the tunnel which he did for some days. This was told to Azhar by Sajjad Afghani. The digging work was being done at night. Sajjad Afghani was in the know of the daily progress. When the tunnel was completed upto 12/13 feet in length, Sajjad asked Azhar to see the progress.

Azhar, accordingly, went to the spot and entered the tunnel. The width of the tunnel was less than the required size for escaping. Azhar was unable to move ahead after 5/6 feet and directed Sajjad to widen the tunnel so that fat man like Azhar could pass through the tunnel. Sajjad told Azhar that first they would complete the tunnel upto the escaping point and then widening of tunnel would be taken up. Fahadullah, a Pak militant was also helping Sajjad and some other Kashmiri militants of barrack no. 6 were engaged in the digging process.

Azhar had visited the digging site 2/3 times. After a few days Azhar was informed by Sajjad that about 23 feet of tunnel had been completed and after digging some more feet they would be able to reach the exit point. Bilal Ahmed told Azhar that he was arranging a guide for the Pak militants to guide them upto the border, after their escape from the jail, but he could not arrange. Masood Azhar, Sajjad Afghani, Fahadullah (Pak militants), Bilal Ahmed Gagloo, Shafatullah Shah and Mohd. Muzaffar Shah (Kashmiri militants) had full knowledge of the tunnel process and escape programme. Other Pak militants lodged in that jail were not aware of the programme. On 27th November 1994, jail authorities alongwith the security forces after entering inside the jail complex started search operations and discovered the tunnel dug out by them and destroyed the tunnel. This attempt also, therefore, failed.

In fact, subsequently, Pakistan militants outside the jail made efforts to get Maulana Masood Azhar and other Pak militants lodged in the jail released when they were taken to the courts or to the hospitals. They could not succeed in this. Another attempt was made to dig out a tunnel inside the Jammu jail and during such attempt to escape through the tunnel on 12.6.99, Sajjad Afghani got stuck up inside the tunnel and on hearing the noise, the jail authorities came and removed him from the tunnel and on account of the injuries, Sajjad Afghani died in the hospital. This was corroborated by Abdul Latif also because Yusuf Azhar, brother-in-law of Maulana had gone to Jammu to guide Maulana and other militants upto the Pak border after their escape from the jail through the tunnel.This attempt also failed. Therefore hijacking was the do or die attempt to get Maulana Masood Azhar released which was undertaken by his brothers and brother-in-law in which they succeeded.

They had also made attempts earlier in this regard. Umar Sheikh and other Pak militants had kidnapped foreign tourists from Paharganj in Delhi in 1994 to force release of the Pakistani militants lodged in the jails including Maulana Masood Azhar. In 1995 foreign tourists were kidnapped from Pahalgam in Srinagar for the same purpose but both the attempts failed. Umar Sheikh was arrested and was in custody in the jail and the trial of the 1994 kidnapping case was going on when he was released alongwith Maulana and Mohd. Zargar in the hijacking case. Investigation was made by the CBI to ascertain whether Maulana and the other two released militants knew about the conspiracy to hijack IC–814 but the visitors register of the jails, letter and parcels register and telephone register of the jails and questioning of those who visited them in the jails during the relevant period did not throw any light on this.

They were in the jail and there was nothing to show that they knew about the hijack plans to get them released. Maulana was in the jail till 31.12.99 but no charges were filed against him. It may be mentioned here that the hijackers were demanding for the dead body of Sajjad Afghani, in Kandahar for release of the hijacked aircraft and the passengers etc and this confirmed his death. There was information that after leaving the aircraft, the hijackers and the three released militants met Osama bin Laden to pay their respect and had dinner with him. This could not be confirmed. It is to be noted that the Taliban had its Headquarters at Kandahar and therefore it was a safe place for militants like Osama. Here it may be mentioned that there was a news item in the *New York Times* that the American security forces had recovered the ticket counterfoils, boarding card stubs of the hijackers on the hijacked flight and a handwritten list containing names, during raids in Kandahar. But the FBI did not hand over them to the CBI. When I alongwith Loknath Behera visited Kabul for questioning Taliban Foreign Minister Muttawakkil, we wanted to go to Kandahar but were told that there was no airport there and nobody was there. In the meeting held in Dhaka in the first week of September 1999, chief hijacker had told Abdul Latif and 5 others present that the hijacked aircraft will be taken to Afghanistan and he had talked to Taliban minister and they will get full support. There was also information that before landing of the aircraft, the ISI chief in Kandahar was in touch with Taliban leaders. When questioned Muttawakkil gave vague replies and many times said that Mullah Omar, chief of Taliban may know it.

There was also some information that there was a red bag in the cargo hold of the aircraft and the hijackers were trying to open it but could not and later on, after they left, the same was taken away in the Pajero jeep of Mr. Muttawakkil. This also could not be confirmed. According to the pilots, the hijackers while escaping had advised them to leave the aircraft immediately as they had kept some gifts in the aircraft. But Capt. Rao, the pilot who had brought the aircraft to Delhi on the next day, stated that he remained in the aircraft itself and could not confirm any such information. All these will become clear only when one of the hijackers is caught. Therefore investigation remains to be done in this case to ascertain the involvement of others in the hijacking.

It may be mentioned that after release in this way, Maulana Masood Azhar formed a dreaded militant outfit called Jaish-e-Mohammad. Within a short period of time it gained strength and power and became a threat to India. Reportedly they were involved in the J&K Assembly attack and Parliament attack case.

Umar Saeed Sheikh

Ahmed Umar Saeed Sheikh alias Rohit Sharma alias Amir Sohail alias Arvindan alias Umar, S/o Saeed Ahmed Sheikh, R/o 16 Deyr Court Gardens, Wanstead, London, 2BU, UK, a British national born on 23.12.73 in London was a student of London School of Economics. His parents who were originally from Lahore, Pakistan had settled in UK. His father was a businessman dealing in ready-made garments. Umar did primary education from Nightingale School and secondary education from 'Forest School' in London and thereafter shifted to Pakistan alongwith his parents, brother and sister. He studied in Aitchison College, Lahore for three years and obtained school certificate 'O' Level. In September 1992 he joined London School of Economics in London. In November 1992 he saw the film "Destruction of a Nation" in Bosnia Week. It was a documentary film highlighting the cruelties on Bosnia Muslims by Serbs. It left a deep impression on his mind, according to him. After watching this film, he came in contact with organisation namely "Muslim Aid and Islamic Relief".

He started taking part in rallies and demonstrations urging the Muslim countries to help the Muslims in Bosnia and asking to lift arms embargo in that area. He also attended the talks by various groups/organisations on these issues to help the Muslim refugees. The students of Islamic Societies of various colleges in London got together and decided to do massive conference in the London School of Economics sometime in January 1993. He was one of the organisers and he worked whole-heartedly to make it a success.

The most important speakers in this conference were 'Umar Bakri Mohammed' of Hizbul Tehrir, Yakub Zakir of Muslim Institute (Muslim Parliament), Dr. Shabir Akhtar, Professor at the Cambridge University in England, but nothing substantial emerged out of this conference. In February 1993, he went to Pakistan for a week and took tapes relating to Bosnia issue. In Pakistan, he met Ameor-ul-Aziam, Secretary of Information of Jamait-i-Islam and distributed the tapes in order to highlight the Bosnia issue in Pakistan.

In March 1993, he came back to London and met Arshad Khan who was running an institution "CONVOY OF MERCY" and started working with 'CONVOY OF MERCY.' Arshad told him that he will be taking necessary aid to Bosnia. In April, Arshad Khan took 5-6 trucks, loaded with aid articles to Bosnia and Umar Sheikh accompanied him upto Split in Croatia and fell sick and was too ill to accompany the convoy to Bosnia and stayed back in a house in Split. While at the Bosnia border, he met some Mujahidins who were going to Bosnia. There were many agencies which were involved in the aid work. There he met one Abdul Rauf alias Mohd. Ali, a Harkat-ul-Mujahidin man waiting at the border to go to Bosnia. Abdul Rauf told him to undergo arms training in Afghanistan and gave him the contact number of Maulana Sayeed of Lahore, Pakistan and also gave him a recommendation letter.

After about a month, Umar Sheikh went back to London. He started motivating people in England and also got his passport renewed. His parents were annoyed with him as they wanted him to complete his education before doing anything else. He tried to get back into the Academy to prepare for exams, but continued attending talks by various groups especially Hizb-i-Tahrir. He left the aid work and wanted to do something towards jehad and he made up his mind in this direction. He had a clash with his parents and finally left his family to work for jehad.

In April 1993, he went to Pakistan and met Maulana Sayeed in a Madarsa in Lahore and gave him the letter which was given to him by Abdul Rauf. Thereafter he met his relations (uncles *etc.*) in Lahore and told them that he was going to China on tour and did not disclose his real aim/motive to his relatives. He also met leaders of Jamait-e-Islami and Dr. Israr and decided to work for Harkat-ul-Ansar group since he found them more sincere than other organisations. He stayed in the Madarsa in Lahore for about a month and half, got training on city tactics. One Maulana Abdulla also came there and he gave an idea of a plan of kidnapping some foreigners inside India in order to facilitate release of the militants of his organisation lodged in jails in J&K. A group of 15 boys were arranged for training in Afghanistan under the leadership of Hassan Mafia, for this.

The group reached, Afghanistan via Islamabad. It was a road journey. The training camp was located in Khost. He met Nazir Khan, who was undergoing training in that camp. After two weeks in Afghanistan he fell ill and had to leave for Lahore and stayed for some days with his relatives. After he recovered from the illness he went back to Afghanistan for 'Jandulla' (four months) course, which is given to those who dedicate their lives to jehad. He was given training in handling and use of small and heavy arms. Ex–SSG men from Pakistan named Saleem, Abdul Hafeez came and taught the subject "Special Arrangement". The members of Jandulla were joined by 40 or so permanent members of Harkat-ul-Mujahidin. SSG men introduced new things/subject such as Formations, Raid and Ambush Tactics, Repelling, Blastings, Field Craft, Intelligence tactics and survival etc.

In December 1993, Maulana Abdulla (head of Tashkeel Harkat-ul-Ansar) came to the camp in Afghanistan and met Umar Sheikh and asked him whether he would help their organisation in getting their comrades namely Masood Azhar, Najrullah Khan and Sajjad Afghani freed from Indian jail. He agreed. Maulana Abdulla told him that they had almost succeeded when two Britishers were taken as hostages in Kashmir and only because of lack of communication an unconditional release of the hostages was made. He said that if the same is done inside India, they may succeed in getting release of their comrades.

Umar went to Islamabad where he was told that visa will not be issued for a month but by that time his passport expired. He met Maulana Abdulla in Islamabad who instructed him to go back to the camp and become an instructor. Umar told him that his passport will expire and also that he would like to go to UK and encourage people for training in Afghanistan.

In January, 1994, Umar went back to England after staying some days with his relatives in Lahore. From January 1994 to April 1994, he encouraged people to go for training and at least to undergo martial arts training. During this period he collected funds for the people undergoing training in the camp in Afghanistan and got his passport renewed and obtained visa for Pakistan and India. In May, 1994 he went to Afghanistan via Pakistan and after refreshing his knowledge for a couple of weeks started instructing a class for the 40 days course. In June 1994 Maulana Abdulla again came to the camp and told him to go to India for kidnapping foreigners in Delhi, to help in getting their comrades freed.

On July 26, 1994, Umar Sheikh arrived at IGI Airport by a PIA flight from Lahore, Pakistan. He went to Connaught Place by hiring an autorickshaw. He has been instructed in Pakistan to spend the first night in some good hotel to keep away from any suspicious followers and then contact two phone numbers in Delhi. He was to ask for a "Farooq" as instructed by Maulana Abdullah. The subject booked a room in Hotel Holiday Inn, Connaught Place, Delhi in his own name "Ahmad Umar Saeed Sheikh" and gave his passport number. It was a costly hotel. He did not know that he had picked up a very expensive hotel and realised that his money would be exhausted soon. Therefore, he decided to contact Farooq straight away. He phoned both numbers from the hotel. Both answered that there was no Farooq there and that they had never heard of him. This made him worry even more and he thought whether to contact Maulana Abdulla in Islamabad but decided not to do it. He went out in search of an STD booth but they had all closed.

He phoned his uncle's house in Lahore from the hotel since he was feeling lonely. Next day he tried both the numbers again but got the same reply. He came to know that one number is that of Naseem Guest House. He checked out from Hotel Holiday Inn and decided to go and find Naseem Guest House, perhaps Farooq would be there under some other assumed name. Somehow he had the notion that this guest-house was in Azadpur. He recalled Maulana Abdulla saying that they were Azad Kot numbers. He asked people and went to Azadpur by bus with his luggage.

In Azadpur he could not find any Naseem Guest House. He phoned Maulana Abdulla from an STD booth in Azadpur and told him that he was absolutely lost and fed up. Maulana Abdulla told him to call again after sometime which he did. Maulana Abdulla told him to go to Jama Masjid and find the Muezzim called Mehmood who sold hats in a shop nearby and ask to be taken to Farooq. Then he went to Jama Masjid. It was Zohar time and he only just prayed. After the prayer he was searching for the address of Muezzim called Mehmood and he met a person.

He had never seen him before but his appearance and manners made him suspect that he might be the man. He approached him and asked him whether he knew the Muezzim. He asked him why he wanted to see him. Umar felt reassured and said that actually he was looking for his friend called Farooq and the Muezzim would know him. That person left saying that he would return after 10 minutes. When he returned he asked Umar as to who has sent him to that place. Umar told him Maulana Farooq (as instructed by Maulana Abdulla). Maulana Farooq Kashmiri? asked that person and when Umar nodded, that person shook hands with him and introduced himself as Sultan alias Yusuf alias Mehboob. Sultan took him to a guest house in the Jama Masjid area and booked a room in the name of Yusuf and wrote that they were from Darul-Aloom Deoband. In this hotel Umar spent the night of 27th July 1994. After they checked in, Sultan became much more friendly. Umar asked him if Zubar better known as Shahji had arrived and Sultan said not yet but he would come soon.

Sultan was pleased to hear the name of Shahji and told Umar that they had fought many battles together in Afghanistan. They had lunch at Karim Hotel and then Sultan rang up Pakistan from a local STD booth. He spoke to Maulana Saadat who was the head of HuJI. Umar also spoke to Maulana Saadat who asked him to wait patiently since some setback had occurred and Shah Saab will not be arriving soon. They went back to the guest house and chatted for a while. Sultan was from Punjab in Pakistan and had instructed/trained several militants. Umar asked him about the conditions in India and Sultan said that they were not doing anything effective because Farooq (who was from HuM) and himself were not getting on well and they did not know who was incharge amongst them and they did not have any clear directions from Pakistan. Umar asked Sultan what they had in terms of weapons and he said that he has some grenades also. He asked him where the stuff had come from but he was evasive. Later on Umar came to know that all the weapons had come from Kashmir but by which route and other details he did not know.

Later, in the evening Sultan brought Farooq to meet him. Farooq was reluctant. They had dinner and then Farooq left. Next day *i.e.* on 28th July 1994, Sultan took him to a place in Sadar Bazar near Kasabpura. It was the first floor of a house and included two rooms, a bathroom and a kitchen. It was in dilapidated condition. Sultan asked him to stay there and that he or Farooq would be visiting every now and then and that he should not venture out too much. If asked, he was to say that he is a Kashmiri. Over the next few days Umar visited many places in Delhi. He managed to persuade Sultan to take him to the place where he lived and Sultan took him to a house in Hazrat Nizamuddin. At that time Sultan, Farooq and Nazir were staying there. Nazir was a Pak national who had come via Nepal from Pakistan in order to go to Kashmir. They sat down and discussed the steps to be taken. Sultan and Farooq wanted to wait until Shah Saab arrived before starting anything. Umar told them that they should purchase a house in Delhi and procure arms etc. They told him that the money that had been sent to them from Pakistan had been taken away by some Ashraf Darr who had betrayed them after the arrest of Maulana Masood Azhar. Umar wanted to see Darr. They reminded him that the instructions they had received from Pakistan were that he should concentrate on the job for which he was sent namely kidnapping and not interfere in what they were doing.

Umar went to that house a couple of days later and met Karrie and Amin there. Both of them left soon. Umar asked Farooq and Sultan if they had purchased/brought the stuff he had asked them to. They had not. This annoyed him. It seemed they were not taking him seriously. Therefore, when Farooq mentioned that five chaps had run away from Kashmir and one of them had arrived in Delhi, he was eager to meet him hoping that it would be someone more ready to put some effort in the assignment. Farooq told that the Muezzim knew where he was staying and would take Umar there.

It was a day or two later that Farooq and Umar met Siddiqui. They were at Jama Masjid. Umar had just completed the prayer when Farooq called and introduced Siddiqui as his old student. Siddiqui was tall, thin and was in bad shape. He said that he had spent the past 10 days sitting in Jama Masjid. They had dinner and went to a house in Sarai Kale Khan–beyond the reservation office. Siddiqui also known as Saifur Rehman was told to stay there. Farooq told Umar that Amin was living there. A few days later Umar took Siddiqui to Azad Market and the latter started living there with Salauddin.

In the end of August 1994, Umar was told by Sultan (in Ganda Nala House, Nizamuddin) that someone wants to meet him the next day at Jama Masjid. Many people had come to that house in his presence but nobody was introduced to him. Therefore, Umar thought that it must be Shah Saab. Umar went to Jama

Masjid next day and waited. Shah Saab came there. He told Umar that their travelling and meeting etc. has exposed the outfit and warned Umar not to get out of the Nizamuddin house till he comes there and meets him.

After a few days Shah Saab came to the Ganda Nala hide-out with Sultan and another person whom Umar had never seen before. Farooq, Nasir and Umar were present. They had lunch together and then Shah Saab wanted to talk to Umar alone. They went outside and sat on a mat. Shah Saab told Umar that his responsibility was to kidnap the foreigners. American citizens should be the first target and next were Britishers and then French. Umar was asked to go to Agra in a tourist bus and note down all the stoppages of the bus and movement of the tourists. Accordingly, Umar went to a travel agency near Hotel 55, Connaught Place and booked the ticket for the next day. Then he went to Azad Market hide-out and spent the night with Salauddin and Siddiqui.

Next morning at about 7 AM Umar Sheikh got into the Jayco Travels tourist bus outside Hotel 55. There were no foreigners, only Indian tourists were in the bus. However, since the bus was only half full, they transferred the passengers to another bus. This second bus was air-conditioned and had a few foreigners. Most importantly one of them, an Israeli came and sat next to him. He introduced himself as Akhmir. Umar talked to him and tried to invite him to some place.

When they were returning, the bus broke down. When a van came from behind, they stopped it and one Iranian couple, Akhmir and Umar Sheikh got into it and asked the driver whether he could give them a lift to Delhi. The van was coming to Delhi and the driver agreed. They got down at Ashram Chowk which is about 10 minutes from Hazrat Nizamuddin. The Iranian couple took an auto rikshaw and went to their hotel. Akhmir and Umar took an auto-rickshaw. Umar told that he would get down at Hazrat Nizamuddin. Akhmir was to go to his guest house in Paharganj. When the auto rickshaw approached Hazrat Nizamuddin, Umar planned to kidnap Akhmir. He quarrelled with the driver and told Akhmir that the driver was asking for ₹ 500/- and if they did not pay he will take them somewhere else and they would be in trouble. Akhmir immediately got down from the rickshaw. Umar also got down. They were quite near to Hazrat Nizamuddin Markaz. Umar told Akhmir that he had a friend staying nearby and he would give a lift and thus brought Akhmir to the Ganda Nala house and knocked at the door. It was two in the morning. Farooq opened the door and Umar and Akhmir went upstairs. Shah Saab, Sultan and Nasir were sleeping in the room alongwith another person unknown to Umar. Umar told Shah Saab that he has brought one Israeli and all they had to do is to overpower him. Shah Saab looked at Akhmir and got angry and shouted at Umar that he will get them killed and directed him to take and drop Akhmir at the hotel. Umar told Akhmir that his friend has refused and they went in a auto-rickshaw to hotel Hare Rama, Paharganj. Umar could not get a room in the hotel as he told that he is a foreigner but had no passport with him. Therefore he went back to the Hazrat Nizamuddin house.

Next morning Shah Saab asked him to visit tourist interest places in Delhi and see if he could establish friendship with tourists and the next meeting was arranged in Jama Masjid. Umar found this friendship business difficult and told Shah Saab next day that it is difficult. Shah Saab told him to keep trying. Next day, Umar went to ISBT and when he saw a foreigner wandering about, he asked him where he was going.

The foreigner replied Dehradun. Umar told him that he was also going to Dehradun and sat with the foreigner in the bus. His name was Richard and he was a British student who had arranged to have some teaching experiences at Doon School, Dehradun. By the time the bus reached Dehradun he had not only initiated a friendship but also put forward the idea of spending time together while, touring India. Umar came back to Delhi.

On arrival at Delhi, Shah Saab called him to Maulana Azad's grave and told him to concentrate on diplomats and foreign technical persons working for Indian Government. Umar told Shah Saab to include Salauddin and Siddique also in the team. Sultan and Shah Saab were living near Turkman Gate. This was around second week of September 1994. Umar and Nasir were living in the Ganda Nala house hide-out. Farooq and Karrie were living in some other house nearby. Amin was living at Sarai Kale Khan hide-out.

Umar concentrated on diplomats in Chanakyapuri but did not succeed. The security was tight. It was round about third week of September 1994, when Shah Saab told Umar that he had arranged a hide-out in a remote area off Saharanpur and Umar should shift Siddiqui and Salauddin there. The idea was to take foreigners there and keep them in custody. Next day all the four, Siddiqui, Salauddin, Sultan and Umar went to Saharanpur by bus. Sultan had put two pistols inside a flask which was put in the bag of Umar. From Saharanpur bus stand they took cycle rickshaws and went to the place called Khata Kheri. Umar was not happy with the hide-out.

Umar stayed for the night with Salauddin and Siddiqui in Saharanpur and told Sultan that he would not go back with him to Delhi but would go out on the 'hunt' straight away to bring Richard from Dehradun. On the next day Umar went to Dehradun and met Richard at the School. Richard was involved with School activities and he could not take time off to visit his relatives. So Umar returned to Saharanpur, spent another night there and then returned to Delhi the next day and went to Sarai Kale Khan hide-out as instructed where Farooq met him the next day and took him for the first time to the hide-out of Shah Saab. Umar told Shah Saab that these efforts will not succeed and they should adopt snatch method. Sultan was tired and said that the effort to kidnap son of a VIP did not succeed. Then it was decided that Umar would continue his efforts for another four days and if it fails then Umar will adopt the snatch method.

So, next morning Umar went to Paharganj and checked in Ankur Guest House giving an address of Bombay. It may be mentioned here that after Richard had refused to accompany him, Umar had gone to Mussoorie and checked most of the Hotels there but due to agitation at that time there were no foreigners. He had stayed at a hotel in front of the mosque there. Next morning he had gone to Wood Stock School, an American School situated even higher up and applied for job of a teacher. He did this partly because if he got it, he could easily bring one of his co-teachers down to visit his relatives and kidnap him. But he did not get the job. While in Paharganj he practised how to befriend foreigners. He opened the idea of visit to a village. He convinced Rhys Urzel Partridge and

Graham Fox. They had many common interests i.e., chess, travelling and writing. Both were fascinated with the village visit.

On 28th September 1994 Umar met Sultan alias Giasuddin alias Yusuf near Tilak Bridge as planned. This was the first time Umar saw the Maruti van DID-9016 and driver Saeed, whom Sultan had brought with him. They drove to a car park near Turkman Gate where Shah Saab, Karrie, Abdul Rahim also joined them. Farooq was also picked up on the way and they went to India Gate lawns. They prayed Magrib. The driver did not pray.

Then they sat down and Umar told them that two chaps are ready and he has invited them to visit the village. After discussions, Shah Saab instructed that Sultan would accompany Umar and the foreigners, and after reaching Saharanpur where Salauddin and Siddiqui were waiting, Sultan would be incharge of the operation and will chain the foreigners and Umar will keep away. Then they made a collective prayer for the success of the operation. Thereafter, they took soft drinks and left. Umar went to Paharganj and checked into Krishna Guest House and met Graham Fox and Rhys upstairs of the restaurant. Umar played chess with Rhys and told him that the village elders might not appreciate a girl accompanying them. However, next day Graham said that he was sorry he and Kate had changed their programme.

On 29th morning Umar took Rhys to Nirula Hotel, Connaught Place, Delhi. Driver Saeed and Sultan alias Yusuf were waiting inside the Maruti van DID-9016 as planned. Rhys and Umar sat inside the van and set off to Saharanpur at about midday. They stopped on the way near Cheetal and had lunch. They reached Saharanpur after sunset and went to the house. Umar told Rhys that they would have to wait there till the servants come from the village which was about a kilometer away and inaccessible by vehicle. Sultan alias Yusuf came and knocked at the door. Siddiqui opened it. Sultan told him to take the luggage inside which he did. Umar alongwith Rhys went inside and sat inside the bar room. Umar told Rhys their actual plan and asked him to cooperate till they negotiate with the British and Indian Government. Rhys got angry. Then Sultan, Siddiqui and Salauddin came inside brandishing the two pistols. Sultan growled "you are under arrest". Siddiqui and Salauddin said "Hands up".

They chained Rhys's ankle. In the night Umar explained the purpose to Rhys who was too scared. Umar took the passport details of Rhys the next morning and reached Delhi. He stayed in the Sarai Kale Khan hide-out as instructed. Next morning Umar got a message from Nurul Amin that Shah Saab would meet him in Nizamuddin market in an hours time. Accordingly, Umar met Shah Saab there. Shah Saab instructed him to hunt for an American. Umar told him that he had talked to another British chap 'Trevor' and Shah agreed that he should be tried first. Accordingly, Umar contacted Trevor and came to know that he is in YMCA Delhi. Umar went to YMCA and met Trevor who was pleased to see Umar. Umar tried to invite Trevor outside but Trevor had other engagements.

Umar noted that the place was booming with foreigners. So, next day after checking the usual places in Paharganj, he returned to YMCA and joined in a game of scrabble. It was late afternoon. By evening he had established rapport with a chap thought to be American and had told him about the village story. Later on during conversation, Umar found that the American had been teaching English to Tibetan refugees voluntarily and was leaving India because of lack of funds. Umar turned to him and said "Hey I needed someone to teach English at my village school". He was happy at the prospect especially since he mentioned monetary consideration but said he had a few things to do in Delhi first. So Umar agreed to meet him a couple of days after and confirm the details.

Umar thereafter initiated a conversation with an American named Daniel Skinner and slowly came up with the idea of visit to a village. On hearing the story, Daniel agreed to accompany Umar the next day. So next morning, on 5th October 1994, Umar told Shah Saab at the Markaz the latest development. Those days Umar was meeting Shah Saab at Hazrat Nizamuddin Markaz every morning and used to pedal the cycle rickshaw from Hazrat Nizamuddin Railway Reservation office himself. Shah Saab was pleased. He told Umar to return to the Markaz at 1.00 PM where Amin would be waiting for him. Shah Saab told that he would go and wait for them in Saharanpur.

At 1.00 PM Umar went to Markaz from where Nurul Amin took him to the van which was not far off. Karrie and the driver were there. They went to YMCA. Umar got down and told the driver to return after half an hour. When Daniel Skinner and Umar came out with Daniel's luggage, the driver came 15 minutes late. They sat inside the van and started off for Saharanpur but before an hour had passed Daniel wanted to get out for cigarettes. The driver stopped the van and Daniel got off with two bags and said he thought he would better stay in Delhi for a few days more. "What is the matter" Umar asked in a surprised tone. "I have only known you for two days and all of a sudden I am in a car with you" and he left. Umar told the driver that they had changed their programme and that now he would go to Saharanpur alone.

Driver was surprised. In Saharanpur they parked the van in the bazaar and went to the house in a rickshaw. The driver was taken along since he was very ill. Siddiqui opened the door and Umar took the driver inside the house who immediately laid down on the rug. Umar went to the inner room and told Shah Saab that he suspected the driver. At this Shah Saab told him not to worry about the driver and he knew what Umar was doing but Umar did not realise it.

Umar talked to Rhys, who calmed down considerably. Umar told him about the American and Rhys was pleased that someone had outsmarted Umar. Next morning Shah Saab left. It was around 6th October,1994. Before leaving Shah Saab instructed Umar to stay safely in Saharanpur for a few days as the American may report the incident. He was not to venture out of the house. So for the next few days before he left for Delhi, there was Siddiqui, Salauddin, Umar, Sultan who guarded Rhys. Around 10th October, Umar came back to Delhi and stayed in Sarai Kale Khan house and met Shah Saab in Nizamuddin Markaz the next morning. Shah Saab again instructed to find an American.

Umar went on searching for Americans in Delhi University, JNU, YMCA, Paharganj etc., but did not find an American. He told Shah Saab about this and Shah Saab told him to look for Britishers and French persons. Umar went to Paharganj area where he bumped into Graham Fox. He asked Umar how it had all been and he said terrific. Rhys had thoroughly enjoyed himself and was now in Manali. Later, they went to Hare Krishna restaurant, where they met Paul Beufamm Rideant and Chirostopher Miles

Crosten. He did not have to go through the old village story because Graham told it for him in good faith. They played a game of chess and then Umar offered Paul and Chris (who had just arrived in India) to take them to see the Red Fort in Delhi. They agreed and Umar took them to see Dusshera Festival. He managed to take them right through to the VIP Section and they were thrilled as well as convinced that Umar was from a well-connected Indian family. That night they arranged to meet the next evening at Hare Krishna restaurant.

Next morning Umar told Shahji at the Markaz Hazrat Nizamuddin that two Britishers were in the pipeline, did he want them? Shahji answered affirmatively and it was arranged to meet next morning. Umar was to make necessary arrangements, in the meantime. Umar went to Hare Krishna restaurant in Paharganj, met them and casually mentioned to them that he was going down to his village the next day, would they be interested in accompanying him? They agreed and Umar arranged to meet them (Paul Benjamin Ride and Christopher Miles Crosten) the next morning in the hotel where they were staying.

So, next morning at the Markaz Umar told Shahji about the programme and it was decided to pick up the foreigners from the Railway Station near by. Umar had the van arranged in a couple of hours and made other arrangements. Next day at the fixed time Umar went in the arranged van driven by driver Abdul Saeed to New Delhi Railway Station from where the two foreigners were picked up and they proceeded to Saharanpur. On the way they talked about women etc. At Saharanpur the door was opened by Siddiqui. He saw that Umar was accompanied by two guests and so he immediately called others to be alert. There was Sultan, Salauddin and Maulana Saab. The same drama as before was made. Two pistols were used. Sultan also threatened with a picture of AK-47. The two, Chris and Paul were shocked to see Rhys about whom they had talked on the way. Rhys was rather pleased that he was not alone. Both the new comers were also chained.

Next day after taking their passport details and assuring them that he would do his best to expedite the matter, Umar Sheikh returned to Delhi and met Shah Saab at the Markaz. Shah Saab told Umar to make one last attempt for one American and if it fails they could declare on the three held by them. Shahji also told that he had arranged a house in Ghaziabad so it should be easy for him this time. Umar told him that he would go next morning to Vasant Kunj and check for Michael.

Next morning *i.e.,* 18th October 1994, Umar went to Vasant Kunj and this time managed to go inside the apartment and met Michael. He was an adamant type of chap and Umar felt that it would be virtually impossible to convince him to go anywhere. Therefore he came back and told Shahji that they should adopt the grab method on Michael. Shahji told Umar to check the area and movement of Michael and select the proper area for the grab so that public may not intervene. It was decided that Amin would take Umar that evening to Vasant Kunj area on a motor bike. After the meeting Umar went to Paharganj area. His mind was fixed on Michael task so he did not mind about the foreigners around. He just sat in a Café (opposite Ankur Guest House) and ordered a drink. The person sitting in front of him started talking to him and to his surprise Umar realised that the foreigner was an American named Bela Nuss.

Bela Nuss was staying at Ajay Guest House, Paharganj and was about to leave India. He was a lonely sort of fellow. Umar told Bela Nuss that he was staying in Galaxy Guest House and introduced as Rohit Sharma from Bombay. After the conversation it was agreed to meet later. Umar immediately went and booked a room in Galaxy Guest House in the name of Rohit Sharma from Bombay. In the evening Umar met Amin in the market and then two of them went to Vasant Kunj area on motorcycle and they noted various activities there and also verified the location of the nearest police station etc and Umar decided that morning was the better time for the job. Umar thereafter returned to Paharganj and found that Bela Nuss has left a message for him saying that he should meet him next day in the afternoon.

Next morning Umar Sheikh went to Markaz and told Shahji that he could postpone the kidnapping of Michael since he had found another target. In the afternoon Umar met Bela Nuss and they had dinner with Pizza in Connaught Place. Umar told Nuss that he was having dinner with an Indian family the next day and asked Bela Nuss whether he would like to come along. Bela Nuss was delighted to come.

Next day Umar met Shahji at the Markaz who took him for the first time to his room in Nizamuddin behind the tomb. Farooq and Amin were present there. Amin was sent to get food and Umar told Shahji that he had befriended Bela Nuss, an American and he had called him to meet outside in the evening. Shahji told Umar that Salauddin and Siddiqui have been called to Delhi and were at the Sarai Kale Khan house and he can choose one of them for help and Farooq will also help him.

Umar suggested that Salauddin would be the best to act as son of the rich Indian so projected. Shahji then sent Farooq to buy a *burqa* (women's black dress). He told Umar to put it on the American since there would be a check post on the way to the house in Ghaziabad. Umar slept for few hours while Shahji and Farooq went out and made arrangements. When Shah Saab returned he told that the driver would be there in a couple of hours. Shah decided that he and Siddiqui will also be in the team and they will take a lift on the way. Later on Amin returned to the house but Farooq did not.

Shahji, Amin and Umar left the Hazrat Nizamuddin house and went to the petrol pump behind the Markaz. The driver was there alongwith the van. Then they went to Hazrat Nizamuddin Railway Reservation Office and Amin went and called Salauddin. Umar and Salauddin wore good dress. Amin did not return. It was getting late and was about 6 PM so Umar told the driver to drive fast. They dropped Umar at the New Delhi Railway Station. Umar went and checked out of Galaxy Guest House, took his small Air bag from the room and went to find Bela Nuss. Bela Nuss met him at the Railway Station and both of them went to Narula, Connaught Place where the driver and Salauddin were waiting in the van. They got into the van and left for Ghaziabad. On the way Salauddin talked respectfully. Shahji and Siddiqui were waiting near Ghaziabad Check Post. The Van stopped and they got in. Umar told Bela Nuss that they just wanted a lift to a nearby place. All of a sudden Bela realised that they were leaving the city and questioned them. Shahji pulled out the pistol with silencer and pointed the gun at Bela Nuss whereas Umar held Bela Nuss's hands. Siddiqui went to the back side of the van and slipped the burqa on to Bela Nuss so that outsiders may not see.

Shahji was still not satisfied. So Siddiqui gagged his mouth with a scarf. Shahji told the driver to drive fast which he did. On Shahji's instructions Salauddin got down and a few seconds later the van took a U-turn and then went into a lane and then inside the gate of the house. Shahji told to hurry up. They got off from the van and went inside. Karrie was there. Bela Nuss was dragged into a room on the right side and Siddiqui chained his ankles. The arrangement was already there. Umar talked to Bela Nuss and took his passport details. Bela Nuss was stunned. Thereafter Shahji, Umar and the driver went away in the van. Umar was dropped near Sarai Kale Khan. This was 20th October.

Next morning Umar met Shahji at his place, as instructed. Shahji informed Umar that he had contacted Pakistan and asked for the money to be sent before declaration of kidnapping was made so that if things got rough he need not wait for the money to make their escape. Shahji said that they should have correct addresses of the Embassies etc., for sending letters and therefore sent Umar to find out contact addresses and telephone numbers of the Prime Minister of India, concerned Ministries, the BBC, the Voice of America and the Embassies of USA and UK.

The BBC and VOA contact details were collected from the British and American Embassies respectively. Getting details of other agencies was difficult. Umar went to Capital News Agency in Connaught Place and obtained useful information. When Umar returned, Shahji told him that he had received information that Rhys had tried to escape from the Saharanpur house and the people there were alarmed. He said that two of them should go there and talk to the foreigners. Accordingly, Shahji and Umar went to Saharanpur by hiring a taxi from the taxi stand near Ajmeri Gate and paid ₹ 800/- as taxi fair. They arrived there in the evening. In the house there were Sultan, Maulana Sahib, Usman and a chap whom Umar had never seen before who was introduced as Khan Sahib. Khan Sahib spoke to him in Punjabi and told that he had heard a lot about him (Umar) in Lahore. Shahji then spoke to the Britishers which was translated in English by Umar. Shahji told them that the purpose of keeping them will be solved soon and they need not be afraid because they would be freed whether their objectives are met through them or not. He also told them that it may take a month at the most. Next morning Shahji told Umar to go to Chandigarh and obtain the name and address of the owner of Piccadilly Hotel because he was a VIP and they should concentrate on his kidnapping also if the kidnapping of the foreigners was not sufficient.

Accordingly, Umar went by bus but fell asleep and forgot to take the ticket and therefore was fined. In Chandigarh he stayed at Hotel Piccadilly that night in his own name and as a British national. He told the hotel staff that he would like to book the whole hotel for a wedding and thus obtained the name and address of the owner and thereafter he came back to Delhi. Shahji said that they could write the letters now and dictated the letter which was translated into English. It was 25th October. By afternoon they had written three letters. Apart from the names of three militants namely Maulana Masood Azhar, Nagrulla Khan and Sajjad Afghani for whose release Umar had been working all the way from Pakistan, Shahji added the names of three more persons to confuse the Indian authorities.

Umar told Shahji that these letters could have been sent even without kidnapping these persons and therefore photographs of those kidnapped should be affixed on them. Shahji asked how they could get the photographs developed, then Umar told him about the Polaroid camera and Shahji agreed and gave him ₹ 5000/-. Umar went to Palika Bazaar and purchased a polaroid camera and as directed went to Saharanpur. With Maulana Sahib and Khan Sahib at the background holding a newspaper and a photograph of AK-47, photographs of the persons in custody in chained condition were taken and Umar came back to Delhi.

Shahji sent Farooq to Ghaziabad to take the photograph of Bela Nuss. Thereafter, Shahji and Umar made adjustments in the letters for the Photographs fixed and mentioned the deadline for accepting the demand as 72 hours starting from the midnight of 26th October. Then Umar went to Kashmiri Gate and sent one letter by speed post and then went to Daryaganj for faxing another letter to the Prime Minister and asked the owner of the shop to turn his face since the contents were confidential. Next day he went with Farooq and posted the remaining letters from Connaught

Place and then returned to Shahji. It was going to be waiting time and Umar was forbidden from moving out of the house for the next couple of days. Umar stayed with Shahji. Farooq had gone somewhere. Amin was with them and used to arrange food etc. Every morning Shahji went out and on return used to say that he had phoned to Pakistan and comrades/militants had not been freed.

On 29th October, Shahji told Umar that the threat should be repeated and therefore he wrote letters to BBC, VOA, *Hindustan Times*, British and American Embassies threatening to kill the hostages, if the demand for release of Maulana Masood Azhar and others was not accepted immediately. Shahji added some more names to confuse the authorities even more. Next day which was a Sunday, Shahji instructed Umar to go to Meerut and post the letters. Accordingly, Umar went to Kashmiri Gate and hurriedly got the letters posted except those to the BBC and the *Hindustan Times*. Next morning Umar went to drop both the letters alongwith Nurul Amin.

Amin was behind him to see whether everything goes on correctly. They went to Hazrat Nizamuddin (East) and found that BBC office had moved to Rafi Marg. They went to Rafi Marg and gave the letter to the receptionist girl who was sitting at the Reception at BBC office and Umar told the girl. "Tell the Editor I want an answer by 3 PM". They left the building quickly and went to *Hindustan Times* office at K. G. Marg, Delhi and gave the letter to the Public Affairs Manager of the Chief Editor and told him to give it to the Chief Editor. The said officer started opening the envelope so Umar speedily withdrew from the room and went downstairs. Amin and Umar got into an autorickshaw and went to Okhla hide-out to show that place to Amin. On the way near Hazrat Nizamuddin they met Siddiqui and then all of the three went to Okhla by bus.

This hide-out was in the Hazi colony in Okhla, which he had arranged for one month but hardly used. Amin went away. Siddiqui and Umar stayed there. They talked about Afghanistan, Kashmiris, Bosnia and England. They talked about Shahji and the other comrades and the time which they spent together in India. It was just after sun set that Shahji and Amin arrived. Shahji told both of them to get ready. Amin went back. Shahji told that the American has stopped eating and they should go to Ghaziabad and convince him that it is a matter of few more days only. He talked to Siddiqui for some time. Siddiqui was supposed to be in Sarai Kale Khan House. Thereafter all started for Ghaziabad in the van. When they reached near Shahji instructed to get down and told the driver to return at about 9 PM. They got down on the main road and got into the lane. When they reached near the house they were stopped by an armed policeman, who shouted at them to raise their hands. The policeman tried to drag Umar to one side by the collar on which he got furious and started hitting him. The policeman also hit him. His other comrades Shahji and Siddiqui ran away from the spot and he was caught by the police.

During investigation it was found that on 31.10.1994, a police party headed by Station Officer Satya Dev Yadav of Police Station Masuri near Ghaziabad had gone to Nai Basti, Masuri in connection with the investigation of a theft case. Since they found a person running suspiciously, they moved towards the house from which the person had jumped out and run away. They found the door bolted from inside and nobody responded, they broke open the door and entered the house. An American national was found chained inside the room with a spike.

He was unchained and brought to the police station. On his statement, FIR was registered. Police officials were posted near the house to watch the visit of the persons who had kept the American in custody. Constables Sompal and Jagpal Singh saw three persons approaching the house of Sufi Anwar, where the captive was held. They tried to catch them when two of the three managed to escape by firing at the constables but one person whose name was disclosed by him as Umar Sheikh was caught. He was brought to the police station and another FIR was registered. On questioning, Umar Sheikh gave the Maruti Van number as DID 9016 and the police tracked it and seized it from Abdul Rahim and Mohd. Sayeed. On interrogation of the three persons, it was found that three British nationals were kept as hostages in a house in Saharanpur. Immediately, the police surrounded the said house. In the firing which took place, one militant and two police officials were killed. Other militants managed to escape. The three British nationals were rescued. After interrogation and investigation, Nazir Khan, Narul Amin, Mahmood alias Ayub, Naser Mohd. Sodozey, Abdul Rahim, Mohd. Sayeed, Umar Sheikh etc., were prosecuted. Finally, the Supreme Court of India, after hearing the arguments, convicted the accused whereas Umar Sheikh was released on 31.12.99, before the final judgement, in exchange of the passengers, crew and the hijacked aircraft IC–814. (Subsequent to his release, Umar Sheikh was involved in many terrorist activities including kidnapping and murder of Daniel Pearl, American journalist in Pakistan).

Mustaq Ahmed Zargar

Mustaq Ahmed Zargar alias Latrum, S/o G.R. Rasool Zargar, R/o Jamia Masjid, Goni Mohalla, Srinagar studied upto 4th class and then learnt to operate Lathe machine and worked in a shop till 1985. According to him, in 1985, during curfew, while he was going on the road, he was picked up by the police and he remained in jail and was released after a month. His father expired while he was in jail. After release he again started operating lathe machine.

During detention in Central Jail, Srinagar he came in contact with Zahoor Ahmed Sheikh, Mukhtiar Ahmed Baba and Mukhtiar Ahmed Sufi Ali, R/o Anantnag who had contacts with People's League and he took interest in that party. After release from the jail, he started attending the meetings of the party. In 1988, one day he came across said Zahoor Ahmed Sheikh near Lal Chowk, Srinagar, who asked him whether he is interested in having training in arms etc., across the border for subversive activities in India. He readily agreed. He told about this to his neighbour Irfan-ul-Hassan and asked him whether he was also interested in this. He also agreed.

Two-three days later during the same month August 1988, he alongwith Irfan-ul-Hasaan met Zahoor Ahmed Sheikh near Lal Chowk, who took both of them to the house of Ghulam Nabi Bhatt, R/o Trehgam, Distt. Kupwara (real younger brother of JKLF founder leader Maqbool Bhatt who was lodged in Tihar Central Jail, New Delhi during 1982-83). They stayed for the night with Ghulam Nabi Bhatt at Trehgam whereas Zahoor Ahmed Sheikh left in the evening for Anantnag.

Next morning Ghulam Nabi Bhatt detailed his younger brother Zahoor Bhatt to take and hand over them to Ghulam Nabi, guide at Rashanpura (Kupwara). Accordingly, they were taken and handed over to the guide who took them to Muzaffarabad, Pakistan Occupied Kashmir (POK) and there to the house of Raja Muzaffar, a JKLF leader. All of them stayed there for two nights. Then Raja Muzaffar detailed a youth to take them to Rawalpindi, Pakistan Occupied Kashmir (POK). The said person took them to the house of Dr. Farooq Haider, another JKLF whip, in Rawalpindi. There they met Amsa Ulla Khan and Rashid Hasrat who made arrangement for their training. They were taken in a closed jeep by persons. Front seat was occupied by one Assad besides the driver. After 4/5 hours of journey by jeep they reached a training camp comprising of 3-4 tents. One tent was used as a kitchen, the second was occupied by the Instructors and the third was allotted to them.

In that camp they were given seven days training in assembling, dissembling and familiarisation of components of AK-47 rifles, LMG and pistol. After seven days training they were escorted back to Rawalpindi to Farooq Haidar's house. After night's stay there they were sent back to Raja Muzaffar's house at Muzaffarabad (POK). From there they were taken to Attmujim, Pakistan Occupied Kashmir (POK) to the house of Ghulam Mohd. Wani with one sack bag each containing arms and ammunitions which included 2 AK-47 rifles with 4 magazines, 400 cartridges, by the guide Ghulam Nabi. Then they were taken to the LoC by the guide who had one AK-47 rifle. Bread for en route consumption was also taken. They crossed the Line of Control and reached Rashanpura, district Kupwara. The guide took one sack of arms and ammunitions from them and told them to deliver the rest to Mohd. Magbool Bhatt. He told them to catch the bus for Srinagar and accordingly they reached the road and then by bus to Srinagar. Two days later Ghulam Nabi Bhatt's younger brother Zahoor Ahmed Bhatt reached Batmaloo and on instruction from him, they delivered the remaining two bags to him.

After about two months, probably on 16.10.1988, after motivating Zahid Ahmed, R/o Zaina Kadal and Mukhtar Ahmed, R/o Magdoom Sahib near Hari Parbat, Srinagar for undergoing arms and subversive activities training in Pakistan, Mohd. Zargar entrusted both of them to Zahoor Ahmed Bhatt who sent them across the border through the guide. After receiving the training, while they were crossing the border in December 1988, they were nabbed by the security forces alongwith the arms and ammunitions.

In March/April 1989 (during the Holy month of Ramzan) Zahoor Ahmed Bhatt met him and Irfan at Idgah Srinagar. Ashfaq Najid Wani, Javed Ahmed Mir, Mohd. Yaseen Nasik and Abdul Namid Sheikh were there. There was a discussion that the Congress and the National Conference parties were thinking that the militants would not be able to indulge in any such activities and they finally decided to fire shots in the air the next day which was a Friday, in Khanyar and Nohatta areas to convince their ability to do whatsoever they wanted to do. Accordingly on Friday they fired shots in the air from Jama Masjid, Nohatta and in Khanyar area. The people assembled for offering prayer, on seeing this and in support of that danced, lifted them up and shouted slogan *"Hum Naya Chahte hain, Azadi"* etc. The police personnel also fired shots from their positions and therefore they escaped from there.

On Id-ul-Fitr day in May 1989 he alongwith Irfan, Shabir Ahmed Biedu, Tariq Ahmed, R/o Soura, Mustaq Ahmed Khan, R/o Naid Kadal, Shoukat Ahmed Bakshi, R/o Batmaloo contacted Zahoor Ahmed Bhatt R/o Trehgam and told him about the firing incident and wanted to cross the border to escape from the police. He entrusted them to the guide who took them across the border through Uri sector and they reached District Bagh (POK). He contacted Raja Muzaffar at Muzaffarabad (POK) on telephone and told him about the youth brought from the Valley and they took tea in a stall in Bagh Bazaar. After sometime Raja Muzaffar came and took them to his house and sent Shabir Ahmed Biedu, Tariq Ahmed, Mushtaq Ahmed Khan and Shoukat Ahmed Bakshi for undergoing training in the camp in handling arms and ammunition. Zargar and Irfan stayed with him for about 10 days. On return of those persons from the camp, Raja Muzaffar gave two AK-47 rifles, 2 pistols to them and sent them with guide Sher Khan who brought them via Mendhar and then by bus to Jammu. They stayed in a hotel whereas Sher Khan went back. Next day they reached Srinagar by a taxi.

In the same month, 2-3 days after Id, in July 1989, Irfan was nabbed at Khanyar by the security forces and the two bags of arms and ammunitions brought by them were also seized. Zargar managed to evade till September and then he alongwith Shabir Ahmed Biedu, Latif Ahmed Khan, R/o Nawa Kadal and Manzoor Ahmed Khan, R/o Khanyar contacted Zahoor Bhatt who entrusted them to guides Rashid Khan and Gulzar, R/o Kupwara. The guides took them through Shallu Bhatt, District Kupwara and crossed the LoC to Boodh Nihal (Pakistan). Boarding bus from there they reached the house of Raja Muzaffar at Muzaffarabad, Pakistan Occupied Kashmir (POK). The later introduced them to Col. Assad and Maj Tariq (both ISI officers). They narrated about arrest of Irfan. Raja Muzaffar told them that they will be supplied with more weapons. Zargar and Shabir Ahmed Biedu stayed there whereas Latif Ahmed Khan and Manzoor Ahmed were sent to the camp for training. On their return, Raja Muzaffar gave four AK-47 rifles, 4 pistols and 200 cartridges for each weapons which were put in bags. Carrying the same, escorted by guides Rashid Khan and Gulzar, they crossed over to India via Shallu Bhatt and reached Srinagar. The weapons etc., were kept with Mansoor Ahmed, except one pistol each which they kept with them.

In January 1990, couple of weeks after abduction of Dr. Rubaiya Sayeed (d/o the then Union Home Minister Mufti Mohd. Sayeed) for which JKLF had owned the responsibility, Zargar and Shabir happened to meet Javed Ahmed Mir, R/o Zander Mohalla, Habba Kadal and Ashfaq Majid Wani of Maharaja Bazar. They told Zargar about having claimed responsibility for the abduction and issued press release demanding release of five of their activists Sher Khan, Javed Ahmed Zarger, Nor Mohd. Kadwal, Altaf Ahmed Bhatt and Abdul Hanif Sheikh in lieu of her release. Zargar abused them for not including the name of Irfan and asked them to include Irfan's name but they refused. On this, Zargar told them that he will not work with or for them. Thereafter, Zargar along with Shabir Ahmed Biedu, Tariq Ahmed, Mushtaq Ahmed Khan, Latif Ahmed Khan, Muzaffar Ahmed Sofi, R/o Anantnag floated independent militant group and named it as Al- Umar Mujahidin.

They wanted to increase their strength and therefore, he alongwith 16 members crossed over to Pakistan with the assistance of guides Ahmed Shah and Rashid via Shallu Bhatt during February 1990. Zargar told the guides about the split with JKLF and forming of a new outfit. The guides took them to Chehlpul, Muzaffarabad (POK). Zargar contacted Maj. Tariq of ISI and informed him about this and about the 16 new recruits.

Maj Tariq assured help, paid ₹ 5000/- in Pakistan currency and accommodated them there in a house. Next day, Maj. Tariq sent the 16 associates for training. Zargar locked the house and went and stayed with Maqbool Illahi at Muzaffarabad (POK) who was known to him. On arrival of those 16 associates, they stayed in the house arranged by Maj. Tariq. By then due to tight security checking at the LoC they could not cross over and stayed there. They celebrated Id-ul-Fitr at Chehlpul and stayed on there. Many of the youth undergoing training at Muzaffarabad joined Zargar's outfit there and their strength went up to 35.

One day in July 1990 Maj. Tariq of ISI visited them and gave ₹ 20,000/- which included ₹ 10000/- Indian and ₹ 10,000/- Pakistan currency for purchasing necessary items and they purchased the same. In the same month Zargar with 35 associates crossed the LoC via Lipa valley and reached Handwara. The guide introduced them to Ghulam Nabi Waza, R/o Handwara. From across they had brought with them arms and ammunitions including 26 AK-47 rifles, 2 LMGs, 30 Pistols, 30 grenades, 10 Walkie- talkie sets which they kept with Waza as advised by the guide for safe keeping. They visited Mohd. Afzal's house, who was friend of Shabir Biedu. After sometime, Shabir also came there and Zargar told him everything when Shabir asked Waza about the weapons. Waza told them to go after 2-3 days and collect the weapons etc. and then he went away.

Two days later Zargar sent Khalid Bashir, R/o Biaripura to bring the weapons etc., and he went in a truck and brought some of them to Mohd. Afzal's house. About 2/3 days later Tariq, R/o Habba Kadal was nabbed by Army personnel, on whose tip off Army raided Mohd. Afzal's house to nab Zargar and others but they managed to escape. But the Army succeeded in recovering the remaining arms and ammunitions which included 19 AK-47 rifles,

2 LMGs, 30 grenades, 10 Walkie-Talkie sets. Mohd. Afzal was not there and on coming to know of the raid, he also absconded.

Keeping the re-organisation of the outfit in mind, after discussions, Zargar appointed Shabir Ahmed Beidu and Tariq as Dy. chiefs of Al Umar, Sajjad Ahmed Kachru, R/o Ali Kodal as finance controller, Idris Khan, R/o Qahwa Mohalla, Khanyar as Intelligence chief, Shabir Hussain Khan code name Bitta Khan, R/o Saj Giripura Square as military adviser, Prof. Tariq, R/o Biaripura as publicity chief of Al Umar and Muzaffar Sofi, R/o Anantnag as district commander of Al Umar, district Anantnag. Thereafter a meeting was convened for discussing about the arms and ammunitions brought from across which had been seized by the Army and the need to procure more weapons. As agreed Shabir Ahmed accompanied by Tariq and three others of Saura crossed over to Pakistan for getting arms.

Mohd. Afzal requested Zargar to include him in the outfit but Zargar refused stating that he is a family man and will not be able to function as a militant and keep away from his family for days together. Two weeks later in October 1990 Shabir Ahmed with 30 youth including the four associates he had taken along with him came back via Kangru with 22 AK-47 rifles, three LMGs and three rocket launchers. Mohd. Afzal complained to Shabir Ahmed about Zargar's refusal to take him. Shabir compelled Zargar to include Mohd. Afzal but Zargar did not agree. On this Shabir Ahmed declared that he will form a separate outfit and thereon alongwith the 30 Pakistan trained militants who came with him formed an outfit named Al Umar Commandos and also retained the remaining arms and ammunitions smuggled from across the border.

In November 1990, Zargar sent Naeem-ul–Haq, R/o Chhota Bazaar, Habba Kadal, Srinagar code named as Naeem to Pakistan with a letter to Col. Assad and Maj. Tariq of ISI informing about the loss of arms and ammunitions given by them due to Army raids and requesting to supply more arms etc. to the outfit. A month later Naeem came back after getting training and alongwith 30 more trained Pakistani militants. He expressed a desire to open a unit of the outfit in Pakistan Occupied Kashmir (POK) so that they could get more Pakistan trained militants and weapons etc. Zargar readily agreed and 2-3 days later, Naeem crossed over to Pakistan Occupied Kashmir.

In the beginning of January 1991, while Zargar alongwith Tariq Ahmed Sheikh, R/o Mahrajganj, Srinagar and Mushtaq Ahmed Khan, R/o Naid Kadal was walking around Jama Masjid, he saw Farooq Ahmed Khan, R/o Mir Mohalla, Jama Masjid, whom he did not like and he fired at him with his pistol injuring him in his leg and they escaped from there. Two days later on the instructions of Shabir Hussain alias Betta Khan, the Al Umar military adviser, both Tariq Ahmed Sheikh and Nazir Ahmed Tani, R/o Chhota Bazar, Habba Kadal, Srinagar strapped an explosive device on Qasim Billa, R/o Habba Kadal, a police informer which exploded and Qasim Billa died on the spot. Zargar and his other associates came to know of this next day from the newspapers. The outfit owned responsibility for this.

Few days after, when Zargar and few associates were walking near Jama Masjid, a woman aged about 30/32 years wanted to talk to him. A boy aged about 10/11 years was also with her. When Zargar went to her, she told him that one person has been harassing her but she felt shy to explain it. Then the boy told Zargar that Mohd. Syed Koasa, R/o Nohatta, Srinagar, taking advantage of her strained relationship with her husband, had allured her assuring of better life in case she eloped with him and thus, took her to a room and had sex with her which was secretly videographed by Koasa. Using that video, the said person has been blackmailing her and forcing her to have sex with him.

On hearing this, Zargar was enraged and promised the woman that the said person will be taught a lesson so that in future none may dare to outrage the modesty of a female. Getting this assurance, the woman and the boy went away. Zargar discussed this matter with Betta Khan and then told him to nab and produce the said Koasa before him at their hide-out in a Kashmiri Pandit's abandoned house in Mohalla Rainwari. As directed, Shabir Hussain Khan alias Betta Khan nabbed and produced the said Koasa before him. Zargar had told his associates about this. When questioned, Koasa denied these allegations even though he was tortured. Then Zargar asked his associates to leave Koasa and he went and sat by his side, gave him a cigarette, a cup of tea and told him about his connections with Maulvi Farooq's Action Committee and promised to save him if he tells the truth, otherwise he will get severe punishment. On this promise, Koasa confessed his crimes of alluring women and girls and indulging in sex with them, preparing porn videos of sexual intercourse with them in different compromising positions. He also disclosed the place where he had concealed the said video cassettes.

Zargar asked Shabir Hussain Khan alias Betta Khan to go to that place with Koasa, search and bring all those cassettes. Accordingly Betta Khan with some associates went with Koasa and brought the cassettes, TV and the VCR. The cassettes were viewed by them which showed that Koasa was indulging in such illegal activities with women and girls including the women who has complained and also the said boy. They felt that Koasa needs to be eliminated but wanted to seek the opinion of Maulvi, after discussions. Accordingly, Betta Khan was sent to Maulvi to ascertain the adequate punishment to be given to Koasa according to the doctrin of Quran. On return, they conveyed the advice of Maulvi that according to Islamic law Koasa deserves death penalty. Zargar ordered to execute Koasa which was carried out by Betta Khan and associates at a place with a pistol.

During April 1991, some days before Id-ul-Fitr, Jamshed Khan R/o near Jamia College, Newal, Srinagar, chief of Al Madad-Yalgar Ali (militant outfit) was kidnapped by JKLF activists to compel him to disband his outfit and merge with some other outfit. Zargar discussed this with Noor Mohd. Nalwal, the then Dy. chief of JKLF outfit, near Jama Masjid. Zargar asked Nalwal to free Jamshed Khan and allow him to merge with any outfit of his choice after release. Nalwal agreed and the next day Jamshed Khan was released by the JKLF. About two day of his release, Jamshed Khan met Zargar and offered to merge with Al Umar which was welcomed by Zargar. Accordingly, Jamshed Khan along with 20/25 associates merged with Al Umar with their arms and ammunition which included 16 rifles, a rocket launcher. Zargar gave the weapons to Betta Khan who distributed them. Jamshed Khan was inducted as one of the Dy chiefs of Al Umar.

On last Friday preceding Id-ul-Fitr (April 1991) accompanied by Idris Khan, Khalid, R/o Biaripura and Latif, R/o Nawa Kadal, Zargar went to Palpade near Bemina Police colony, in order to see Hassan Dar, the then chief of HM militant outfit. Members of HM had seized weapons from Al Umar members in Rural areas by force and Zargar had protested. Al Umar's strength was less in rural areas and more in Srinagar, compared to Hizbul Mujahidin. Hassan Dar had asked Zargar to meet him at that place to sort out this problem. When they met Zargar warned Dar that if they continue to do that, then Al Umar will seize weapons from HM militants in Srinagar.

On hearing this, Hassan Dar assured not to repeat such things as they felt that fight between two groups will not be in the interest of militancy. Same evening on return to Jama Masjid, Zargar learnt that his men headed by Shabir Khan alias Betta Khan, military adviser had attempted to kidnap divisional commander, Kashmir, Wajahat Habib Ulla from Jama Masjid area but failed in view of police encounter resulting in the death of police official and injury to two civilians. Zargar was angry as it was not planned by them and therefore expelled Manzoor Ahmed alias Jag, R/o Jamia Masjid and Shofait of Rajouri Kadal but kept in abeyance any action against Shabir Khan, the military adviser.

About one month later, after Id-ul-Zuha in August 1991, under orders from Shabir Hussain Khan alias Betta Khan, the military adviser, Shofait R/o Zaina Kadal and Manzoor of Chanyar entered the house of Shafi Pir, ex-MLA (NC), R/o Lal Bazar, Srinagar and shot him dead firing shots from their pistols. He was on the outfits hit list. After the incident Shabir Hussain alias Betta Khan, the military adviser reported to Zargar about this.

In the middle of September, 1991, Shabir Hussain Khan alias Betta Khan ordered G. Gandhru, R/o Hazratbal Shrine, Srinagar to kill Shiekh Sadiq, ex-MLA of the same locality, cousin of NC Chief Dr. Farooq Abdullah as he was on the hit list of Al Umar. Accordingly, G. Gandhru shot dead Sheikh Sadiq and the outfit Al Umar owned the killing and a press note was also released to the press. In the end of September/beginning of October 1991, G. Gandhru, group commander, Al Umar with some outfit activists as per dictum of Shabir Hussain Khan alias Betta Khan waylaid and shot dead Hussain Din, NC MLA, R/o Hazratbal outside his home and Al Umar claimed responsibility and issued a press release.

In October 1991 Al Umar military adviser Shabir Hussain Khan alias Betta Khan shot dead Nake Waza alias Rias, the MLF activist, R/o Nawal, Srinagar for his extra-marital relations and having an affair with a girl of his locality. Al Umar claimed the responsibility by issuing a press note. Thereafter during those days when negotiation were on for securing release of Dorai Swami, the ONGC Chairman and in lieu of his release militants were released including Javed Shalla, chief of Akhwan-ul Musalmaan, Raja Waza code name Wajid Javed, military adviser of that outfit was unhappy and joined Al Umar. Zargar appointed him as military adviser replacing Betta Khan as action against him was kept in abeyance earlier. Betta Khan was named as Dy intelligence chief.

About 5/6 days thereafter, on the orders of Zargar, Kobari alias Khali Mumtaz, R/o Saribal, Lal Chowk, Srinagar, the district commander of Al Umar, Srinagar with others of the outfit kidnapped Tasadaq Dev, R/o Haider Pura. Two days after, Purna Nand, Dy SP was kidnapped. Nazir Siddiqui, R/o Camurwari, a mediator contacted Zargar for release of the Dy. SP against release of 4/5 militants. Thinking that the Dy SP is a VIP, Zargar did not release him. About one month later, they kidnapped Hamid Ulla Khan's (Governor's Advisor) younger brother Mohd. Shafi Khan from his house in Anantnag. About a month later the security forces (army) conducted a crack down operation in Chak Dhara area, where Al Umar was active, during which the Dy. SP escaped.

About 10-15 days later, Nazir Siddiqui acting as mediator negotiated for the release of Hamid Ulla Khan's brother Mohd. Shafi Khan and accordingly Zargar released him and in lieu of that seven militants including Muzaffar Shafi of Anantnag, Manzoor Ahmed Khan of Baramullah, Altaf Ahmed Bakhei of Handwar, Latif Ahmed Shalla of Saraf Kadal, Manzoor Ahmed Wani of Nohatta and Shakeel Ahmed Mathi, R/o Saffi Kadal were released from jail. There was gang war between Al Umar and JKLF and shoot-outs and deaths on both sides. The Masjid intervened and there was a cease-fire. During same month, *i.e.*, March 1992 they kidnapped Prof Sharma of Srinagar University and shifted him to Anantnag and handed over to Tariq, district president of Al Umar for safe custody. Two days later they kidnapped Professor of Regional Engineering College, Srinagar and kept him in custody in Anantnag.

On 14/15.05.1992 when Zargar and Riaz Ahmed alias Lala were sitting in the park of Jamia Masjid, Azad Ahmed alias Piran, R/o Sraf Kadal, came there and met him . He invited Zargar for dinner. After sometime, Zargar came across Qayoom Dar, Azad Ahmed Wani, R/o Pora near Jamia Masjid. Alongwith them, Zargar went to the house of Azad Ahmed around 8PM. They had meal there. In the meantime, Javed Ahmed and Latif Ahmed Shalla came there. After meal, around 11.30PM, while Zargar was offering prayers, BSF personnel cordoned off Azad Ahmed alias Piran's house, raided the place and nabbed all of them namely Zargar, Riaz Ahmed Shah alias Lala, Qayoom Dar, Azad Ahmed Wani and Azad Ahmed alias Piran whereas Javed Ahmed and Latif Ahmed managed to escape. They were blindfolded and taken to Shahnaz Hotel. The BSF personnel did not know who was Zargar. When asked, Zargar gave his name as Fiaz Ahmed R/o Saffa Kadal taking the clue from Piran who pointed out Zargar as his brother-in-law Fiaz Ahmed.

Next morning they were taken to interrogation centre and interrogated. During interrogation they identified Zargar and they were happy that they have captured Al Umar chief Mushtaq Latram. Senior officers promised to lodge Zargar in Central Jail, Srinagar if he directs for the release of those kidnapped by the outfit. Ashraf alias Lally Zargar was brought by the police and later on mother of Zargar was also brought so that the message for the release could be sent by Zargar to his men. Accordingly, Idris and Iqbal Zargar, released those in their custody. Zargar remained in the Interrogation centre and thereafter in JIC, Srinagar and thereafter shifted to Kot Bhalwal in Jammu. He was released from that jail, taken to Kandahar and handed over to the hijackers.

The above background of the three persons, as disclosed by them earlier, shows their importance and clarifies why the hijackers wanted their release in exchange of the hostages and the aircraft. It will be of interest to the public to know these details. This will definitely pose a question whether we are alert in this country? Whether our Intelligence agencies were aware of these activities of the militants. It is because of their contribution to militancy that these three were selected to be released. Maulana was to be released but the other two were selected out of the remaining 35. It is clear that the hijackers had a long list from which they selected these 35 names besides that of Maulana Masood Azhar. In this connection, the news that the American forces had recovered a big handwritten list along with counter foils of tickets of hijackers during raids in Kandahar became very relevant but the concerned agencies in America did not hand over them to the CBI.

Chapter 7

Nithari Necrophilic Killings

Necrophilia is the sexual attraction to corpses. In medical terms, Necrophilia is sexual attraction to, or sexual contact with dead bodies. According to experts, it is a rare disorder that has been known since ancient times. According to Herodotus, the ancient Egyptians took precautions against necrophilia by prohibiting the corpses of the wives of distinguished men or of beautiful women from being delivered immediately to the embalmers for fear that the embalmers would violate them as it actually happened in case of a woman, who had just died. The dead bodies were delivered after 3-4 days when they had decomposed. According to a legend, King Herod had sex with his wife Marianne for seven years after he killed her. Jonathan Rosman and Phillip Resnick (1989), after review of 122 cases (88 from the world literature and 34 unpublished cases) postulated that the following psychodynamic events could lead to necrophilia:

- The necrophilic develops poor self-esteem perhaps due, in part, to a significant loss;

  (a) he is very fearful of rejection by women and he desires a sexual object who is incapable of rejecting him and or

(b) he is fearful of the dead and transforms his fear of the dead by means of reaction formation into a desire for the dead,

- He develops an exciting fantasy of sex with a corpse, sometimes after exposure to a corpse.

From their sample study of Necrophilics, they reported that:

- 68 percent (pc) were motivated by a desire for an unresisting and unrejecting partner;
- 21 percent by a want for reunion with a lost partner;
- 15 percent by sexual attraction to dead people;
- 15 percent by a desire for comfort or to overcome feelings of isolation; and
- 11 percent by a desire to remedy low self-esteem by expressing power over a corpse.

Even in its truest form, necrophilia can be quite varied, ranging from simply being in the presence of a corpse to kissing, fondling or performing sexual intercourse or cunnilingus on the body. The presence of other paraphilias or personality disorders, however, can manifest in more grotesque or sadistic elements such as mutilation of the corpse, drinking the blood or urine, or homicide ("necrophilic homicide" or "necrosadism"). The latter is the most disturbing extreme end. Although the act of murder itself may generate the subsequent sexual frenzy, research has determined an alarming rate of homicide in order to obtain a body for subsequent sexual violation.

Rosman and Resnick found that 42 percent of their study sample of necrophiles had murdered in order to obtain a body. In all cases, there is undoubtedly sexual preference for a corpse rather than a living woman. When no other act of cruelty/cutting into pieces etc., is practised on the corpse, it is probable that the lifeless condition itself forms the stimulus for the perverse individual. It is possible that the corpse, a human form absolutely without will, satisfies an abnormal desire, in that the object of desire is seen to be capable of absolute subjugation, without possibility of resistance. According to Dr. Jonathan Rosman and Dr. Phillip Resnick, there are three basic types of "true" necrophilia:

- Necrophilic homicide, which is murder to obtain a corpse;
- Regular necrophilia, the use of corpses already dead for sexual pleasure;
- Necrophilic fantasy, envisioning the acts but not acting on them.

In their study of 122 cases, more people fit into the second category than the other two. More than half of them worked in a morgue or some other aspect of the funeral industry.

In fact, in another paper, J. Paul de River documents the case of an Italian grave digger who began to masturbate as he worked whenever he had to bury a beautiful young woman. To help him achieve climax, he would touch the corpse. In time, he began having sex with the dead when no one was around. When caught with his mouth on the genital area of a deceased woman, he admitted to having violated hundreds of corpses. De River diagnoses him (and all necrophiles) as a psychopath. He cites another case of a mortuary worker who would expose and then touch his penis against the thighs of cadavers as he worked on them. He was soon having sex with four or five corpses every week. With one adolescent girl, he sucked both blood and urine from her, and badly wanted to chew on parts of her body. Instead, he bit her buttocks and then sodomized her.

Reportedly, necrophiles are primarily male (about 90 percent), but one female apprentice embalmer claimed that during the first four months of her employment, she had sex with a number of corpses. She admitted that she could not achieve satisfaction with the living, in part, because she had been molested once and later raped. She could express herself to corpses without fear. While she did not engage in penile penetration, another female mortician did and she managed it by devising a pump that fit under the skin of the penis.

Contrary to common belief, say Rosman and Resnick, most necrophiles are heterosexual, although about half of the known necrophiles who have killed were gay. In only about 60 percent is there a diagnosed personality disorder, with 10 percent being psychotic. The Nithari killing cases fit into this category of necrophilia. Opinions obtained from clinical psychologists and psychiatrists, by the CBI during investigation, confirmed the above definitions and descriptions of necrophilia. A human form absolutely without will, satisfied an abnormal desire, in that the object of desire is seen to be capable of absolute subjugation, without possibility of resistence. Mutilation and eating of flesh of the killed women is categorised as necrophagia.There were large number of missing cases in Noida, Uttar Pradesh, specially in the Nithari area over the years. Although reports were made to the police, no cases were registered and in some cases, out of pressure, missing reports were entered/made in the General Diary of the police station. The experience of the public show that tracing of the missing happened to be rare.

In some cases, the victim is tracked to a particular point on account of last seen information but in blind cases no such tracking could be done. The relatives of the victims had to put pressure for getting an FIR registered for investigation. The detection of the Nithari missing cases is due to such effective persuation by Nand Lal, father of missing Payal alias Deepika of Sector-19, Noida. During such investigation 17 more missing reports were also converted into FIRs. On recovery of skulls etc., another FIR was also registered with regard to it and in total 19 cases were registered and transferred to the CBI in January, 2007. Investigation by the CBI disclosed the following:

Moninder Singh Pandher, a businessman dealing with sale of JCB machines in Noida, Uttar Pradesh was living in house no. D-5, Sector-31, Noida since February 2004. His wife was in Chandigarh. Surender Koli, S/o Shankar Ram Koli, R/o Village Magru Khal, PS Jolly Khal, District Almora, Uttarakhand, was working as a servant with Moninder Singh Pandher since July, 2004. Pandher would leave the house for work or otherwise and therefore, Surender Koli used to be alone in that house. As there was sudden demand for JCB machines on account of large scale construction activities, he had brisk business of sale of these machines and earned good money. He started going to night parties and came in contact with call girls. Pandher used to frequently bring call girls to the house and spend the nights with them. Surender Koli used to prepare food and take it to the bedroom of Pandher and on many occasions he had seen the girls lying naked on the bed of Pandher. This created an urge in the mind of Koli to release his sexual pressures. When this went on and he could not get relief, standing at gate and looking at the women and girls passing on the road, he developed a mental and sexual perversion. He developed a tendency to have sex with non-resisting female to satisfy his urge. Detailed evidence of a call girl racket and supply of girls to Pandher and his activities falling under the Immoral Activities (Prevention) Act came out during CBI investigation. Evidence of efforts made by him to save his reputation by bribing the police officers, etc., also came up and he was charged for these activities. However, the cases are under trial.

Surender Koli had an abnormal tendency of alluring girls and women into the house through deceitful means for killing them and raping them. Thereafter, he would carry the bodies to the bathroom located on the first floor of the house which was for his exclusive use. There he would dismember the bodies with a knife and dispose of the body parts in the gallery behind the house and in the drain running in front of the house, in a clandestine manner, when nobody could see him. In some cases, Surender Koli would eat the flesh of the victims. He would indulge in these inhuman and diabolical acts, when he was alone in the house. Lonliness had contributed to his negative mental condition.

During the period February, 2005 and April, 2006 Surender Koli murdered and sexually abused eight women and children and disposed of their dead bodies as mentioned below:

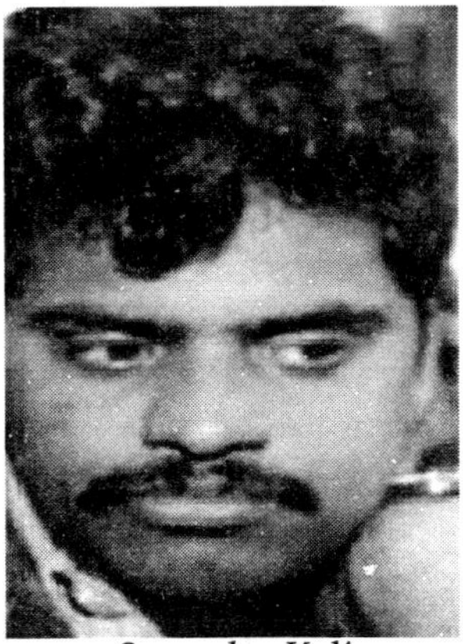

Surender Koli

In February 2005, when accused Surender Koli was alone in the house, he lured Rimpa Haldar into house D-5, Sector-31 Noida, and when she came in, he strangulated her with her own chunni and killed her. He also tried to rape her. Then he took the dead body to the bathroom on the first floor, cut the body into parts, packed the parts in polythene bags, threw the head and some bony parts into the back side gallery and other parts into the drain in front of the house. Clothes, chappals were thrown into the back side gallery.

In this case, he cut the left breast and flesh from the arm, cooked it in a cooker and ate it. This was the first case as disclosed by him. It was found that Rimpa aged about 14 years was missing since 08.02.2005. After about a month, he lured another girl Bina Haldar inside the house. In the drawing room, he strangulated her with her own chunni, killed her and attempted to rape her. Thereafter he took the dead body to the bathroom on the first floor, dismembered it and disposed off the body parts as mentioned above. In this case also he cut the breast into pieces, cooked it along with flesh from the arm and ate it. Bina Haldar aged about 13 years was missing since 15.03.2005. Thereafter, he allured a female child named Payal, who was playing in front of house no. D-5, Sector-31 Noida, into his house, throttled her, killed her and attempted to rape her. In the month of June 2005 accused Surender Koli called Jyoti, inside and then strangulated her with her chunni, killed her and attempted to rape her. After 5-6 months, one evening, accused Surender Koli lured another child into the house, blocked and closed its nose with his hand, killed it and when he removed the clothes, he found that the child was a male. He dismembered the body in the bathroom, ate pieces of liver of the said boy with salt and disposed off the skull into the backyard and body parts into the drain (nala) in front of the house. The name of the child was Harsh and he was aged three years and was missing since 23.02 2006. After a few days, he lured Rachna into the house, strangulated and killed her and attempted to rape her. The girl was aged eight years and was missing since 10.04.2006. A few days later, he lured another girl called Pushpa, strangulated and killed her and attempted to rape her. The girl was aged ten years and was missing since 19.04.2006. A few days thereafter, he lured another child inside the house where he strangulated and killed the child. When accused Surender Koli removed the clothes of the child, he found that the child was a boy. Later on, he came to know that the name of the child was Max as there was announcements in the area. The boy was aged eight years and was missing since 27.04.2006. He took the dead body of aforesaid victim to the bathroom located on the first floor of the house and disposed off in the manner mentioned above.

Payal alias Deepika, aged 27 years, resident of Sector -19, Noida was one of the girls who used to visit the house of accused Moninder Singh Pandher. Few days before her death, she spent a night with Pandher. On that occasion, Koli had asked for her mobile number telling that he would introduce her to other clients and she had given the mobile number to him.

On 5.5.2006, Moninder Singh left for Chandigarh to see his ailing father who was admitted in hospital and expired on 8.5.2006. Surender Koli was left alone in the house. He called Payal twice on her mobile phone on 6.5.2006 at 5:42 and 5:44 PM from the PCO booth located near House No. D-5, Sector 31, Noida. The owner of the booth had heard Surender Koli talking to a woman. Surender Koli had asked Payal to come to the residence of Moninder Singh Pandher. She first expressed her inability but later on agreed to visit on 7.5.2006 to which Surender Koli agreed. Koli had deliberately avoided using the residential telephone of Moninder Singh Pandher to avoid detection.

On 7.5.2006 at about 4 - 4:30 PM, Payal after informing family went to the house of Pandher with her mobile phone. While leaving, she was wearing a greenish blue print kurta with white background and sky blue colour salwar and plastic chappals. She carried her small red coloured purse. Payal left her house in a cycle rickshaw. After leaving her house, she had a talk with her boy friend in Mumbai on his mobile phone at 16.30 hours and told him that she was heading for Sector-31, Noida. Surender Koli was alone in the house. He was waiting at the gate. He allowed her to enter and followed her inside. On entering, she sat on a cushion chair. She was familiar with the house. Koli went behind, pulled her chunni, strangulated her with it. She struggled and then died. Koli checked whether she was alive. On finding no resistence he undressed her and raped her. According to him, he was successful in raping her. After that Koli further tightened the chunni around Payal's neck and after making sure that she was dead, he carried her dead body to the bathroom, cut her body into pieces with a knife and packed the body parts in polythene bags. Late in the evening, Surender Koli threw the skull, clothes, slippers packed in polythene bags into the gallery at the back side of the house and other body parts in the drain running in front of the house. He also took away Payal's red coloured purse with 30-32 rupees in it and SIM card as also her Nokia mobile phone. Surender Koli used the aforesaid set of Payal with new SIM cards subsequently procured by him. This helped in tracking the mobile set.

On 07.05.2006, when Payal did not return home till late in the evening, her family started searching for her. On 08.05.2006 Nand Lal, father of deceased Payal, went to the house of Moninder Singh Pandher and met servant Surender Koli in the house. On being questioned about the whereabouts of Payal, Surender Koli turned pale and went inside the house saying that he did not know anyone by name of Payal. On 09.05.2006 Nand Lal talked to Moninder Singh Pandher on his mobile phone who told him that he was in Chandigarh. On being confronted with the fact that his servant Surender Koli had called Payal to his residence on 07.05.2006 from where she had not returned, Moninder Singh Pandher told him that he did not know anything about her. Later on, repeated efforts by Nand Lal to contact Moninder Singh Pandher on his mobile proved futile. As mentioned above, Pandher's father had died in the hospital in Chandigarh.

Nand Lal again visited house no. D-5/31 Noida and showed the photograph of Payal to Surender Koli but the latter deliberately and intentionally did not identify her. Since Payal had gone in a cycle rickshaw, Nand Lal made enquiries at the cycle rickshaw stands with rickshaw pullers by showing the photograph of Payal. Amar Haldar, a rickshaw puller told Nand Lal that on 07.05.2006 he had ferried the woman seen in the photograph from Sector 19 to Sector-31 and had left her in front of house no. D-5, Sector 31 Noida. He had also told him that after alighting from the cycle rickshaw, the woman had gone inside the said house.

To trace Payal, Nand Lal went to Police Chowki located in Sector-26, Noida [Nithari] and met SI K.P. Singh, Chowki In-charge and sought his help. SI K.P. Singh sent some policemen to house no. D-5, Sector-31 Noida and called Surender Koli for questioning. When Moninder Singh Pandher, who was in Chandigarh, came to know of it, he immediately sent his manager to secure the release of Surender Koli. Due to his intervention, the police let Surender Koli off. When Nand Lal insisted for registration of an FIR, the SI sent him to Sector-20 Police Station for the above purpose. Nand Lal went to Sector-20 Police Station, where he met the SHO and narrated the incident regarding the disappearance of his daughter, but no case was registered.

When the police did not take any concrete step for recovery of Payal, Nand Lal, met SSP, Noida and complained of police inaction in the matter. The SSP then directed the SHO, Sector-20, Noida to take necessary action in the matter. Thereupon a missing person report was registered at the Police Station *vide* GD entry no. 31 dated 29.06.2006. When nothing concrete emerged, Nand Lal filed a petition in the Court of CJM, Gautambudh Nagar on 24.08.2006, for registration of FIR by the police. The CJM vide his order dated 27.09.2006, directed the SHO, PS Sector 20, Noida to register an FIR and commence investigation forthwith. Pursuant thereto, FIR no. 838/2006 under Section. 363, 366 IPC was registered on 07.10.2006 against MS Pandher and Surinder Koli at PS Sector-20, Noida and investigation thereof was entrusted to SI Simarjit Kaur.

In the last week of November, 2006, while travelling from Sector-37 to his residence, accused Surender Koli inadvertently left behind the Nokia phone of deceased Payal along with SIM card bearing no. 9871215328 in the rickshaw of Satlaren. Satlaren kept the mobile phone in his bag from where it was taken out by Mantu, who lived in the same quarter with Satlaren. The mobile was taken from Mantu by Sanoj alias Saroj, another rickshaw puller, who used SIM card no. 9871496595 in the said instrument. This SIM card belonged to Birender, a friend of Sanoj. On 03.12.06 Sanoj sold the mobile phone to one Arun for ₹ 800/- and purchased a Tata mobile phone. Arun used SIM card no. 9999098088, purchased in the name of his father Radhey Shyam, in the said mobile instrument. On 22.12.2006, the mobile phone was seized by the local police from Arun.

With intent to avoid further interrogation/possible apprehension by the Noida Police, Surender Koli suddenly left Noida for his native place in Almora district on 25.12.2006. The Police summoned him back to Noida for questioning. The Noida police arrested Surender Koli and Moninder Singh Pandher on 29.12.2006 in this case. On questioning by the police, Surender Koli confessed to have deceitfully called Payal to house no. D-5, Sector-31, Noida, killed and raped her.

He also confessed to have dismembered the dead body and thrown her body parts into the gallery behind the house and the drain running in front of the house. He also disclosed that he had thrown the slippers of deceased Ms. Payal into the backside gallery of the said house. On the basis of disclosure made by Surender Koli on 29.12.2006 under Section 27 of the Evidence Act the police recovered the slippers and red colour purse of Payal and the knife used by accused Surender Koli for dismembering the bodies of Payal and other victims. Importantly, on the disclosure made by the accused, the local police recovered 15 skulls and a number of bones and clothings of the victims killed by accused Surender Koli.

The clothes so recovered were shown to the family members of the victims and on their identification, the police registered separate FIRs as mentioned above. On the request of the Government of Uttar Pradesh and orders of the Central Government by way of notifications, the CBI took up investigation of these cases. On taking up investigation of the 19 cases, the CBI arrested Surender Koli and M.S. Pandher and interrogated them in different cases. It was found that though after missing of Payal, police summoned accused Surender Koli for questioning, accused denied his activities of alluring children and women, killing and raping them and in spite of being questioned by the police, accused Surender Koli lured and killed in the same manner Deepali (aged 12 years), Nisha (aged 11 years), Aarti (aged 7 years), Anjali (aged 25 years), Pinki Sarkar, Nanda (maid servant who worked earlier in the same house and was aged 25 years) and Madhu (aged 20 years) upto November 2006. As this was a complicated case and first of its kind, and the investigation was to be carried out with the assistance of forensic scientists, the CBI involved the well-known forensic experts in the country, in the investigation. During interrogation by the CBI, accused Surender Koli admitted that his first victim was Rimpa Haldar whom he killed in February 2005. He was standing at the gate when she was passing. He asked her whether she wanted to work as a maid servant and when she said yes, he told her to meet the madam, inside. When she came in, he followed and once she was inside the house, he closed the door and told her that madam is inside the room.

She was looking at the room. He pulled her *chunni* from the back and she fell back, he strangulated her with the *chunni* though she struggled. He tightened the *chunni* and she died. After finding that she was not responding, he removed her clothes and made attempts to rape her. He went on trying but could not. This was his first crime. She was found missing in that month only which confirms the statement of Surender Koli. Thereafter, he carried the dead body to the bathroom on the first floor, dismembered the dead body with a knife, threw the skull, clothes, chappals into the back side gallery and the body parts into the drain running in front of the said house. He also cut the left breast and flesh from the arm of the dead body of Rimpa, cooked it in a cooker and ate it.

During detailed questioning by the CBI, Surender Koli made further disclosures about throwing of bones, body parts into the drain etc. and that all places were not searched earlier and properly. The disclosure made by him before the CBI was recorded and he was taken to the spot. With the assistance of forensic experts from All India Institute of Medical Sciences, New Delhi, State Forensic Laboratory, Andhra Pradesh, Central Forensic Science Laboratory, New Delhi etc., the CBI searched and scanned the drain in front of the house upto a long distance with sophisticated equipments, in the presence of Surender Koli and recovered the following materials:

- 73 pieces of bones of different sizes from the gallery at the back of house no. D-5, Sector-31, Noida;
- 53 polythene packets containing biological material/soft tissues/human bones etc., from the drain in front of house no. D-5, Sector-31, Noida;
- Bunch of hairs;

- Several pairs of shoes/slippers of different sizes and dirty, torn muddy clothes of different sizes etc from the back side gallery.

On 13.01.2007 accused Surender Koli made another disclosure statement offering to point out the specific spot in house no. D-5, Sector-31, Noida, where he strangulated and killed Payal, the cushion chair (out of many chairs) on which Payal urinated on being strangulated, the spot through which he threw the dead body parts, clothes, chappals of the victims to the enclosed gallery at the back of the house and also the specific openings through which he had dumped the other body parts of the victims in the drain running in front of the said house. In furtherance of the said disclosure, accused Surender Koli pointed out the abovesaid places and also got recovered the cushion chair on which Payal was strangulated.

On 18.01.2007 accused Surender Koli made a further disclosure that he had also used an axe to cut the dead bodies of the victims, which was covered in a polythene and hidden by him inside a bush in the complex of the house and when he was taken to that place, he pointed out and got the said axe recovered. In furtherance of this disclosure, the said axe was recovered on 18.01.2007, on pointing out by accused Surender Koli.

Experts from Forensic Science Laboratory, Agra, had conducted a detailed inspection of the scene of crime and after due examination submitted a report about it. During the course of investigation the local police had forwarded the skulls, bones, clothes, knife etc., recovered from the premises of house no. D-5, Sector-31, Noida, to FSL Agra for expert opinion. The skulls and other materials required scientific processing/cleaning, individualisation and post-mortem examination before subjecting them to DNA extraction and profiling test, the CBI obtained the orders of Chief Judicial Magistrate and retrieved those materials and thereafter alongwith the bones, biological materials etc so recovered by the CBI, forwarded them to All India Institute of Medical Sciences, New Delhi. The examination was a mass scale operation which also required large number of forensic experts to assemble at a place. It was necessary to identify the various bones and then individualise with reference to its age etc and the skull. This could be done by forensic anatomy experts. Processing and post-mortem examination were to be done by the forensic medicine experts. Biological materials were to be processed and then identified. Then they were to be subjected to DNA extraction test. The forensic experts of AIIMS, New Delhi processed the items scientifically. Processed skulls could be shown as below:

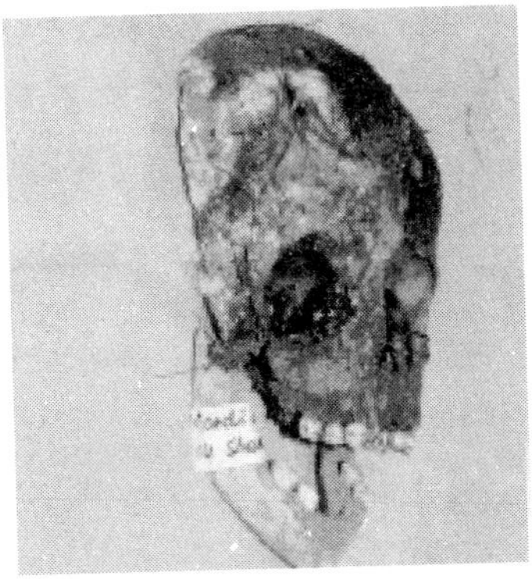

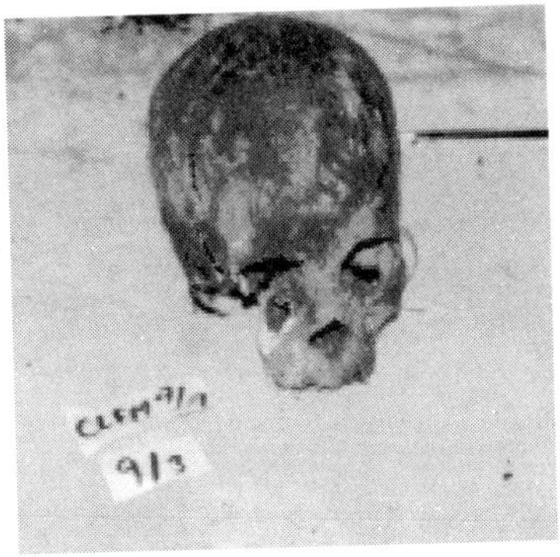

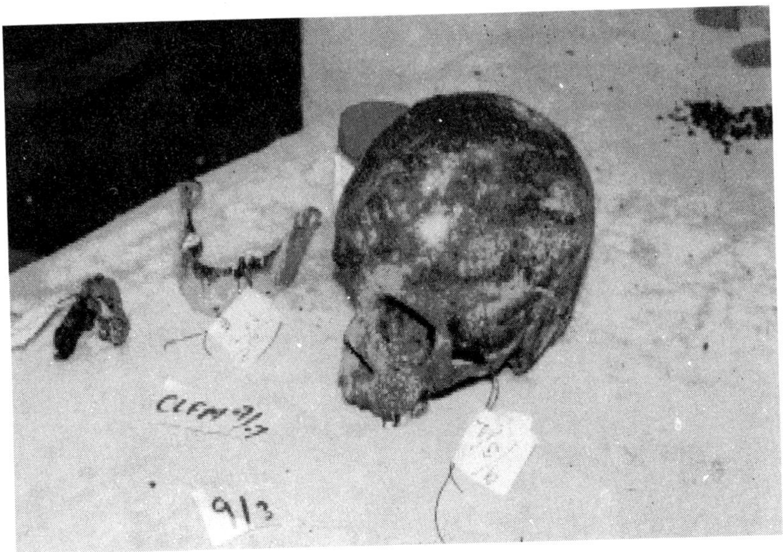

The bones after scientific processing, without any damage to them could be seen as follows:

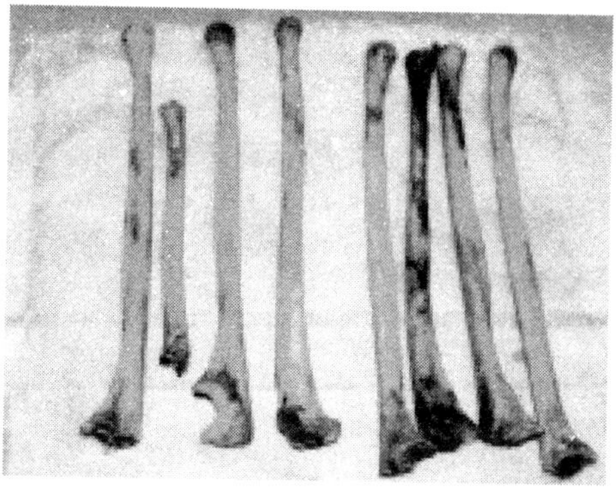

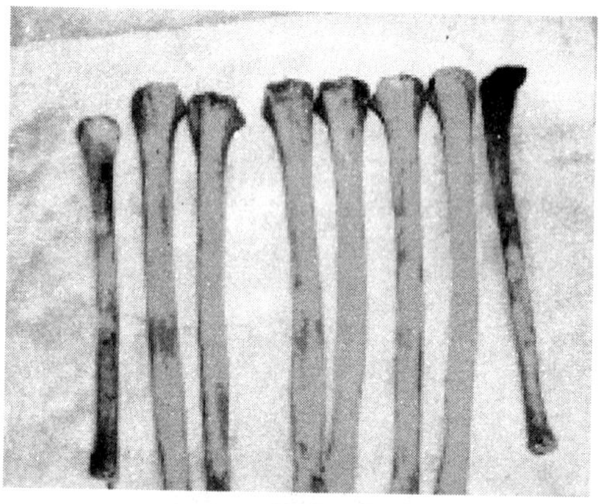

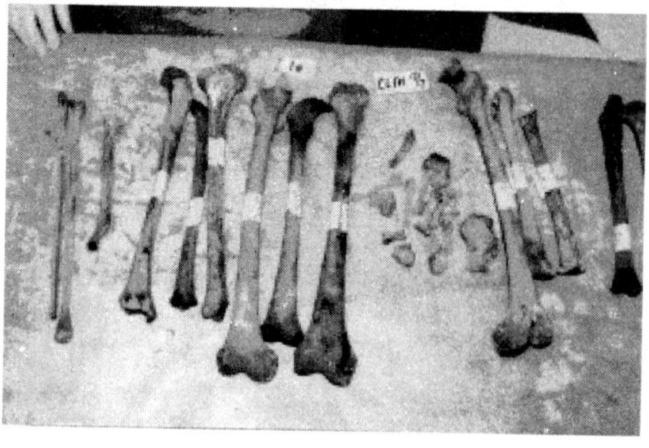

The biological materials recovered from the dirty drain in front of the house, after scientific processing looked as follows:

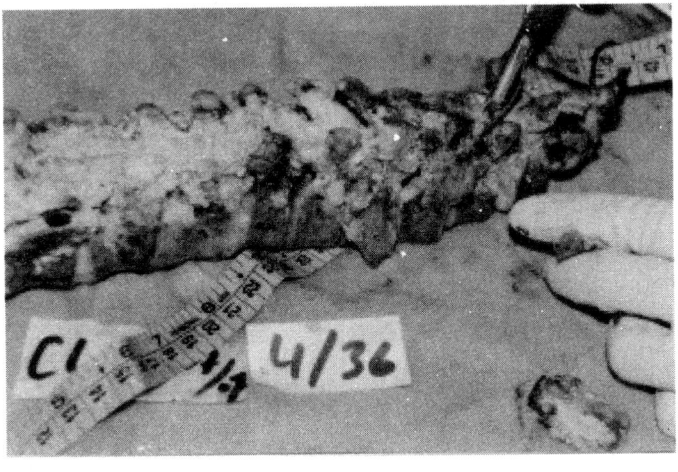

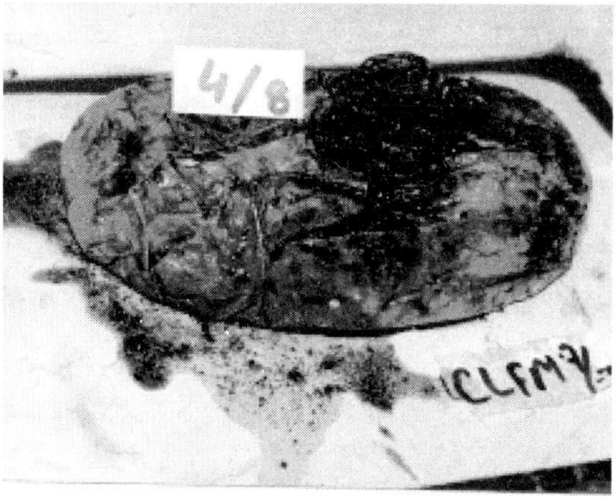

SL

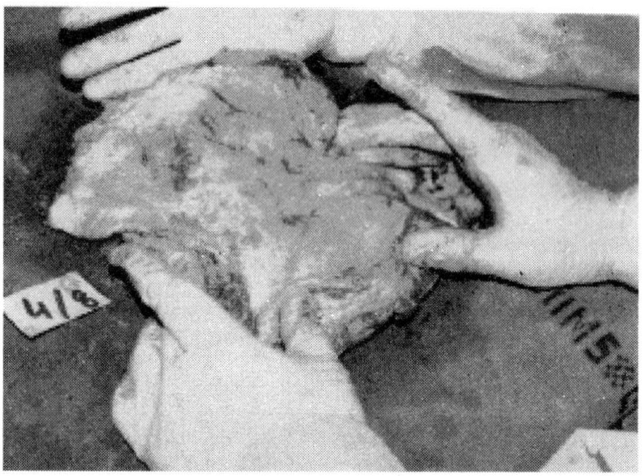

Though AIIMS had also started the DNA profiling facilities, but on account of mass scale work involved, it was felt that only the Centre for DNA Fingerprinting and Diagnostics, Hyderabad could handle the work as it is a reputed Institution in this field. It was also decided that the AIIMS experts and FSL, Andhra Pradesh scientists will assist them for early completion of the examination, as the accused were in custody. It may be mentioned here that in a case of murder etc., the limitation period for filing of charge-sheet against the accused in custody is 90 days from the date of custody. Accordingly, all the materials were transported to

CDFD, Hyderabad for DNA test. With the assistance of AIIMS experts, blood samples of relatives of the missing ladies and children were taken and transported to CDFD, Hyderabad. After due examination, All India Institute of Medical Sciences gave a report opining that dismemberment of soft tissues and bones in various exhibits could have been caused by sharp edged weapon. All the soft tissues and bones, barring a few and the bunch of hairs, were confirmed to be of human origin.

After examination by forensic experts of AIIMS, the skeletal remains were referred to CDFD, Hyderabad for DNA profiling and matching with the DNA extracted from the blood samples of the relatives of the missing persons. The CBI took blood samples of relatives of the missing persons, with the assistance of experts from AIIMS, which were forwarded by AIIMS to CDFD, Hyderabad. After DNA extraction and profiling, CDFD, Hyderabad submitted a report confirming the identity of eight victims only. They could generate DNA from the said eight skulls only and matched the profiles with the DNA profiles of relatives of said victims. From the rest of the skulls and other items no DNA could be extracted. From the skull of Rimpa Haldar, DNA could be generated and the profile matched with the profile of blood samples of her parents and her identity was established. Similarly, the identity of seven more skulls was also established.

After examination of all possibilities of confirming identity of the skulls, the remaining skulls were forwarded to Central Forensic Science Laboratory at Chandigarh for digital superimposition test. The said laboratory after such test, fixed the identity of five more victims. This test is not a conclusive test as the DNA test. In these cases, the clothes of the concerned victims were identified by the parents before the Magistrate and both the pieces of evidence confirmed the identity with reference to the evidence of missing and the confession of Surender Koli. Besides this, in three more cases, the clothes of the victims were identified by the relatives which corroborated the confession of Koli and missing reports etc.

The clothes of the victims, the knife and the axe recovered during the course of investigation were forwarded by the CBI to CFSL, New Delhi, for scientific examination. After due examination, CFSL, New Delhi opined that blood stains of human origin were found on some of the clothes. CFSL also opined that the knife, recovered from the said premises on the disclosure of accused Surender Koli, was a strong, sharp knife and it was possible to cut the human tissues with it. Regarding the axe (*kulhadi*) recovered by CBI, on 18.01.2007, on the disclosure of accused Surender Koli, the CFSL has also opined that it is a strong and sharp one and it is possible to cut the human body tissues with it.

Accused Surender Koli and Moninder Singh Pandher were subjected to polygraphy test (Lie Detection Test) at CFSL, New Delhi which indicated that Surender Koli was telling the truth regarding various killings etc. Pandher's answers that he was not involved, was also found to be correct. No deception was found.

During investigation accused Surender Koli and Moninder Singh Pandher were referred to the Directorate of Forensic Science, Gandhi Nagar, Gujarat for Psychological Assessment, Polygraphy, Narco Analysis and Brain Mapping tests. After the scientific tests, the aforesaid Laboratory opined that the Narco test conducted, on the permission given by the court, indicated that the confession made by Koli regarding killing and raping the women and girls were correct. It also indicated that Pandher's statement that he was not involved in the killings was correct.

During his interrogation, accused Surender Koli had described the precise manner in which he used to dismember the bodies of the victims. In order to ascertain the veracity of his admission, Director, AIIMS, New Delhi was requested to constitute a Board of Experts, including experts from Forensic Anatomy Department to subject Surender Koli to a test to ascertain whether he is speaking the truth. Whether he could have cut the bodies in that manner. The board was requested to examine him, talk to him and conduct the test, independently without the presence of any CBI officers. Accordingly the Board of Experts examined Surender Koli at AIIMS, New Delhi. Reports and video cassets received from the Board, subsequently, indicated that the forensic experts could individualise the bones etc with reference to the skulls, analysing the age, identity of various skeletal remains and had thus, assembled them scientifically, to make out dead bodies through forensic anatomy tests as shown below:

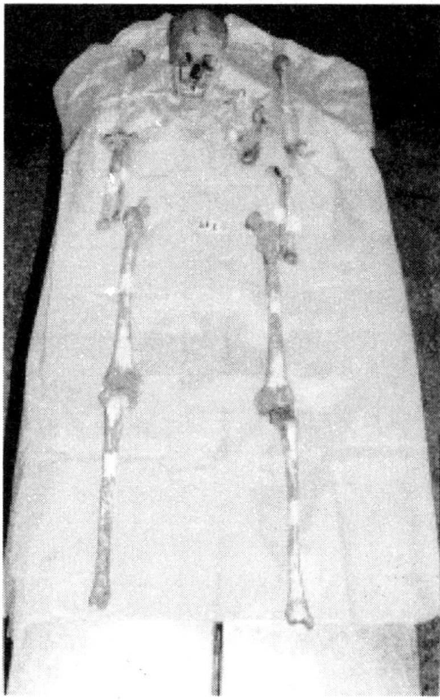
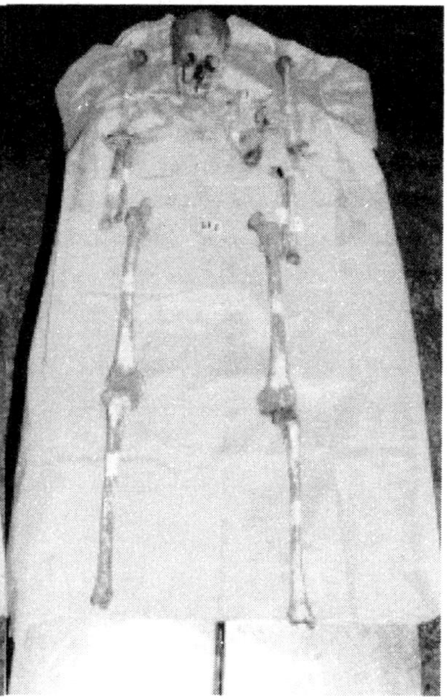

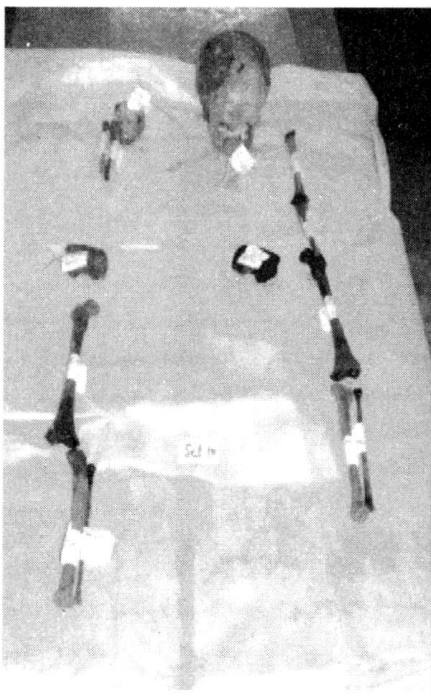
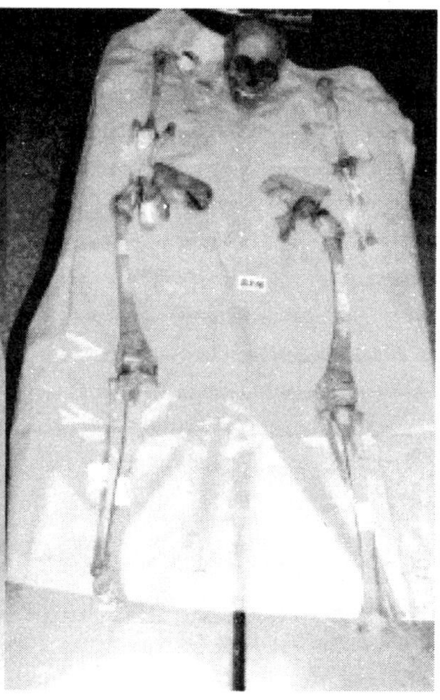

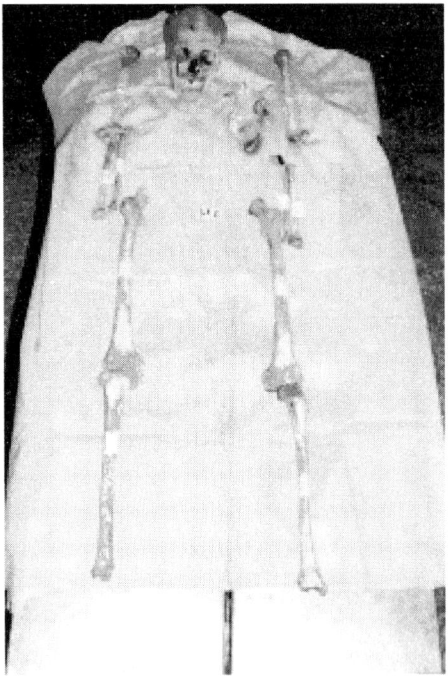

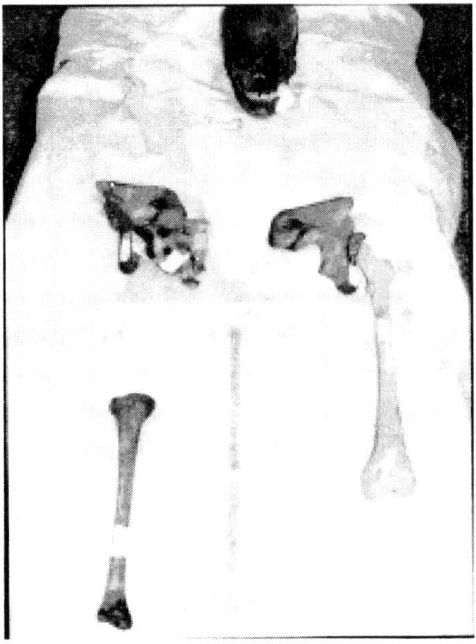

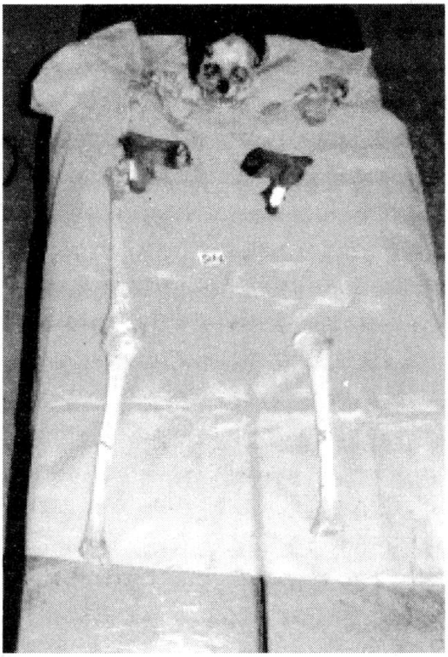

Surender Koli on being shown the skeletal remains, by the independent Board, as above, had identified the three small skeletal remains as could be that of Harsh aged about 3-4 years, Max aged about 6 years and Rachna aged about 8-9 years. Surender Koli was also shown various exhibits like hairs, hair clips, rubber bands etc., which were found on the skeletal remains, by the Board and he told the experts that they could be that of deceased Nanda, Pinky, Rimpa and Madhu. On examination of the style of hairs like its length, density etc. Surender Koli recognised them to be that of the victims Rimpa, Payal etc. These were the findings of the independent forensic experts board which forms part of the case records proved. Surender Koli, during interrogation, had explained the way he used to cut the dead bodies. He appeared to be an expert in cutting the dead bodies without damaging the body much like in the case of a brutal cutting of the dead body. He explained various joints which could be separated without much difficulty or medical instruments. When asked, he had told that, in the hills they used to cut the goats during festivals and he knew the art. To confirm whether it could be done like that, it was found necessary to subject him to a practical test wherein he could be tested by an independent forensic expert, without presence of

CBI officers and any pressure on him. It was felt that a crime investigation process, in this era of sophisticated crimes required the assistance of such forensic science tests and evidence, in the interest of logical and proper investigation.

On verification, it was found that unidentified dead bodies were also used by the hospitals to give practical training to the medical students and for conducting researches without intentionally tampering with the dead bodies. Such an experiment was found to be necessary in and for a criminal investigation to arrive at the truth in public interest and to render justice to the victims. With this genuine intention and idea in mind, AIIMS was requested to constitute a Board of Forensic Experts in the concerned fields including forensic anatomy and also preserve an unidentified dead body, before its disposal and test the capacity of Koli in dismembering as stated and explained by him. He was to mark with a piece of chalk on the dead body, the way in which he used to cut the bodies of the victims, before the independent board, without the presence of police or CBI officers. Accordingly, the expert board was constituted by AIIMS and one unidentified dead body was preserved before disposal. Accused Surender Koli was forwarded to the Board. Subsequent report and video received from the Board showed Koli was asked by the Board of Experts to outline with a chalk, on cadaver, the way he used to dismember the dead bodies of the victims. The report and video received from the board showed that Koli had voluntarily marked the way in which he had cut the bodies of the victims, as shown below:

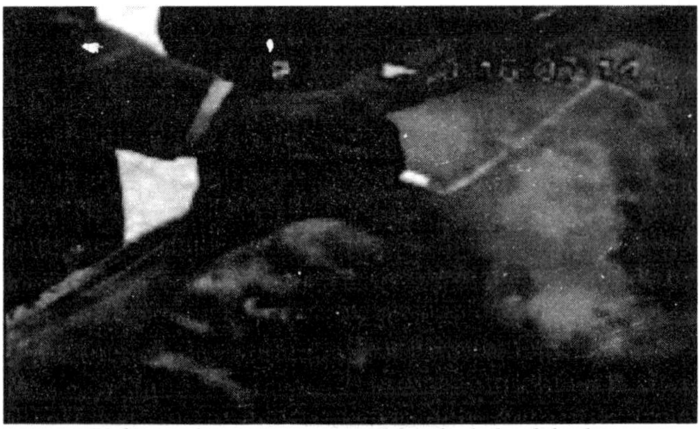

Koli marking on an unidentified dead body.

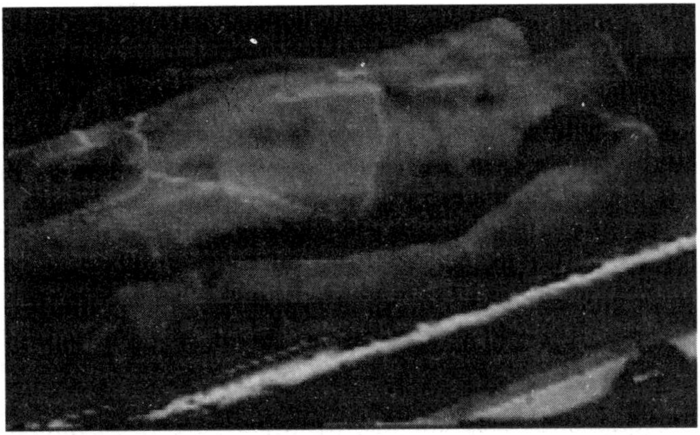

The outlines marked by accused Surender Koli were further correlated with the dismembered parts of bodies recovered, by the Board. The Board opined that:

"Cut marks with clean cut margins at upper and lower ends of various bones of skeletal remains are consistent with the area marked for dismemberment of the body. Surender Koli also told that it took about three hours to dismember the body, which is possible".

During interaction, the experts informed that the manner in which accused Surender Koli marked on the dead body, the way he used to cut the bodies of the victims is exactly how it is mentioned and explained in the Medical books.

To ascertain whether Surender Koli is suffering from any madness and whether he knew what he was doing when he committed all those acts, he was examined by an independent Board of Psychologists, Psychiatrists, Forensic medicine experts etc. constituted by AIIMS. The Board after Forensic Psychiatric Assessment of both Koli and Pandher, over a period of few days, opined in respect of Surender Koli that:

> "..... On the basis of history, sequential examinations, psychological testing, EEG and MRI brain, the Board opines that the accused Surender Koli is suffering from Necrophilia (ICD Code F 65.8) and Necrophagia. He does not suffer from psychotic disorder or any

> other psychiatric illness except for necrophilia, a type of paraphilia, a sexual perversion disorder. He was fully conscious at the time of the alleged commission of crime and also aware of the consequences of the act. There is nothing to suggest from the assessment that he is not fit to stand the trial".

Regarding Moninder Singh Pandher the Board opined that:

> "....... On the basis of history, sequential examinations, psychological testing, the Board opines that the accused Moninder Singh Pandher has suffered from Alcohol Dependence and Opioid Dependence (currently in remission). He does not suffer from any psychotic disorder or any other psychiatric illness. He is aware of the criminal charges he is being investigated for. There is nothing to suggest from the assessment that he is not fit to stand the trial".

All these forensic experts reports were produced and proved in the court in the presence of the accused and his counsel and judicially analysed by the courts. The CBI made detailed investigation in the field and the area contacting various people when Reena, aged 21 years; Pratima, aged 26 years; Mehnaz, aged 7 years; Poornima Haldar, aged 13 years of Nithari stated before the CBI that accused Surender Koli had also tried to allure them into the house no. D-5, Sector-31, Noida, on different pretexts but they did not go inside the house.

In many complicated and professionally committed crimes by any accused, it was experienced that without the assistance from the accused it will be difficult to unravel the truth and complete the story. Just like in the hijacking case, without the truth from the mouth of accused Abdul Latif, which was voluntarily made, it would have been difficult to unravel the whole picture as to how the conspiracy was hatched and what preparations were made and who were the persons involved etc. Similarly in this case there was no eyewitness account and last seen together evidence. How the women and children were allured inside the house and what happened thereafter will not be clear and proved without a confession from the accused. Therefore, in this case and in all such cases where such evidence is needed to prove the case, the accused is asked whether he would like to state the truth before a Magistrate. In many cases it was experienced that the accused refuses to make any statement before a Magistrate because it will be used against him in the trial. In some cases the accused comes forward to speak the truth before the Magistrate. There is provision under Section 164 CrPC permitting recording of the confession by the Magistrate. Such confession should be voluntary so as to be admissible under law. It is to be mentioned that if an accused confesses before a Police Officer it will not be admissible as per Sections 25, 26 of the Indian Evidence Act except those falling under Sections 27 and 32 of the Act.

Coming back to this case, it was felt necessary to get the confession of accused Surender Koli recorded by a Magistrate as the accused volunteered before the CBI that he would like to unburden his guilty feelings and would like to tell the truth in the court. Therefore, he was produced before the court in New Delhi. The court sent him to judicial custody. Later on the CBI came to know that the accused Koli had made a voluntary confession and the Magistrate had recorded it. It also came to notice that the confession was straight away video recorded by the court and thereafter the same was transcribed, explained to the accused Surender Koli and his signatures were obtained. The CBI requested the court and obtained copy of the confession so recorded.

Investigation disclosed that Pandher was not involved in these serial killings and he was charged for the offence under the Immoral Traffic (Prevention) Act and for bribing the police. However, trial in all the cases is going on and the judicial findings will come.

It is significant to mention that copy of the confession recorded by the court and the CD containing the direct recording of the confession of accused Koli by the court which was simultaneously transcribed disclosed that the accused had voluntarily admitted having killed and raped or attempted to rape or so, Rimpa, Payal, Bina, Pinki, Payal (Child), Jyoti, Rachna, Harsh, Pushpa, Max, Deepali, Aarti, Nisha, Anjali, Nanda, Madhu. This tallied with the missing reports. He correctly recollected having raped Payal, Nanda (who had earlier worked in that house) but stated that he had tried to have sex with all he had killed but does not actually recollects whether he was successful or not except with Payal and Nanda. In his confession, he admitted that Pandher did not know about all these things but Pandher used to bring 2-3 girls in the night and they used to drink and have sex and he (Koli) used to prepare food for them. There was a separate entrance to Pandher's bedroom from the main gate and he was not to come inside the house, drawing room, kitchen etc. He confessed that he had lured Harsh and Max and killed them and he came to know that they were boys only when he removed the clothes to have sex with them. It was by mistake. He had cooked and eaten the flesh of Rimpa and Bina and the liver of the boy Harsh. On seeing the red coloured liver of the small boy he could not control and applied salt and ate it. Since he ate more, he vomitted and was to be admitted in the hospital. According to him, he did not eat the flesh thereafter.

After completion of the investigation in the case of the murder of Rimpa Haldar, Payal and other victims, CBI filed charge sheets against Surender Koli in the cases for kidnapping, raping, murder and destruction of evidence of commission of the crime, in the court. The trial of the case of kidnapping, killing, raping and disposal of the body in the form of pieces of victim Rimpa Haldar was completed by the trial court which sentenced him to death penalty which was confirmed by the High Court and finally by the Supreme Court. All the above evidence was provided to the accused, before the trial as required under the law so that he could defend himself.

All the above evidence was produced and exhibited in the courts. Therefore, facts and details of evidence have been disclosed as above. He has been convicted in some other cases which are pending for confirmation by the High Court. Therefore, these cases are not discussed here except references made in the chargesheet, as above, which document is a public document. The case of murder of Rimpa, as above, is a true case of necrophilic killing with necrophagia as Surender Koli also ate the flesh of Rimpa Haldar. As far as Pandher is concerned, confirmation of the sentence awarded to him in one case is pending. It may be mentioned that eight victims were identified through DNA test. Then the remaining skulls were forwarded to CFSL Chandigarh for digital skull superimposition test alongwith the available photographs of the victims and the laboratory, after such scientific tests, fixed to identify of five more victims. Identity of three more victims could be fixed from the identification of clothes and chappals, recovered from the place, by the relatives in the court. Therefore there were total 16 cases pending trial in the court, out of which some have been decided.

Chapter 8

Prosecution

Prosecution of a case is a tough and time consuming job, requiring lot of patience and tolerance. It is more agonising than the process of investigation. The investigating officers, besides investigation, have to handle the trial of a number of cases in various courts. There are thousands of cases under trial and in each branch, cases investigated by it, earlier, remain under trial because the courts take years to finalise a case. The accused has all rights to challenge each and every order in the higher courts and delay the matter. Every year about 1200 cases are disposed off from investigation and that adds to the list of pending trial cases. Since the number of courts does not go on increasing, the cases get piled up. Of course, it is not possible to increase the number of courts every year but the delays could be curtailed by restricting adjournments, disposing of miscellaneous petitions speedily and disallowing delaying tactics. In many cases, the courts hear arguments on cognizance and hear the parties on the point of framing of charges. The order for framing charges itself , invariably, challenged in the higher courts resulting in stay of the proceedings and the decision on it, takes years. It can further be challenged in the Supreme Court and the matter gets stayed. Then, once the prosecution evidence starts either the accused or his advocate falls sick, gets busy somewhere else and the witness goes back. Then on the next date, the witness becomes unavailable for some reason. Even if the witness turns up on the next date, he may not be cross-examined on that date. On the next date, may be that the presiding officer would be on leave. The witness gets fed up and thinks why did he at all opted to be a witness. He is suffering for coming forward to assist the criminal justice delivery system or the process. Nobody takes care of his interest and he is being abused in the courts. The defence counsel starts questioning his reputation, antecedents and abuses him, threatens him. I have vast experience of watching such things. The witness suffers. If the presiding officers participate in the trial, effectively, as required under the CrPC, most of the pending trials will be finalised without delay. There are presiding officers who effectively participate in the proceedings, control the trial proceedings from the beginning, restricts cross-examination by the defence advocate by disallowing all irrelevant questions.

But they have so many cases to handle. There are so many cases wherein the investigation was completed within the stipulated period of 60 days or 90 days, as the case may be as per Section 167 CrPC but the cases are pending for decades. The result is that most of the witnesses become incapable of giving evidence, many expire or become untraceable and many refuse to come and depose in view of many reasons. There are cases where the presiding officers have issued arrest warrants for production of the witnesses, who could not attend on account of some reason. If the police have filed the charge-sheet/ report under Section 173 CrPC within 60 or 90 days, the courts would dispose off the case within 6 or 9 years, at least. This point has not been addressed, effectively, so far. It goes on and on. Justice delayed is justice denied.

Coming back to the Investigating Officers, they have to assist the Public Prosecutors in the court. They have to see that the summons are obtained from the court and served on the witnesses and the witnesses attended the court. They have to assist the Prosecutors in sorting out the relevant documents when the witnesses are examined. The Prosecutors in the CBI have large number of cases with them in various courts and find it difficult to attend all the courts, sometimes. It is the combined effort of both the investigating officer or pairavi officer and the prosecutor which results in successful conviction of a case. The percentage of conviction in CBI is around 65 to 70 percent whereas in most of the States it is reported to be below 30 percent and in some states it is disappointing. This is because of the assistance rendered by the investigating officers and or the pairavi officers to the prosecutors in the CBI, that the conviction rate is high and quality of conviction is also very good. If more special courts are created for the CBI cases, then maximum cases will get disposed off. If the prosecution is separated, then it is difficult to say whether the witnesses could be traced and produced. The conviction percentage rate will definitely go down.

One major problem faced is that the witnesses do not get back the money spent by them to attend the court for evidence against the summons issued by the court. Some meagre amount was fixed as daily expenses for them long back but it was not revised keeping in mind the increase in the travelling and living cost. They are not allowed deluxe bus charges and air-conditioned class charges in the trains. Some witnesses come by air but are not being paid. It was experienced that the courts have no funds to re-imburse the expenses incurred by the witnesses. In many cases the witnesses are told by the court staff that the expenses will be sent by money order but no money order reach the witnesses or are never sent.

In the CBI, efforts are being made to accommodate the witnesses but how far can it go? It is high time that the witnesses are taken care of otherwise why should they come and give evidence? There is no problem as far as the public servants are concerned but the problem is with the private witnesses. According to the status they should be paid. If it is not possible to pay them the airfare, they should be paid at least the A/C fare, ₹ 100 per day as DA and the accommodation charges by the court and the rest of the reasonable amount actually spent by them should be met by the police or the CBI. They are assisting these law-enforcing agencies and therefore they should be taken care of. In large number of cases the trial starts after many years. The witness might have forgotten the incident, facts and actually what had happened and how it happened. It will be too much to expect that the witness will come directly to the court, get into the box and depose all the facts. It will be in the interest of justice that the witness goes through the papers, his statement made years back and assists the court in knowing the facts. If the evidence is based on voluminous documents then the witness has to spend considerable time to go through them before deposing in the court. The witness has to undergo a torture if he is a private person or has retired long back. There is need for appropriate provision for looking after their interest. They should not feel that they committed a mistake by telling the truth and helping the criminal justice system. It is high time we start respecting the witnesses. I have experience of investigating officers and or pairavi officers spending money from their pockets and/or withdrawing from provident funds to handle the witnesses.

There are officers who pledged the jewellery of their wives and spent the money on the trial work. The trial work is neglected. I will be surprised if any supervising officer claims to have undergone the agony of a day-to-day and prolonged trial, except those who were/are the investigating officers and therefore faced the problem. No supervising officer in the CBI attend the court and grasp the difficulties of an investigating and/or pairavi officer or prosecutor in the court.

What is the use of sitting in a room in the office and abusing the field officers and, or questioning them for any lapses. CBI needs supervising officers who know about investigation and the court work besides many other work being carried out by the department. If facilities are provided, every case in the CBI will get convicted. Making the IO or the pairavi officer or the prosecutor responsible without providing required infrastructural facilities will not be the correct or appropriate approach. This requires serious consideration.

Another problem is that statements of the witnesses are written in hand in the courts which take lot of time. Many courts do not have computers. In this era of scientific and technological developments, it is high time that the courts record the statements of the witnesses by such method for early completion of the trial. Most of the delays are on account of inadequate number of magistrates, non-availability of infrastructural facilities, funds etc. There is need to improve the justice delivery system to contain crimes. Similarly, the jails should be deterrent places and should improve the personality of the inmates rather than making it a picnic point for them.

There is no Witness Protection Act in India and they are not being protected. They remain under pressure from the accused and his/their gang. I have experienced in so many cases that witnesses are being kidnapped or their wives or children are being harassed, kidnapped so that they do not depose in the court. What protection is given by the police? It is not possible for the police except in some specific cases on reciept of complaints or orders from the courts. We do not have so much of police force to take care of this. In the National Investigation Agency Act (NIA), there is specific provision vide Section 17 to protect the interest of the witnesses, to keep their identity secret etc in the court. But after the evidence, they have to go back and live at the same place. It is not difficult for the accused or their gang to trace them and harass them. It is necessary to have a Witness Protection Act.

Prosecution is more important and should be conducted effectively and sincerely. In the states, after investigation, the case is dumped in the office of the Prosecutor, as per my knowledge. But in the CBI there is accountability. If the witness does not turn up, explanation of the prosecuting team is called for. If the witness turns hostile, then also explanation is called for and action is taken. So is the case with acquittals and so on. Therefore investigation and prosecution are two sides of the same coin and cannot be separated. Investigation is not the end of the job.

Prosecution is the test to find out the veracity of the investigation. Therefore should be handled by one and the same agency. The tempo, interest and efforts put in the investigation of the case should be continued in its trial also so that the case ends in conviction and the accused are punished and justice is rendered to the victims. Otherwise there is no point in showing so much of interest in the investigation. Well, if the investigation is proper and perfect, it helps in a successful trial of the case by way of conviction. Similarly, if the case is not properly and effectively followed up in the court, the efforts put in the investigation becomes meaningless. Therefore both the investigation and the prosecution are very important in a CBI case. For better output, there is a need for more investigating officers for investigation and trial. Similarly there is need to have adequate and dedicated prosecutors for handling the cases in the courts. In both cases the officers are too inadequate. There is a need to strengthen these two institutions in the interest of effective justice delivery system in the country. At the same time, the salary of these two categories of staff should be at par with their utility to the society and their role in the criminal justice delivery system.

As far as the cases pending in the courts are concerned, the burden is on account of such cases lingering on for more than 20 years or so. There is no significant development in these cases. Justice delayed is justice denied. It is high time that sincere effort is made to consider withdrawal of all such dead cases pending for more than 15 years in the courts, which are not of serious nature, importance or sensitive nature. This will help in reduction of the work load in the courts and also in the organisation. Both these institutions will be able to devote more and result-oriented time on the remaining old cases which are of serious nature and other fresh or existing cases. This will result in more productive work. In the organisation the officers will be able to concentrate more on investigation also on account of reduction of cases pending in the courts. There are special courts for the CBI for trying and disposing of corruption cases. These are not in required numbers. For other cases, the organisation has to depend on local courts which are otherwise over-loaded. Cases can be withdrawn under the provisions of Section 321 CrPC.

Prosecutors' job is very tough. One prosecutor has many cases with him and has to attend many courts. Therefore, he needs the assistance of the investigating or pairavi officer for handling the witnesses and exhibiting the documents and or articles. Therefore, separating trial work from any agency will not be beneficial. There is need for more prosecutors and many fast track courts. Here, I would like to point out that all the sincere efforts made by the investigating officers and thereafter by the prosecutors may not result in success. They may get disappointed, finally because the important accused may get acquitted. The Evidence Act is very old and the principles laid down are age old and really do not suit to the present day crime scenerio. Witnesses can be purchased or threatened not to give evidence. We take benefit of the statement that "benefit of doubt goes to the accused". This is used as a sword to cut the prosecution story. How can anybody be sure that the accused will not tamper with the evidence? He will always try to escape by creating a doubt in the flow of evidence. All efforts are being made by the accused to see that the case does not go well in the court. There are so many instances. I recollect, when the trial of the case relating to blasting of Kutku dam in Palamu, Daltonganj District of Jharkhand and killing of engineers, investigated by the CBI, was going on in the Ranchi court against hardcore MCC Naxalites, the witnesses were badly beaten up and sent inside the court by the accused and they turned hostile.

When they came out of the court, again they were beaten up by the accused and their associates. It was very difficult to operate in this district and the adjoining Latehar district. I also recollect, when this was pointed out to the police, they told us that the accused Naxalites were not in their control and the Naxalites controlled the area. They were helpless. Case ended in acquittal. When the trial in the MLA Ajit Sarkar murder case was going on in the Court at Patna against hardcore criminals Rajesh Ranjan alias Pappu Yadav and others, the pairavi officer reported that all the first seven or so witnesses produced and examined in the court have turned hostile as they were badly beaten up and produced by the accused in the court and the police were not of any help. Then I told him to connect me to the complainant who belonged to CPM and reportedly connected to MCC Naxalite group and I told him to take interest in the case.

It was reported to me, later on, that on the next date onwards, those people from the side of the complainant took charge of the witnesses and also in disguise surrounded the court complex causing the earlier group to flee from the place and the witnesses deposed in the court and the case ended in conviction. The CBI does not have a Commando force or fighting force to take care of such things and we depend on the local police who have their own interest and or problems. Well, when the trial in the Uphar Cinema case was going on, it was reported to me by the pairavi team that the two important witnesses to whom summons have been issued for their evidence are not traceable. I constituted a team and the two witnesses were traced and picked up from a dark store room in Bhikaji Cama Place, in the night as they were secretly dumped there by the accused. They were produced in the court and they deposed correctly. During the trial of Ram Avtar Jaggi murder case in the court in Raipur, the pairavi officer used to report to me that as soon as the list of witnesses to be examined on the next trial schedule is given to the court, they found that the witnesses are not available. One eye witness to the murder could not be traced. Suddenly, on the fixed date the witness appeared in the court directly.

As it was reported that he was not available, the court puts him a question as from where he has come and how did he know of issue of summons and the date in the court? He replied that he had gone to a place in Uttar Pradesh and he had telephoned to his neighbour who told him that CBI people had come with summons for the date and therefore he left that place in the night by bus and straightaway reached the court from the bus stand. Then the court asks him how many hours the bus took to reach Raipur. He answered that he travelled for 12 hours continuously to reach the court directly.

Then the Judge makes an observation that the witness says that he travelled for twelve hours in a bus and directly came to the court but it is found that the witness is wearing a neatly washed and ironed dress which indicates that he is not speaking the truth. The witness turned hostile and whenever he gave a negative reply, he looked towards the place where the accused Amit Jogi and others were standing and smiled. When asked by the Judge, he replied that he is looking at his counsel and telling him to go from the court. The Judge observed that the advocate reportedly came with the witness was standing on the other side whereas the witness frequently looked at the accused and smiled.

After the case ended in conviction in the trial court, the same witness reportedly filed an affidavit stating that his child was kidnapped and kept in custody by the accused to force him not to speak the truth in the court and therefore he lied in the court. In the same case, some of the important witnesses turned hostile but when one eyewitness to the conspiracy deposed truthfully, the accused present in the court turned violent, ransacked the properties, misbehaved with the CBI prosecutors forcing the Judge to leave the court and go to his chamber. A few police persons present could not handle the situation. It is nothing but *goonda* or jungle raj. There are so many such instances. In many cases poor man gets convicted whereas the influential one gets acquitted and gets the 'benefit of doubt'. In the Rungta abduction case, during the trial against Mukhtar Ansari and five others, most of the witnesses turned hostile and the accused were acquitted by the Judge. Subsequently, two absconding accused who received the ransom amount in Patna (but Rungta was not released) were arrested and as ordered, I supervised the trial against them.

We examined the remaining witnesses who were not examined earlier and the new Judge, on the basis of evidence convicted the two accused. Appeal against acquittal and appeal against conviction, in the same case based on same evidence came up before the High Court. A peculiar situation. Here, I also recollect that recently in one of the anti-Sikh riots cases, the trial court convicted five accused and acquitted Sajjan Kumar, Member of Parliament giving him the benefit of doubt. The court observed that he deserved the benefit of doubt as key witnesses were untrustworthy and inconsistent. The court also termed the silence of Delhi Police, despite appearing to be privy to the killings in November 1984, a serious lapse. The court said that the victim Jagdish Kaur who lost her husband, son and three cousins in the riots did not name Sajjan Kumar in her statements to the police or the Justice Ranganath Mishra Commission in 1985.

In this connection I refer to the interview given by Mr. Ved Marwah, who was Additional Commissioner of Police and was asked to probe into the role of police officers during the riots. He stated that the evidence collected by him alarmed the people in question and he was asked to wind up the inquiry. He had completed the inquiry but was to write and submit the report when he received an order to stop his inquiry. The then Commissioner of Police gave him a written order, in this regard and when he asked why the Commissioner just smiled. He said, it was obvious that the men in uniform had vanished from their police stations when Delhi was burning and Sikhs were being killed. This is what I referred to earlier in the book. If the police threatened the witnesses not to speak the truth and did not write what they said, in their statements and there was complete hostility, how can you expect a witness to prove what had happened at that time except making a true statement when he or she gets a chance to state the truth as and when the situation becomes favourable to speak the truth? When our officers approached them they were reported to be shivering with fear and agony while referring to the incident and told the officers that they were not allowed to speak the truth and everybody was against them. As far as the Commissions were concerned, there were many and the witnesses were told that they have to file the affidavits to get compensation and somebody as a volunteer came and got their signatures and they did not know what was written in it. How can we treat them as untrustworthy and inconsistent?

We tried our level best to unravel the truth. Over the decades, I can only convince myself that we should only go by the truth and discard all the negative points. The defence will always bring out something and claim for 'benefit of doubt'. We should not be emotional but should be able to or have the mental strength to realise the truth. We can write pages after pages on these things of prosecution and trial. I spent my career in handling trial of such sensitive cases. In the anti-sikh riots cases when the victims point out the involvement of particular persons, it is in all fairness that proper and fair trial is held, in the interest of justice, irrespective of the status of the accused and this should hold good in every case.

Chapter 9

Arrest

Arrest is another controversial subject. There has been criticism that persons are not being arrested. Arrests are not to be made as a matter of routine. Arrest can be made merely on suspicion but such suspicion should be based on some reason. First, arrest is automatically made if the person is caught while committing a cognizable offence as detailed in Section 41 CrPC. Secondly, when a person is caught redhanded while accepting bribe, he is arrested. Thirdly, we make arrests when there is apprehension that the suspect who is reasonably suspected to be involved in a case may abscond and will not be available for investigation and subsequent trial or he may tamper with the evidence.

Tampering with the evidence either by threatening the witnesses, destroying documentary and other type of evidence will be a strong ground for arrest to prevent such things. Fourthly, arrests are made if there is scope for making recoveries and for getting confessional statements recorded. Interest of investigation and that of the witnesses as well as the need for custodial interrogation to unravel the truth or detect the case are the important factors which govern the arrest. In conventional crimes like murder, kidnapping, rape, dacoity, etc., where we have to collect evidence through the accused and allowing the accused to move freely is not in the interest of proper investigation, we arrest the accused.

Power to arrest is available under Section 41 CrPC. Otherwise, we make arrest to produce the accused alongwith the chargesheet. The problem is if the accused is arrested, the limitation period for filing charge-sheet in the case as mentioned in Section 167 CrPC starts and if the chargesheet is not filed within 60 or 90 days of custody (except in some special Acts where the limitation period is more), the arrested gets the right to be released. In a case involving large number of or voluminous documents, the same are to be scrutinised and scrutiny reports are to be prepared. From the scrutiny reports, pointers for investigation are prepared and then further documents are collected wherever necessary and witnesses are examined to prove the documents, procedures, tenders, quotations, contracts etc. In many cases, we find it necessary to obtain document or handwriting expert's opinion to fix the identity of the accused or prove the signatures or writings.This takes lot of time. Therefore arrests are made when the Agency feels that it would be able to file the chargesheet within the fixed period. Arrest should be made in serious cases.

Selective arrests should not be made. I recollect one recent case in which the accused completely destroyed a family for getting their property, abducted them and kept them in custody, forcefully obtained their signatures on blank papers, tortured them etc with the help of the police in Rajasthan but the accused were not arrested by the CBI. I recommended that they should be arrested. The accused happened to be local politicians. When the chargesheet was produced before the court, the Magistrate refused to accept it without the accused. This order was challenged in the High Court.

It is a futile exercise. Why should we favour the accused? If the accused are roaming around freely, how the victims and the witnesses come forward to give evidence and specially when some police officers are also involved in the case and helped the local politicians in committing the crime. There is a social accountability and we should not be bothered about the status or position of the accused. Impartiality should be maintained in all cases, in all orders to be passed, irrespective of any consideration, status, muscle-money power, political affiliation *etc*. Recently, the High Court Bench at Jodhpur passed strictures against CBI, for failure to arrest an accused. In nutshell, we should not favour any accused.

Besides the point of interest of investigation, arrest of an accused is necessary to generate public confidence, as and when necessary, in the larger interest of the society. Nothing should be done with ulterior motive. But if the accused is arrested then it is necessary that the charge-sheet/report under Section 173 CrPC is filed before expiry of the limitation period. Otherwise, the arrested gets the right to come out on bail. Therefore, there can not be a fixed policy on this as it will and should depend upon its need for effective and proper investigation of the case. But, invariably, the accused should be produced in the court alongwith the chargesheet and that work should not be left to the court. In many cases, the courts have bailed out the accused on the ground that the accused was not arrested during the course of investigation and therefore he will continue to enjoy the same benefit. Courts have refused to take the police report/charge-sheet on record in absence of the accused. Well, if some of the accused are absconding, then courts are requested to issue arrest warrants for tracing and producing them in the court.

Chapter 10

Criticism of CBI

Corruption within

There is lot of hue and cry whenever a CBI officer is accused of any irregularity. A few officers, of negligible quantity, have fallen prey to temptations and have been caught. It is the greatness of this organisation that it has a strong in-built system to track the activities of CBI officers and take appropriate action, unlike in other departments. This system is controlled by the IPS officers. But this system is not used against the IPS officers who are working in the organisation. I do not mean all of them. Many are very good, honest and know their job. Since I am from the cadre, many officers interacted and are interacting with me. They have so much of information about the activities of officers working on deputation with specific details but they do not have a platform to make complaints because it will go against them if they do so. Therefore they have been the victims. Well, anybody indulging in corruption should be punished harshly. Out of greed and on account of their inability to withdraw themselves from the well off society around and on account of dealing with anti-social elements, indulging in frauds, very negligent percentage of officers have indulged in corrupt activities. This is to be condemned. Recently, Vivek Dutt was caught while accepting bribe for favouring in a case under the control of the Delhi Police. How can he do that? The CBI investigating officers, as mentioned above, have so much of information about corrupt officers who worked and are working in the CBI whether it relates to misuse of available facilities and or favouring the accused in any form for wrongful gain or so on. Once, the Lokpal comes into existence, they may find a platform. It will be illogical to say that if they commit any crime the deputationists can be sent back. No need to say anything more as it will amount to be a one-sided comment. Field work is done by CBI investigating officers and they suffer a lot. There are large number of incidents where they abuse the CBI cadre officers who are well disciplined and hard working. They misbehave and treat them very badly. Here again, not all of them. It is absolutely incorrect to say that the CBI is functioning because of deputationist officers. The organisation is surviving because of the cadre officers but they have no career prospects. It is existing because of the hard work put in by the prosecutors. There are inspectors with 18 years of service in the same rank waiting for promotion as Deputy Superintendent of Police. CBI is a specialised agency and should largely be run by the specialised CBI officers only. When Vijaya Rama Rao, Director got the pay scale of Superintendents of Police raised, many IPS officers protested. But when Joginder Singh joined, it was reduced. To say that the CBI cadre officers are corrupt will be a one-sided approach unless you are clear yourself. This should wait till the Lokpal comes into existence. CBI officers have to investigate against joint secretaries and above, against ministers, parliamentarians and so on and therefore they should not be treated as a normal public servant and their pay and emoluments should be separate and higher than other public servants so that they are financially in good position and do their duties boldly and impartially. There is need to enlarge their career prospects also. Within the organisation there is need to have and or cultivate a cordial relationship and team spirit so that there is unity amongst all in the interest of successful completion of all assignments.

Inefficient Handling of Cases

The CBI has been critisised for going slow against prominent politicians like Jayalalithaa, Lalu Prasad Yadav, Mayawati and

Mulayam Singh Yadav. In all these cases relating to disproportionate assets, corruption, Taj Corridor etc., it is alleged that the CBI, from time to time has shown lesser interest and no seriousness in expediting the proceedings. All these cases require to be re-visited when the Lokpal comes up for appropriate action to expedite them. CBI handles sensitive cases like these and other scams, conventional crimes. Law and order is a state subject matter and the Central Government cannot interfere in it unless there is specific provision. Crime is part of law and order. Only sensitive cases and those having inter-state or international ramifications are given to the CBI by the states by issuing a consent notification under Section 6 of the Delhi Special Police Establishment Act, 1946 and the Central Government directs the CBI to take up investigation by issuing a notification under section 5 of the said Act. Besides this, the High Courts and the Supreme Court may direct the CBI to investigate a particular case. Yes, there were cases given to the CBI out of political vendetta whenever the government changed. In such cases, according to the master in power, the CBI has been adjusting its actions sometimes leading to criticism. What can the CBI Director do?.

He does not even have any power to engage a retired investigating officer as a Consultant in a sensitive and complicated case or cases. He can not engage an effective and experienced counsel to conduct trial of a sensitive case or cases in the trial courts and a senior, good counsel in the High Courts and also in the Supreme Court. The Ministry rejects a proposal personally sent by the Director, without having any knowledge or experience of practical difficulties faced by the CBI. Without knowing the field requirements, how can you, sitting in a room, reject the proposal? This is nothing but interference in the working of the CBI.

The Director has no power to approve filing of appeal against acquittal or inadequate conviction in any case and can not move the Supreme Court against the High Court order. In complicated cases, if the Director feels it necessary that the services of the investigating officer who has retired is required for proper trial of the case, he sends a proposal and the expenditure is to be met from the funds allotted to the CBI. The Ministry rejects it and does not allow him to utilise the funds so allotted in a manner he thinks better in the interest of effective execution of the work. When influential public servants are involved, sanction for prosecution rarely given. In fact, when a criminal offence has been committed, there is no need for any sanction because it is not the duty of the public servant to commit crime.

Some Controversial Cases

The CBI handles many high-profile cases and everybody knows that it is never far from controversy. In public, media and in all other circles, it has come under severe criticism specially in the following cases:

Bofors Case

This case involving corruption in purchase of 410 Howitzer field guns valued at $ 1300 millions from Swedish arms firm AB Bofors has been in lime light from time to time since 1980s. It was alleged that these guns were inferior to those offered by a French competitor. It was alleged that the deal was through after payment of commission of $ 40 million which moved from Britain and Panama to secret Swiss banks.

Further, it was also alleged that associates of the then Prime Minister Rajiv Gandhi were linked to alleged pay-offs and Italian businessman Ottavio Quattrocchi, who was close to Gandhi family was behind the deal and the illegal pay-offs and that he used to visit the house of the Prime Minister, frequently. CBI investigated this case and also got the amount of ₹ 21 crores in the London bank account of Quattrocchi and his wife Maria frozen in 2006. It was alleged that Quattrocchi was present in India and the CBI got the Red Corner Notice issued.

But in April 2009, the CBI got that Red Corner Notice withdrawn and allowed Quattrocchi move freely and no action was taken against him. The frozen amounts were got released. Some Defence Ministry officers were chargesheeted in the case but the case was not pursued effectively and nothing happened. The withdrawal of the Red Corner Notice happened about three weeks before the end of the Dr. Manmohan Singh government's tenure, as above and the case was also withdrawn.

I recollect that when Deve Gowda was the Prime Minister, the then CBI Director, Joginder Singh visited foreign countries and on return showed a box, stating that he had brought all the records in the Bofors case. Nothing happened and no Director took any effective steps in this case as is being done in some cases. Whatever it may be, this is a fit case to be revisited when the Lokpal comes up, to take the case to a logical conclusion and fix the responsibility of officers for no effective action in this case and expose them, if any. However, in a recent development, Quattrochi died on July, 13, 2013. Hence, the situation has changed now.

Hawala Scandal

When we were investigating the J&K terrorist cases in 1990-1991, evidence came up showing funding of such terrorist activities by their associates and sympathisers abroad and in India through Hawala transactions. A separate case was registered on this and during the searches, a diary was seized from the house of Jains in New Delhi which contained details of payments made to various political leaders etc including former Union Ministers Ajit Kumar Panja, P. Shiv Shankar, V.C. Shukla, Arjun Singh, Madhavrao Scindia, N.D. Tiwari, former Uttar Pradesh Governor Motilal Vohra, BJP leaders L.K. Advani, Yashwant Sinha, Madanlal Khurana, R.K. Dhawan and so on. Many people were chargesheeted but the courts held that the diary was not a Book of Accounts so maintained during normal course of business and legally not admissble as evidence and the accused were discharged.

When the matter went to Supreme Court in the form of a Public Interest Litigation by Vineet Narayan, Supreme Court laid down guidelines for making CBI autonomous and independent. It was alleged that the CBI did not investigate it properly and thereafter failed to conduct effective prosecution because of involvement of politicians. The Supreme Court directed that the Central Vigilance Commission should be given a supervisory role over the CBI. Inspite of this nothing happened and if the CBI would have functioned as an effective independent agency then all those involved in various scams like 2G, Coalgate, CWG and so on, irrespective of their position or status, would have been in jail. It is not that there was no power. There is need to act effectively.

Priyadarshini Mattoo Murder Case

Priyadarshini Mattoo, a 22 year old law student was raped and murdered at her residence. Santosh Kumar Singh, son of a senior IPS officer was found to be stalking her and was found moving outside her house by a neighbour before the murder wearing a helmet. He had hit her with the helmet. Pieces of the glass shield of the helmet were found at the scene of crime with blood on them. Blood samples sent for DNA test were found contaminated. There was sufficient evidence against Santosh Kumar Singh. But, the question was, whether the underwear and the helmet were examined. The net result was that the trial court acquitted the accused holding that there was deliberate inaction on the part of the CBI to conduct a proper investigation. In the Judgement, the Judge commented on how "the influence of the father of the accused has been there". It is not strange as there are cases where IPS officers are not considered to be the accused. CBI filed an appeal against the acquittal in 2000 and it was lying there. In 2006, in another case in Delhi there was hue and cry and therefore the media highlighted this case also. The CBI filed an application for early hearing in July, 2006. On account of these factors, this case was taken up by the High Court and the accused was convicted for rape and murder and awarded death penalty. The Supreme Court reduced the sentence to life imprisonment. The question is about the fairness and effectiveness of CBI investigation. Since the case is over, there is nothing more to comment on it.

Here, I may mention that conviction by the trial court is always subject to confirmation by the higher courts. Death penalty requires to be confirmed. Other punishments may also be challenged. Recently, in the Ajit Sarkar murder case Rajesh Ranjan alias Pappu Yadav and others were acquitted by the Patna High Court. The matter may go to the Supreme Court now.

Nithari Serial Killings

Nithari serial killing cases were personally supervised by me. We utilised the services of known scientists of the country in this case to recover the body parts, identify each part, segregate them anatomically, subject them to post mortem examination, conduct DNA test and fix the identity of the victims, subject the accused to psychological tests and all types of scientific examinations etc because this is the first such kind of case in the country where the accused killed, raped and also ate the flesh of some of the women. From all type of tests including Lie Detection tests, Psychological assessment tests and Narco analysis tests and other type of evidence, we logically concluded that only Surender Koli was involved in this crime and Moninder Singh Pandher was involved only in one case of Payal, who used to come to Pandher. When Koli was called by the police, Pandher sent his manager and gave money and gifts to police officers to save his own reputation as he was bringing callgirls to his house at nights. He was booked under the Prevention of Corruption Act, Immoral Activities(Prevention) Act and also for attempting to destroy the evidence in the case of missing Payal, which is pending trial. In one case, Supreme Court has confirmed death sentence on Koli and in few more cases Koli has been convicted and sentenced to death which will have to be confirmed by the Supreme Court.

From investigation point of view there was no evidence of involvement of Pandher in other cases and foul smell used to come from the open drainage in front of the house which flows down from a village nearby and even the wife of Pandher, whenever she was present in the house, did not feel the smell of decomposed dead bodies. Koli used to cut the bodies immediately into pieces, pack them in polythene bags and throw them at the back side and parts in the Nala which moved down in the drainage. However, the cases are sub-judice and let the courts decide the cases.

Dawood Ibrahim Case

After Babri Masjid demolition there were bomb blasts in Mumbai. The Mumbai Crime Branch efficiently investigated the case and filed a chargesheet. The case was transferred to the CBI for further investigation to get the accused arrested as they were reported to be out of India. Dawood Ibrahim is one of them. His brother Anees Ibrahim and Tiger Memon are among others. Since the Interpol, India is under the CBI, it was thought, perhaps, that the CBI will be in a better position to interact with the Interpol Headquarter in Lyons and Interpols of Pakistan, and United Arab Emirates where they were reported to be present.

CBI and the Government of India miserably failed to get them though their movements are shown on the TV channels. Dawood and Anees are specifically located in Karachi and Dubai. Since then, they have been involved in large number of terrorist activities against India. Whichever Government comes to power, it is necessary to get Dawood, his brother etc in India to face trial in the concerned cases, according to law. Our diplomatic rapport and or pressure is ineffective. It is almost a failure and rightly criticised.

Sister Abhaya Murder Case

Sister Abhaya, a nun, was found dead in a well in Saint Pius Xconvent hostel in Kottayam, Kerala on March 27, 1992. The case was transferred to the CBI as it was found to be a sensitive case. It came to light that there was sexual scandal going on involving the Church people,inside and Sister Abhaya had seen such an act and therefore the persons involved, to save their and Church's reputation killed her and threw her body into the well. The act of throwing of the body was seen by a witness. CBI went on investigating without properly evaluating the evidence resulting in criticism by the public, media and the High Court. The investigation was conducted by the Central Branch of Delhi and the officers did not know the local language Malayalam. In August, 2008, the Kerala High Court ordered that the case should be investigated by the local CBI branch. The then Director Ashwani Kumar ordered me to constitute a Special Investigation Team, as I had taken charge as Joint Director and the concerned branch had also come under me just then and I constituted an SIT of local branch officers of CBI, Kochi branch. The SIT got the statement of witnesses recorded again and arrested Father and his associates who were charge-sheeted.

Sohrabuddin Case

CBI is being criticised for the investigation being conducted in this case. It is alleged that the CBI is playing politics and wants to fix the Chief Minister of Gujarat in this case as well as in the case of Tulsiram Prajapati and Ishrat Jahan encounter cases. On November 23, 2005, Sohrabuddin Sheikh was travelling in a public transport bus with his wife Kauser Bi from Hyderabad to Sangli in Maharashtra. At 01.30 AM, Gujarat Police Anti- Terrorist Squad stopped the bus and took them away whereas Kauser Bi was taken to a farm house. Three days later Sheikh was killed in a stage-managed encounter on a highway at Vishala Circle near Ahemadabad. It is alleged that two days later Kauser Bi was strangulated and cremated in Illol, the native village of Deputy Commissioner of Police DG Vanzara. The encounter killing was exposed after a few police inspectors boasted about it over drinks with journalist Prashant Dayal. Dayal conducted his own investigation at the farmhouse and then at Illol and ascertained that a burqa clad woman had been cremated there. He published the story in *Dainik Bhaskar* in November, 2006. Sheikh's brother Rubabuddin filed a Writ Petition in the Supreme Court, which ordered for an enquiry by the CID. Accordingly, Ms. Geeta Johri, IPS, the then Inspector General of Police, CID conducted an enquiry and reported involvement of about 10 police officers. On the basis of this, DIG DG Vanzara, Rajkumar Pandian, SP, who was with the Intelligence Bureau and MN Dinesh, SP, Rajasthan Police were arrested. In her report to the Supreme Court, Ms. Johri expressed threat from Amit Shah and others.

Finally, on 12.01.2010, the Supreme Court ordered the CBI to investigate. CBI arrested the police officers and Amit Shah, the then Home Minister of Gujarat and also a Minister of Rajasthan Gulab Chand Kataria etc. Ms Johri submitted to the Supreme Court that the CBI is pressurising her to state the involvement of Narender Modi in the case. It is alleged that Sohrabuddin is linked to Laskar-e-Taiba and the ISI of Pakistan and was also an associate of underworld Dawood gang and he was involved in extortion cases, arms smuggling and murders. He was extorting money from marble dealers and 40 AK-47 rifles were recovered from him. It is also alleged that RK Patni, owner of RK Marbles, Rajasthan had paid ten crores rupees to get Sheikh killed and Patni has connection with Congress leaders. It is also alleged that a year later, Tulsiram Prajapati, an underworld associate of Sheikh, who was a witness to Sheikh's killing was also killed in a fake encounter, which is also with the CBI.

The CBI is also investigating into the killing of Ishrat Jahan. There are so many cases of Gujarat under controversy. There is allegation that all efforts are being made to get Chief Minister Narendra Modi involved in these cases. CBI should not get involved in such attempts to please the bosses. If any CBI officer is involved in fabricating evidence to involve innocent people, the courts should decide these cases fast and strict action should be taken against them by registering cases against them. We have investigated a large number of fake encounter cases of Delhi, UP, Bihar and so on. Public wants that the investigation should be impartial and honest and those involved should be brought to book. In the prevailing circumstances, it appears to be not possible, at present. If the Supreme Court orders to make independent investigation and constitutes a Special Cell in the CBI for the purpose, then only it is possible to bring out the truth. It should be kept away from politics. There may be a large number of such fake encounter cases in other states but not reported. CBI does not have staff to handle hundreds of cases being given to it by many authorities. It is necessary to create 500 more investigating officers to handle all the cases, immediately. It is necessary to fill up the vacant positions and the so created posts for handling the increasing work load. IPS officers who come on deputation should also be made as investigating officers and given these type of cases. In fact, Joginder Singh started it but it was not properly implemented, then and thereafter.

Sant Singh Chatwal Case

Sant Singh Chatwal, an NRI Hotelier businessman in USA was investigated by the CBI on the allegation of conspiring and defrauding Bank of India's New York Branch to the tune of US $ 8,992,815 (₹ 28.32 crore). CBI had filed four chargesheets in this regard out of which he was named as accused in two cases and this was pending for about 15 years. In 2007, he was discharged in one case and the officers upto the rank of Special Director recommended for filing revision in the High Court but on the advice of S.K. Sharma, the then Director of Prosecution, the then Director Vijay Shanker on 30th May 2007 ordered not to challenge the matter. In 2008, Chatwal was discharged in another case and again all officers recommended for challenging the order.

Again, S.K. Sharma, the then Director of Prosecution recommended that there is no material to challenge the discharge and on this the then Director Ashwani Kumar on 10th August 2008 ordered not to agitate the matter. Director of Prosecution is a representative of Law Ministry in the CBI and he carries instructions from there. Sant Singh Chatwal was and is influential but the Directors should take independent decision in all the cases and specially when the officers below who had handled the cases recommend for agitating the matter, he should have agreed, in the interest of the cases and justice and in the spirit of impartiality, integrity and honesty. With the result, Sant Singh Chatwal was honoured with Padma Bhushan by the Government of India. Director of Prosecution should be an outsider and a committee should select one for the post after calling for applications from reputed, experienced and effective senior counsels/Advocates in the High Courts and the Supreme Court and the person who cannot be inflenced by any political party should be put in that post. Otherwise, there is no point in introducing a separate Prosecution Wing. Director, CBI can always disagree with the DOP and there are so many cases where Director, CBI did not agree with their recommendations and that of the Attorney General also. In view of these allegations, it will be appropriate if these cases are re-visited when the Lokpal comes up for possible legal remedies at this stage because discharge is not an acquittal and he can be charged and tried again. Role of officers also needs to be brought to light.

Malankara Varghese Murder Case

Malankara Varghese was the Managing Trustee of Orthodox Syrian Church who was hacked and stabbed to death by hired *goondas* at Perumbavoor on 5.12.2002. It was alleged to be a rivalry between the Malankara Orthodox Syrian Church and Jacobite Syrian Christian Church. The CBI filed chargesheet against Father Varghese Thekkekara, the main accused without arresting him. It is alleged even in the charge-sheet that the accused directly handed over ₹ 55,000/- to a *goonda* gang leader after the murder. The Kerala High Court pulled up the CBI for showing leniency, when the CBI said that the Father was co-operating in the investigation and the arrest was avoided as the matter related to Church and was sensitive. The High Court asked the CBI, whether it is for the first time that a priest is involved in such crimes and does the CBI has a practice of not arresting those who co-operate with the investigation. In fact, wife of Varghese has challenged the leniency shown by the CBI. In all conventional cases, the accused should be arrested and at least at the time of filing the chargesheet. Comments are given in Chapter 9 in the book, in this regard.

Well, CBI has arrested Father and other Church functionaries in the Sister Abhaya murder case and therefore, the allegation gets cleared. But in the Sister Abhaya murder case, the officers involved in the investigation, till the High Court transferred the case, failed to take a proper decision and they were slow and perhaps what the High Court observed appears to be correct. When I became Joint Director on 5th August 2008, the High Court had already passed an order for production of the case diaries as the Narco analysis test report given by Dr. Malini of FSL, Karnataka was in question. Therefore, I instructed the investigating officer to arrange the case diaries, number the pages and make them into proper volumes and get them bound with Index sheets pasted on the volumes. He did a good job.

But about five days before the case diaries were to be produced in the High Court, he came and told me that one volume of the case diaries particularly containing the Narco-analysis report was missing from his table. I directed the DIG and the SP of that branch to cause a search to be made but they did not do a good job. The missing of one volume of case diaries came to the notice of Director Ashwani Kumar through the Special Unit or Vigilance Cell of CBI which is directly under him. They roam about in the branches picking up rumours and such information but they did not collect information about 2G scams, Coalgate scams and so on. When I met him he told me that I have not told him about it and he came to know of it through the Special Unit and he was not happy. I told him that search was being made and it would have got mixed up as the investigating officer was having some other cases also with him and he was getting copies made.

He said that a preliminary enquiry should be registered against the IO. After the meeting, I visited that branch and made all IOs to search for the missing volume. The same was traced at a corner on the top of a box. Then I went and told the Director. A report came up about possibility of mischief by one staff and I told the Director and a PE was registered against him and enquired into but nothing came up. On the fixed date the High Court ordered for investigation by the local CBI Unit.

On the order of Director, I passed an order constituting a SIT of local officers and the case accordingly got transferred to Chennai Zone. I could not do anything in this case, as by the time I took charge, the High Court had already passed an order as there was some demand for it. The public, media etc were agitating the matter.

Bhopal Gas Tragedy

Everybody knows about this case. The main allegations were that the CBI did not charge the accused for offence under Section 304 Indian Penal Code i.e. culpable homicide not amounting to murder and that no action was taken to get Union Carbide CEO Warren Anderson extradited. This case was handled by the Anti Corruption Zone. It is also alleged that ex-CBI Joint Director B.R. Lall has confessed that he was asked to go soft on extraditing Warren Anderson. In fact once the accused leaves the country it becomes difficult to get him back in India.

We have so much of experience in this regard. Unless we have a good diplomatic rapport with that country and we had helped them in extraditing the accused wanted by them from India and the offence is also an offence in that country it will be difficult. Even if the court in that country orders for extradition of a particular person, the final authority to order is the government in power there. It is alleged that he was allowed to go out of the country by some Congress Chief Minister. Accused always take the plea that if he is extradited he will not get fair trial in India, the conditions in the Indian jails are very bad and that the trial takes years in India and so on.

If the government does not agree then there is always a right with the victims to move the High Court or the Supreme Court to pass appropriate orders to the Central Government to make effective and sincere efforts and submit reports of action taken in this regard. Here, I recollect that in the Uphar Cinema case also, we applied Section 304 IPC against some of the accused and they have been convicted. If the accused has the intention or the knowledge that death was likely to be caused by such negligence on his part but does not take preventive steps and allows such lapses to go on then Section 304 IPC should be applied. Final decision is always that of the judiciary. This case may be re-visited when the Lokpal comes up.

2G Spectrum Scam

CBI is also criticised for ineffective investigation in this case or for not probing into the role of all those possibly involved in this scam. 2G is short for second generation Wireless telephone technology. 2G network allows for much greater penetration intensity. It is reported that the three primary benefits of 2G networks over the previous one are that phone conversations were digitally encrypted; 2G systems were significantly more efficient on the spectrum allowing for far greater mobile phone penetration levels and 2G introduced data services for mobile starting with SMS text messages. Further, 2G technologies enabled the various mobile phone networks to provide the services such as text messages, picture messages and MMS. Moreover, all text messages sent over 2G are digitally encrypted allowing for the transfer of data in such a way that only intended receiver can receive and read it.

Well, Radio spectrum is a precious and scarce natural resource of national importance and it was allotted by the government at throwaway prices to private companies through corrupt and illegal means. It is reported that India is divided into 22 telecom zones with about 281 zonal licences in the market. According to the Telecom Policy of India, as and when a licence is issued to an operator, some start-up spectrum comes along with it. Further, the Policy does not have a provision for auctioning the spectrum. No person can say that earlier there was no specific policy and therefore I followed the same procedure.

Because about a decade back only a few were using mobile phones but now millions of people are using mobile phones. Similarly, there are large number of service providers now in the market and they are earning good money. May be long back nobody was interested in the spectrum and only few companies might have been there in the market. That is not the case now. Therefore, in the interest of the country, it was and is necessary to earn more money from the sale or allocation of the precious spectrum. It does not require any technical or financial expertise to decide that the government should have called for the tenders and allotted particular spectrum to the highest bidder. Why should we follow first come first served policy. There should be transparency in the policy, in this regard.

In 2008, 122 new second generation (2G) Unified Access Service licenses were given to private telecom companies at the

2001 price on a first-come-first-served basis. CBI concluded that several rules were violated and bribes were paid by the companies. Similarly, the Report of the Comptroller and Auditor General of India(CAG) also says that several licences were issued to firms with no prior experience in the telecom sector or were ineligible to get it or had suppressed relevant facts. It is also alleged that the cut-off date was preponed from 1.10.2007 to 25.9.2007 and on the same day, DOT announced that those who apply between 3.30 and 4.30 PM on that day would be issued licenses in accordance with the said policy. It is also alleged that companies like Unitech and Swan Telecom got licenses without any telecom experience.

It is further alleged that Swan Telecom got the licence even though it did not meet the eligibility criteria and Swan got licence for ₹ 15.37 billion (US$ 280 million) and then it sold 45 percentage stake to UAE based company Etisalat for ₹ 42 billion (US$770 million). Similarly, Unitech Wireless, a subsidiary of the Unitech Group got licence for ₹ 16.61 billion (US$ 300 million) and later sold 60 percent stake for ₹ 62 billion (US$ 1.1 billion) to Norway-based company Telenor.

According to CAG, the shortfall between the money collected and the money that the law mandated to be collected is estimated to be ₹ 1766.45 billion (US$ 32 billion), based on 3G and BWA spectrum auction prices in 2010. It is alleged that according to CBI chargesheet filed on 2.4.2011, the loss could be ₹ 309845.5 million (US$ 5.7 billion). It is further alleged that, according to Telecom Regulatory Authority of India(TRAI), the government gained over ₹ 30 billion (US$550 million) by giving 2G spectrum. According to the Minister there is zero loss in the allotment. The loss is disputed and requires thorough enquiry.

The Supreme Court on a PIL vide judgement dated 2.2.2012 declared allotment of spectrum as unconstitutional and arbitrary and quashed all the 122 licenses issued in 2008, during the tenure of Minister A. Raja. The court held that A. Raja wanted to favour some companies at the cost of the public exchequer and virtually gifted away important national assets. This is a technical subject matter.There is allegation that the CBI did not probe into the role of other Ministers, Attorney General and private persons like Tatas and also the foreign angle involved and how much bribe was received etc. There is allegation that the then Finance Minister P. Chidambaram had supported the decision of Telecom Minister A. Raja but no investigation was conducted on this. It is also alleged by people having copies (obtained through RTI) of some correspondences exchanged between the Prime Minister Dr. Manmohan Singh/PMO and the then Telecom Minister Dayanidhi Maran that both of them were involved as the orginal Terms of References (ToRs) were diluted and changed to help some private parties and the spectrum pricing was allowed to be decided by the then Minister Dayanidhi Maran and the Group of Ministers so constituted to deal with the matter was not allowed to decide the spectrum pricing issue. These correspondences should be in the file. It is necessary that these are investigated into.

A. Raja wanted to tell some details but he was not being heard. It cannot be that A. Raja only swallowed the crores and others did not and were not involved. Role of these Ministers and all others in the concerned Ministry from Under Secretary onwards should be probed into. It is necessary to further investigate this case, through a Multi Dimensional Monitoring Agency or SIT consisting of CBI officers, officers from Enforcement Directorate, Income Tax, DOT, Revenue Intelligence, Auditors etc so that the investigation is logical and factual, to see that all those who caused loss to the country are punished. This may happen once the Lokpal comes or the government changes. This scam affected the economy of the country and therefore it is against the interest of the country and with that spirit politics should be kept away and all should be arrested and punished, according to law.

Coal Allocation Scam

Coal is another important natural resource in the country like minerals, oil, iron, diamond, gold, water resources, forests, air space, uranium, thorium and so on. The investigation is on. The scam relates to allocation of coal deposits to private companies by the government headed by Dr. Manmohan Singh. In fact during the years 2006 to 2009, when Dr. Manmohan Singh, Prime Minister was also the Coal Minister, maximum coal allotments were made blindly to private companies causing loss of about 10673.03 billion (US $ 200 billion). According to CAG report, 25 private companies were unduly benefited from arbitrary allocation of 57 coal blocks causing a loss of about 1.86 lakh crore. If the Minister in-charge says that he did not know about the allocations, then God save this country. Role of the Minister of State in the Coal Ministry is being reported. The role of Under Secretary and onwards in the Ministry who had processed the matters should be probed and action taken against them. It is important to see whether the government servants or public servants had performed their duty properly and in the interest of the country or not because if they have done it properly, then only you can blame the political leaders who are Ministers. This loss affected the economic development of this country. When the investigation started, how the files for the relevant period, went missing? It is another scandal. How many scandals, how much of loss to the country. These are very serious offences affecting the country and therefore should be condemned and all involved should be brought to book and punished.

It requires deep investigation and there should be a Special Cell for these cases so registered and to be registered. The status report to be filed in the Supreme Court was vetted by the Law Minister Ashwini Kumar and by the two joint secretaries of PMO and Coal Ministry, respectively. There is doubt whether the CBI will be able to investigate the case properly when the sitting Prime Minister himself is alleged to be involved. My answer is No. All scams should be monitored by the Lokpal and there should be a team of officers in the form of a SIT or a Zone or a Cell. Investigation is not an easy task. It is a difficult and specialised work, scientifically and technically.

It needs a team for continuous work and thereafter to follow up the trial work. What does the Lokpal do? It is the investigators, who are to do the job. CBI can do it, if they are allowed to do it freely and if they want to do it. If they take a bold step then they can investigate properly and arrest and take action against all the bureaucrats and the Ministers involved and prosecute all of them in a special court, on a day to day basis. Yes, it requires officers to work not sit in the office and push the files around. CBI should be expanded and it needs many more investigating officers and prosecutors. Whenever important case or cases or scams come what we do is withdraw officers from other branches or cases and put them in that case. This disturbs the quality and quantity also.

There is shortage of officers. For these scams and important murder and other conventional crimes there is need for a big team to work continuously. Investigation should be independently conducted.

This is a serious case and all those involved should be punished irrespective of the status or rank, position. Even Narasimha Rao faced prosecution. What needed is effective prosecution by a special court for early disposal. If we take this casually, they will eat up the country. Nothing remains but whatever remains will also go. With the money which the country would have earned from proper allocation of 2G Spectrum and Coal blocks, the country could have provided free education to poor children, medical facility in villages, drinking water facility wherever it is not available, extended roads upto the villages , provided rice or wheat at fixed quantity free of cost to those below the poverty line and so on and therefore every citizen has the right to ask for strict action against all those involved. There are other cases and all such controversial cases should be reviewed and those under investigation should be properly expedited as and when the Lokpal comes, by the Lokpal or by the CBI itself whether monitored by the Constitutional courts or otherwise.

All these criticisms, details etc. are in the public domain. It is correct that sometimes, for good work done also, CBI is being criticized by some having vested interest. Sometimes the time of decision taken is being criticized whether it is DA case against Mulayam Singh Yadav, Adarsh Society case and so on. There is nothing like clean chit. If there is evidence of involvement of a person, he is charge-sheeted. If a person's name is mentioned in the FIR and no evidence has come up during investigation against him, we do mention it in the report/charge-sheet and request the court to discharge him from the case. If the investigation is not complete, we do mention that investigation against others is continuing. If some allegation comes up against a person during the course of investigation, then it is probed into and mentioned in the report. If there is no involvement of a person, we do mention it specially when some hue and cry is made. You can not drag in a person because some people are making allegations or suspecting. Similarly, if there is allegation and there is suspicion and there is some role of that person, it should be boldly and impartially investigated and action be taken according to law. Favouring anybody will result in criticism and it spoils the reputation of the organisation.

The question is not that the CBI is incompetent but the real point is that it should be allowed to function effectively and properly, according to law. More important to the public is that the CBI should be ready and able to do so honestly and impartially. Here I also recollect a case called as Gutka case. This case requires to be revisited. Accused Dhariwal may be subjected to Narco-Analysis test and the truth will come out which may clarify talk of inappropriate acts.

I had the opportunity to read the book *"Turning Points"* by Dr. APJ Abdul Kalam, former President of India. All would have drawn inspiration from it. The former President said in the book that when he was a child, his father was elected as President of the local Panchayat, somewhere in 1947. One day one person came with a gift and since his father was not there, he asked Dr. Kalam, whether he could keep the gift. On being permitted by Dr. Kalam, he kept the gift on the cot and went away. When his father came, seeing the costly gift, he got angry and did beat Dr Kalam, who started weeping. Later, his father explained the reason for getting angry and advised Dr. Kalam, who was very young, never to receive any gift. He quoted a *Hadith* which said "When the Almighty appoints a person to a position He takes care of his provision. If a person takes anything beyond that, it is an illegal gain". His father further told Dr. Kalam that a gift is always accompanied by some purpose and therefore it is a dangerous thing. It is like touching a snake and getting its poison in return. Dr. Kalam said that the incident remained deeply embedded in his mind and has shaped his value system. Even now, when any person appears before him with a gift, his body and mind shudder. The former President further writes that later in life, he studied '*Manu Smriti*' or the Laws of Manu in which Manu warns every individual against accepting gifts for the reason that it places the acceptor under an obligation to the giver and ultimately results in making a person commit immoral or illegal acts. The point does not need any more explanation as it is self-explanatory and all should be able to understand, the advice contained therein. I leave it to the readers to grasp it.

Chapter 11

Conclusion

Frankly speaking, the personal experiences, spanning a period of decades, cannot be summarised in a few pages. Every incident or transaction cannot be explained in one book. Nothing mentioned above is in the form of any complaint. Reputation of the department is of utmost importance. Therefore, no attempt is made to harm the reputation of any officer.

Any exposure referring to incidents inappropriately handled tarnishes the image of this great organisation. People who have given their life to this organisation will definitely feel hurt. Like my other colleagues, I do feel that many times actions of the department indicated inappropriate handling of some cases and or matters. The reputation and credibility of any organisation mostly depend on the personality of the person who heads it. If the investigation establishes the involvement of a person in a case, whether it is fraud/scam or any other offence, then he or she should be investigated irrespective of his position or status as in the case of any other person placed in the same situation, action according to law should be taken against him/her. Law does not recognise politics in the course of investigation. The organisation needs courage to work in accordance with law and tell the concerned to refrain from interfering in the process of investigation or functioning of the CBI.

There is need to amend the DSPE Act, 1946 (as amended), to make it clear that if the permission requested for by the CBI for investigating into the involvement of joint secretary and above is not issued within 3 months then it will be considered as not refused. Even in cases wherein it was refused within that period, the CBI should move the High Court and get an order for investigation. If there is any specific allegation against any minister or above, the investigating agency should look into that aspect and question the concerned, whether it be the Prime Minister or any other Minister. The final decision should always be on the basis of evidence, as in case of any public servant or any other citizen of the country. In many cases I did feel the pressure on the senior officers. Whether it was from higher ups or outside the department was not known. Whether it was self-created for personal gain or to make somebody happy, was not known. But, after having worked for years, I could make out that the senior officer's order or instructions in many times was not in the interest of the case. When Dera Sachha Sauda cases were being investigated, I felt that there was pressure from some young Members of Parliament from Haryana etc. including Mr. Navin Jindal and they had visited the CBI Headquarters. On instructions from above, I had to instruct the officers at Chandigarh to go to Sirsa to examine the involved person. Though it was informed that the person will make available himself only for half an hour, I did not restrict the officers and they were free and took time and grilled him for more than 3 hours. Now, the same MP is being questioned in the Coalgate scam. In nutshell, do not care for anybody while you discharge your duty but do your duty without being influenced. There will be pressure from parties having vested interest. I investigated large number of sensitive cases in which the progress was monitored by the Constitutional Courts and as directed by the courts, we had filed and used to file progress/status reports before the said courts. Such progress/status reports were never vetted by the law officers, forget the Attorney General, Solicitor General or Additional Solicitor Generals and or the Ministers. Before the matter came up in the court, those law officers or Standing Counsels used to be briefed for making submissions. It is a report of investigation containing the progress made during the period in question.

Some law officer said that it is not a report of investigation. It is not correct. Forget about showing it to a minister. As per law, it is the investigating officer of the case or his superior officers (as per Section 36 CrPC) who can only handle such reports. There is no provision permitting the Government or such law officers to vet such reports. Specially when the allegations are against the Government in power, it should not have been shown to them. Even if you have shown, on instructions or under pressure, then it should have been mentioned in the report filed alongwith the changes, if any, made by anybody in the report. But if we resort to such things where is the question of honesty, impartiality or fairness in the investigation? The action has destroyed the reputation of the organisation and demoralised the honest officers. When the time comes, the authority in power should order a fresh investigation in all the controversial cases handled and action should be taken against all persons involved in the case. Now, there is full support of the order of the Supreme Court. Therefore, who ever is involved should be exposed and action should be taken against him whether he is Secretary, Minister, PMO officer or anybody.

Though, the investigation is done by the investigating officer of the CBI, the final decision is taken on the order of senior officers. Therefore, the system requires that if the investigating officer and his immediate supervising officer and two law officers give an unanimous specific opinion in any case or point, if the final authority differs, then there should be a detailed discussion amongst all and a legally viable final decision should be arrived at and recorded in the file. This will prevent malpractices. Somebody suggested that there should be a separate Prosecution Wing so that such things may not occur. Where do you get the Director, Prosecution and other senior prosecutors and so on?. They are appointed by the Government. It applies to any organisation whether Central Vigilance Commission or any other. Retired government servants are appointed to handle such Institutions and how can you be sure that it will be independent? CBI is celebrating its Golden Jubilee. In one of the dinner parties, it is reported that, addressing the CBI officers, the Minister in-charge instructed the officers to do good work and said that the Government will reward good work and gave example that a former Director has been appointed as Governor and some other Directors were given some other posts. Politicians corrupt the system. Therefore, everything depends upon the personality of the Chief. It may be mentioned here that after the Justice Liberhan Commission on Ayodhya submitted its report, the then Union Home Minister asked the CBI to investigate into the role of persons mentioned by the Commission except those already charge-sheeted and see that some of them are chargesheeted in the court. But, after thorough examination, the CBI politely declined to do so.

Recognise the contribution of the CBI investigating officers and prosecutors and give them the necessary power in the working process. Do not treat them as second citizens in the department. Provide them all required facilities and free atmosphere for impartial investigation and prosecution. There are about 200 inspectors waiting for promotion for a long period. There is urgent need to promote them. There is stagnation because of wrong policies in deputation, giving seniority to those who have come on deputation and dumping the organisation with officers on deputation. 75 percent of the officers in the rank of SsP should be from the CBI cadre either recruited as Sub Inspector or by the UPSC as Dy. Supdt. of Police. 50 percent in the rank of DIGs and 25 percent in the rank of Joint Directors and Additional Directors (if anybody becomes eligible) should be from the cadre including the directly recruited Dy. Supdt. of Police (by the UPSC). Of course, such promotions should be on the basis of merit only with due regard to seniority. This will take care of the problem. There should be 4 posts of special directors/additional directors to look after the 3 investigation divisions and one to look after the Administration, Policy Division including Vigilance and Intelligence, Technical Cell including the Central Forensic Science Laboratory, Co-ordination Division, Training Academy and connected offices.

There is no limit for expansion of this organisation. There is lot of scope for keeping watch on the availability and utility or misutilisation of our natural resources. It may be water resources, coal, natural gases, oil, petrolium products, metals and minerals like diamond, gold, silver, iron, manganese, magnesium, zinc, lead, copper, aluminium, antimony, uranium, thorium and so on. We have plenty of them. Many of these resources might be misutilised. There is need for a proper and effective audit and subsequent effective action to conserve these assets so that disgruntled elements may not take advantage of the failure to safeguard them for the benefit of this great country. Economy generated from these natural resources will help in the development of this country. Every citizen has the duty to preserve them and report misutilisation of these precious items to the CBI or any other concerned agency for appropriate action and for punishing those involved. There is need to expand and strengthen the Economic Offences Division of the CBI which deals with anti-smuggling, drug trafficking, arms trafficking, counter-fieting currency, stamps, black money related work, so that it can contribute effectively and significantly towards improvement and development of the country's economic situation. Black marketiers and black monied people need to be brought to book.

There is criticism that the CBI is partial or dishonest. In some cases, it might have been. But the fact is that it is not an independent department but is controlled by the Government with regard to funds for any activity, for filling up the vacancies, for infrastructural facilities, for raising or fixing the tour allowances of the investigating officers and below, for giving promotions to the deserving and eligible officers and for everything including development of the career of these officers and for increasing the strength of the investigating officers and the down below. Director, CBI should be a Secretary to Government of India rank officer. He cannot be subordinate to the Department in the Ministry. One can see an under secretary in the ministry turning down the proposal sent by the Director. Director does not have power to appoint special counsels to handle an important or sensitive case though there is acute shortage of prosecutors in the CBI. Director should have the power to engage a senior lawyer to handle important cases in the High Court or Supreme Court.

Officers have to travel a lot and therefore enough funds under the Head-"TA/TE" should be made available. There are hundreds of cases where the investigating officers do not get their travelling allowance bills paid for months together. Since there are vacancies in the rank of investigating officers and the total strength has not been increased, the Director, CBI should have the power to appoint retired and efficient officers as consultants to handle the cases. This is specially required in cases of important nature so investigated by the officer before his retirement. The functioning of the CBI should not be viewed as a routine or a casual work.

Further, Director, CBI should have full authority to send officers for training abroad and for the purpose of investigation to be conducted abroad. Provide about 500 more posts of investigating officers in the rank of inspectors, deputy superintendent of police and additional superintendent of police (if this post is still retained). Similarly create at least 500 more posts of prosecutors to handle the trial work etc. Increase in the work load, on day to day basis requires it and do not keep the posts vacant. Make their career an enjoyable one. Give priority to promotions wherever and whenever they are due. Develop a CBI cadre, at least now, in the interest of the organisation. The facts narrated above will be of much relevance to thousands of investigating officers and to many of the supervising officers. Fact is a fact, irrespective of the fact whether anybody accepts it or not. No effort has been made to malign anybody. The system requires a complete change. CBI cadre officers have no other option but to complete their career in the organisation. If there is transparency and impartiality by all in the organisation, this will be the best investigating agency in the world. Let us all join together to work with boldness, impartiality and in accordance with the law. Let us not play politics in the investigation and trial of criminal cases. The whole department needs to be sanitised to function within the ambit of law only without worrying about any sort of interference whatsoever. Let this be the 'VOICE OF CBI'.

Index